# Romancing with Revolution

## Life and Works of Faiz Ahmed Faiz

# Romancing with Revolution

## Life and Works of Faiz Ahmed Faiz

Zaheer Ali

AAKAR

Romancing with Revolution: Life and Works of Faiz Ahmed Faiz
*Zaheer Ali*



First Published 2020

ISBN 978-93-5002-629-8



*Published by*
**AAKAR BOOKS**
28 E Pocket IV, Mayur Vihar Phase I
Delhi 110 091 India
aakarbooks@gmail.com

*Laser Typeset at*
Sakshi Computers, Delhi

*Printed at*
D.K. Fine Art Press, Delhi

For

**Madhuri**

# Contents

# Preface

This book is the outcome of a series of conversations that I had over a period of five years with a very dear friend, Afaq Khan, who sadly died in February 2019. He had taught all his working life teaching Political Science to the postgraduate students and though he was fairly conversant with literature and literary trends, in particular, of Urdu literature, he was sceptical about the efficacy or impact of literature on the socio-political life of the people. In an extremely illiterate society like ours, his argument seemed logical. Conceding the reasonableness of the thrust of his point of view, I would bring in a caveat emphasising the role of the elite in reforming people and occasionally leading them to the path of socio-political change. Even if we discount the instances from world history, we can cite a few tangible examples from modern Indian history. The contributions of social reformers from Raja Rammohun Roy to B.R. Ambedkar in reforming Hindu society is difficult to ignore. True, most of them were not litterateurs but at least some were men of letters and the fact that almost all of them made excessive use of journalism bears testimony to the fact that the written word did prove effectual in changing social norms and also for preparing the ground for political transformation. Among the Muslims the contributions of Syed Ahmed Khan, Altaf Husain Hali and many more colleagues of Khan and later Muhammad Iqbal are prominent examples that through their poetry and prose they, to some extent, emancipated Indian Muslims from the feudal norms and values. In the twentieth century Faiz's poetry did the same.

This book encompasses the life and works of Faiz Ahmed Faiz, one of the most significant poets in the history of Urdu literature. He started as a romantic poet and then embraced leftist progressive ideology that had its sway over the litterateurs of almost all Indian languages in the mid-1930s. The Progressive Writers Association, to which Faiz belonged, was much more dynamic and all-pervading than similar associations of other Indian languages. We must not lose sight of the fact that when Faiz had just begun writing poetry in the early 1930s the national freedom movement was at its peak. The Communist Party of India was incepted but remained banned under the imperialist rule. The declaration of the Communal Award by the British Premier, Ramsay McDonald, in 1932 had hugely polarised Indian society on religious lines and the genie of the 'two nation' theory was out of the bottle and dancing all across the country. In these emotionally surcharged conditions, Faiz sought inspiration from the Bolshevik Revolution and had a vision to transform the excessively graded society into an egalitarian one. It is obvious that his vision remained unfulfilled but what is important is his dream, His poetry sings the praises of various dimensions of his revolutionary dream.

Faiz was an exceptional man not only because of his excellent poetry but for various facets of his personality. After doing his Masters in English literature and also in Arabic language and literature he started teaching first at a college in Amritsar and then at Lahore. Then, during the Second World War he joined the army as Captain and after the war opted for retirement when he was Lieutenant-Colonel. Shortly before the partition of the country he was appointed the Chief Editor of *Pakistan Times* and at the same time he was also the Managing Editor of the Urdu daily newspaper *Imroz.* In the fourth year of the newly created state of Pakistan he was arrested and sentenced to almost five years imprisonment for a crime he did not commit. Then in the late 1950s during Ayub Khan's dictatorship he was again arrested for no rhyme or reason and incarcerated for less than a year. After his first arrest he hardly had any regular job. It was the valiant efforts of his wife Alys who pulled them through the most difficult times. She worked as a teacher and then as a journalist to pay the school fees of two growing daughters and meet all the other expenses. Nevertheless, it was the magnanimity of Faiz that he did not whinge against anyone or allow any bitterness to flow into his poetry. In his *Kuliyat* (collective works) one can barely find even a couplet in protest against the absolutely unjust and prejudiced treatment dealt out to him by most Pakistani rulers. I could discern a trace of an aggrieved expression that too in a much milder tone in one poem in which he addresses his homeland. The poem is *Hum to Majboor-e Wafa Hain*, which is translated in this book. The two lines quoted are:

*Hum to majboor-e wafa hain magar aye jaan-e jahan*
*Apney ushshaq se aisey bhi koi karta hai*
We are powerless owing to love but O my darling
Does anyone treat one's lovers like this?

The life and poetry of this remarkable man and one of the finest poets is extremely relevant in today's India where the fascist forces are on the ascendancy. They have deeply penetrated most of the institutions, state as well as non-state, and, therefore, it hardly matters if they control or lose power, they remain a compelling and ominous force in India in the times to come. Faiz has been in confrontations with the dictators in Pakistan throughout his life. His power was his resolve to defeat the unjust, undemocratic and authoritarian forces to establish a democratic and egalitarian social order. His means were his activism and his poetry. In present-day India we are face to face with fascism. Remember, organized fascism is far more threatening and treacherous than authoritarian rule. We too have to resolve to defeat the forces of hatred. For this we can seek inspiration from the life and poetry of Faiz Ahmed Faiz. This is the foremost justification for the publication of this volume.

**Zaheer Ali**

Vasai
March 13, 2019

# Acknowledgements

More than a few persons deserve my gratitude for their mentoring, valuable inputs, encouragement, meaningful assistance and well-grounded camaraderie without which this book would not have been published. The late Afaq Khan was a cherished friend. It was just to contradict his, otherwise reasonable scepticism about the efficacy of literature in transforming society that I had started writing this book. Regrettably, he is no more to see the full thrust of my counter-argument in the form of this tome. I will always treasure his words and apprize his memory. I sincerely thank Ibrahim Rungla who is my mentor, guide and friend. He has a superb command over both English and Urdu. His invaluable suggestions from time to time have helped me enrich this volume. Among friends I must thank Zia (S.M. Khan), Munawwar Ali, Sibtain Naqvi, Muhammad Fayyaz, Flory D'souza, Shaista Khan, A. Sattar Basra, Surendra Jondhale, Manohar Sahasrabuddhe, Mohammad Wajihuddin, Khan Shameem, A.G. Khan, Muqueem Khan, Waseem Khan and Lateef Quraishi who have always been around to lend me whatever support I may perhaps ask for. Among my younger friends, I am grateful to Noorjahan Momin, Fareed Khan, Neetin Sonawane, Rishi Kelkar, Sanjeev Dewalwar, Shandon Fernandez, Shuja Shakir, Sameer Khan (Farooq) and Sameer Akhtar (Khan) for making available the books and magazines that made my job much simpler. Among my family members, besides my wife to whom I have dedicated this work, I must also thank my son Zeeshan, and my two brothers Syed Hamid Ali and Syed Khalid Ali and my sisters, Naeema and Shameem (Fahim) for their crucial and wide-ranging support. Lastly, I must express thanks to the publisher, K.K. Saxena and his son Rahul for taking a keen interest in the publication of the book.

**Z. A.**

# Chapter 1

## Faiz's Father

Fathers and sons are much more considerate of one another than mothers and daughters.

**—Friedrich Nietzsche**

I cannot think of any need in childhood as strong as the need for a father's protection.

**—Sigmund Freud**

The backdrop was lush green and deserted except for a dozen cows and goats grazing leisurely in the vicinity and a lone, five-year-old shepherd boy sitting under a tree on a boulder supervising the cattle for that was his job. Suddenly, the serenity of the environs was shattered by the sound of some kind of a bell. The shepherd boy rose with a jerk and ran towards the source of the sound. Now, one could notice a small, non-descript building at a short distance from where the sound was emitting. Simultaneously, one could also see boys of the same age of the shepherd boy and a few older ones entering the building. The shepherd boy stopped quite close by the building, forlornly staring at the boys who wore cleaner and better clothes and enjoying teasing and poking at each other. The building was that of a primary school and the boys were its students residing in nearby villages, many of them coming from the village, Kala Qadir that was also the village of the shepherd boy.

The pain in the eyes of the shepherd boy revealed the miserable financial condition of his father who could not afford to send his son to school and instead he was forced at a very tender age to tend the cattle of the villagers for earning his daily bread.

Kala Qadir was a tiny village named after two brothers, Kala and Qadir, who had been the earliest residents of the village that subsequently bore their names. Beyond this no one in the village or in the entire district knew who they were and what feat they had performed that induced the successive generations of villagers to honour them by naming the tiny hamlet after them. Before the partition of the Indian subcontinent, Narowal *Tehsil*, under whose administrative jurisdiction the village of Kala Qadir fell, was a subdivision of Gurdaspur district. After the demarcation of boundaries of India and Pakistan, Gurdaspur town became part of independent India, while the *Tehsil* of Narowal found itself in Pakistan and was attached to the district of Sialkot. Presently, Narowal enjoys the status of a district in the northeast part of Pakistan's province of Punjab.

Our shepherd boy was born in a destitute Muslim family of the village where almost all the residents were engaged in agriculture. The Muslim identity of the shepherd boy's family was comparatively new for his forefathers belonged to the Chandrabansi Jat community tracing their descent from Sen Pal, a Rajput rajah of Saharanpur. In the tradition of the newly acquired faith, the shepherd boy's grandfather was named Sarbuland Khan and his father as Sahabzada Khan. The shepherd boy also had a majestic name, Sultan Muhammad Khan. The family had been residing in Kala Qadir for the last two generations working mostly as landless peasants. The family was so poor that Sultan's parents would snuff out their lamp quite early in the evenings to save on oil. It was like the proverbial lamp of all the destitute people that served as a profound metaphor for a despondent heart in one of the couplets of Mir Taqi Mir:

*Shaam hi se bujha sa rehta hai*
*Dil hua hai charagh muflis ka*

It gets extinguished early in the evening
The heart has turned into the lamp of a destitute

Though born to the impoverished parents, Sultan was a very healthy and attractive child who would grow into more than a six-foot tall young man. However, that was to happen later in the future. In his childhood, Sultan, despite having a healthy constitution and attractive features had to submit to the wishes of his parents and the villagers to care for the cattle to earn his food. He was barely five years old when he was entrusted with the job of a shepherd that made him wake up quite early in the morning, collect cattle from different houses of the village and take them to the periphery of the hamlet where the school was located. This was the routine that he was engaged in for quite a few months. Had there been no school in the vicinity where he was taking the cattle, Sultan would have led a much quieter existence as a shepherd boy. The school, its bell and the commuting of the boys with slates and books in the cotton bags, however, would always make him fidgety as the feeling grew within him that he was missing something extremely valuable. He was too young to analyse the hierarchical and exploitative structure of society to know that he belonged to the lowest financial strata of the village community whose progenies were not supposed to be in school but to serve those who could afford to send their children to seek education. He was also too young to realise the significance of education in the rapidly changing India of the nineteenth century. These thoughts obviously did not cross the mind of the little Sultan. Yet, he would always become restless whenever he heard the school bell and see the boys of his age entering the school building. As Sultan would tell his son much later that he envied those children. His heart would wrench every time he saw those young boys going in and coming out of the school building.

Though the job of tending cows and goats was not very arduous for the young Sultan, the restiveness that confronted him daily because of the presence of the school was unbearable. In the end, the young Sultan made up his mind to put an end to the wrenching of his heart. One fine morning when all the students had entered the school building and had taken their seats in the class, young Sultan left his cattle, gathered the courage and barged into the school building. He was tense with emotions and with the fear of the unforeseen consequences of his action. The teacher, on seeing the shepherd boy asked: "Why have you come? What do you want?" The innocent Sultan replied with exceptional courage: "I want to study." The teacher was a kind soul. He had also noticed the steely resolve for study in the eyes of the young Sultan. He allowed the shepherd boy to attend the school daily. The young boy was ecstatic. For the first time he experienced thrill and unbound joy. The unexpected turn of events transformed him in a state of mind that he was to interpret in future to his sons that "he was mad with happiness."

Even after the permission of the school teacher to attend the school regularly, there appeared no perceptible change in the routine of the shepherd boy; he would still rise quite early in the morning, clean his teeth with black coal-powder, wash his face, hands and feet, would partake his breakfast that his doting mother would give him, which invariably consisted of half a bread of corn or millet, a leftover of the previous night and a small piece of jaggery. By this time his father would also start preparing to go to the fields and without fail caution his son to be watchful of the cattle and should never lose sight of them. The young Sultan would promise to do so while munching his bread. Having finished his breakfast, he would fasten a piece of cloth round his waist for his lunch—again another dry piece of corn bread, and a small piece of jaggery would be wrapped in it, say *khuda hafiz* to his parents and run out of the small shelter, made of low-rising mud walls and a roof of a thick layer of dry hay. He would go from one house to the other gathering cows and goats and finally when his herd was complete would take it to the grazing field. The slight change in the routine was that now he would leave the cattle in the grazing field and despite the promise made to his father that he would always keep an eye on them, would enter the school building and sit at the back of the class.

The young Sultan, despite all odds—he neither had a slate, the textbooks or notebooks nor did his admission to the school have sanction from the villagers—turned out to be a brilliant student. The news of Sultan attending school spread without delay in the village and some conceited and swollen-with-pride type of *zamindars* might not have approved the idea of the shepherd boy of the village sitting along with their sons in the class instead of tending their cattle for which he was being compensated with his daily bread. Two things, however, went in favour of Sultan. First, the wholehearted support of the school teacher who had seen that Sultan was an extremely gifted child and second, Sultan never showed any laxity or tardiness in taking the herd for grazing each morning and no cow or goat ever went astray. Sultan always stood first in his class. The Standard IV examination was conducted at the provincial level. Sultan topped the provincial merit list and consequently was awarded the scholarship to pursue middle school education. In fact, it was Sultan, who for the first time put the name of the village of Kala Qadir on the map of Punjab by his extraordinary academic feat. It was a moment of pride for his teacher, the school and the entire village.

Nonetheless, there was a hindrance to be dealt with before Sultan could keep pursuing his education. There was no facility of middle school education in Kala Qadir. It was in Maddo village that was located quite a distance away from Sultan's village. The precarious financial condition of Sahabzada Khan would not allow him to let his son go to pursue further education for in that case Sultan would have to give up the job of tending cattle that was the source of income and some support to the household. Eventually, Sultan promised to give away the entire amount of his scholarship (Rs. 2 per month) to his father and thus sought the permission from him to join the middle school. The villagers also approved of the arrangement and young Sultan joined the middle school. Now, every morning Sultan had to walk eight miles for going to and coming back from the school of Maddo village. Neither the scorching heat of the Punjab summers nor the disconcerting rains that would make the village road quite mud-spattered could douse

Sultan's burning desire for studies. Many of his friends from the primary school had discontinued their education and would be found loitering or playing in the streets of the village. They would frequently entice Sultan to join them in the fun and frolic. Sultan, however, never lost sight of his mission. He was once again among the toppers of the final examination of the middle school.

Now, another obstacle appeared. There was no high school in the entire district. The facility was available only in Lahore. The very thought of going to Lahore and fending for himself in the big city was quite frightening for Sultan. At this point of time his teachers came to his rescue. They informed him to seek admission in the high school located in Mochi Darwaza for it was adjacent to Cheeniyonwali Masjid where the students from the destitute families would be provided with free lodging and boarding facilities. Sultan made up his mind to go to Lahore. By now his father was convinced that his son would become a '*bada isua*'(important person) if he was allowed to pursue education. Though, most villagers were opposed to the idea of Sultan going to pursue high school education in a big city like Lahore, for Sultan, the only thing that mattered was the consent of his parents. He wrapped a few books that he possessed by then, a couple of millet breads and jaggery in a sheet of cloth and embarked on his journey on the way to Lahore.

The twelve-year-old Sultan was first awestruck by the tumult of the big city for it was a new and thrilling experience for him. The urban mayhem, however, did not make him go astray or lose focus from the purpose of his trip to the big city. He reached Cheeniyonwali Masjid shortly before the morning-prayer. Having finished the obligatory ablution (*vuzu*), he said his prayer and when the congregation thinned, he approached the imam (the one who led the prayer) with bated breath. Sultan was aware that it was going to be the most crucial interview of his life because the imam's approval or disapproval would be crucial for his future. The mosque had quite a few tiny rooms (*hujras*) on its campus which were mostly made available temporarily to the impoverished travellers to the city who could not bear the cost of lodging in regular hotels. Sultan, however, was going to request for free allotment of a room for a minimum of three years that was going to be his duration of high school education.

He greeted the imam who was still sitting on his prayer mat murmuring the holy verses on his rosary (*tasbih*). Replying to Sultan's greeting the imam looked at the boy questioningly. Sultan introduced himself by mentioning his father's name and the name of the village. The imam rose from the prayer mat and put his rosary in the side pocket of his long flowing tunic (*kurta*). Putting a hand on the shoulder of the newly arrived visitor, the imam led him out of the main building of the mosque and asked, "So you want a room to stay? But you are just a boy...what brought you to the city?" Then Sultan told him the real reason of his visit to Lahore. He informed him about his poverty-stricken family, told him about his excellent academic track record and, most importantly, made the *imam* isuali his indomitable determination to pursue education. The imam was a sharp person. He could immediately discern Sultan's aptitude and passion for education. He not only allotted a *hujra* to him but also promised to help him seeking admission in the high school of Mochi Darwaza. Sultan was a meritorious student. He got the admission in the school smoothly. Boarding was also not a problem because the wealthy residents of the neighbourhood would send food for lunch and dinner for the destitute dwellers of the *hujras*.

Being an occupant of a room of a mosque, Sultan turned quite religious. He would say his prayers without fail, would recite the Quran in a charming tone, observe fasts during the month of Ramzan, would sweep the entire campus of the mosque and would always be available for whatever errand the imam or the prominent persons of the locality would assign him. His piety, deferential manners and courteous temperament made him quite popular among the residents of Mochi Darwaza. The life of relative comfort, however, did not make Sultan forget his poor parents. After saying his night prayer (*isha*), he would head to Lahore railway station and work there as a coolie till midnight. Though he was barely twelve years old but his physical constitution was quite strong. The money he would thus earn as a coolie, he would send to his father. The imam of the mosque would treat him like his own son. The significant thing was that Sultan himself was quite contented with his daily routine.

On a Friday, the counsellor of Afghanistan, Sardar Amir Muhammed Khan came to the mosque for the noon prayer. The imam introduced Sultan to the counsellor. At this time, Sultan could speak Persian and English effortlessly. He conversed with the counsellor in both languages. The diplomat was enormously impressed by the teenager's exceptional proficiency in the two languages. He straight away appointed Sultan as his English tutor. It was the defining moment in the life of young Sultan. Though he felt somewhat embarrassed to be the teacher of a much older person who was also a dignitary. The gracious and easygoing personality of the counsellor, however, helped Sultan overcome his initial discomfiture and he proved his worth as a tutor. Shortly, the counsellor also assigned Sultan the job of translating Persian documents into English.

The counsellor was a loyal devotee of Imam Rabbani Shaikh Ahmed, a sixteenth century saint of the Naqshbandi orders whose mausoleum—Rauza Sharif—is located at Sirhind (a town presently in India). He would frequently visit the mausoleum. Later, he started taking Sultan along with him to Sirhind to pay homage at the mausoleum of the saint. On one such visit, when Sultan was busy saying his night-prayer in the mosque adjacent to the mausoleum he fainted and befell unconscious. In that state he saw in the reverie that the saint of Sirhind foretelling him that one day he would be appointed a minister in Afghanistan. On gaining consciousness a wry smile appeared on his lips considering the good tidings and his actual state of being at that time—a tiny room of a mosque for the residence, a bed of straw and a few earthenwares. He resumed saying his prayer.

Thereafter, when the counsellor was summoned by the King of Afghanistan, Abdur Rehman Khan, to Kabul, he took Sultan along with him and presented the young man before the monarch extolling highly his intelligence and command of the English language. The ruler of Afghanistan was on the lookout for a competent and dependable person to translate his letters and messages with the British who were the political masters of India at that time. He thought that Sultan would be the ideal choice for the job for three reasons: first he had a mastery over both Persian and English languages; second, he was a foreigner so he could not get involved in court conspiracies and third, he was a young man who would be an ideal companion for his son, Mir Habibullah Khan, the heir apparent to the throne. The king first appointed him the official translator of the court. His job was to translate royal letters addressed to the British from Persian into English and render the English letters of the British into Persian. He was so good at the job that before long the monarch appointed him the *Mir Munshi* (Chief Secretary) of Afghanistan. The post of Chief Secretary carried tremendous prestige and enormous powers. Sultan was also drawing a substantial salary besides receiving frequent rewards and valuable gifts from the king and other nobles. He had also become a friend and tutor of Habibullah Khan who later ascended the throne of Afghanistan.

Sultan Muhammad Khan was now a rich and powerful person in Afghanistan. The monarch, Abdur Rehman Khan, gave his niece Sair Jan, the daughter of Sardar Muhammad Rafi Khan, in marriage to him. Now, he had become a member of the royal family of Afghanistan and in addition to the post of Chief Secretary was also given the additional charge of the ministry of intelligence. Sair Jan, however, could not survive long. She died two years after the marriage and was buried at a serene place, Buddh Khak, five miles from Kabul. The royal court and conspiracies go in concert. The growing prestige and powers of Sultan Muhammad Khan provoked some courtiers to plot against him. Sultan was a vulnerable target for his foreign origin. At that time there was a lady doctor of British origin, Dr. Lillias Anna Hamilton, serving as the royal physician in Afghanistan. She had a friendly association with Sultan because he was the only one in the court with whom she could interact well because of his command over English. She got wind of the conspiracies that were being hatched against Sultan and cautioned him to be on his guard for royal patronage might not last forever. She warned him about the conspirators who could achieve their aim sooner or later. In her opinion Sultan should think about his future that could only be secure in the country of his birth, India. She advised him to deposit all his riches in her London bank account and should seriously make attempts to flee from Afghanistan. Sultan himself was not oblivious of the intrigues against him. He saw the soundness of the lady doctor's advice and handed over all his movable assets. Shortly afterwards the lady left for England. Much later she wrote a novel, *A Vizier's Daughter*, wherein a 'fictional' account of Sultan Muhammad Khan's days in Afghanistan was interspersed with the fictional tale of the protagonist of the novel, Gul Begum.

Since, no other authentic record of Sultan's days in Afghanistan exists, it is appropriate to construct the missing part of the story of Faiz's father on the basis of Dr. Hamilton's novel which depicts almost a realistic version of Sultan Muhammad Khan's life as Chief Secretary of Afghanistan. Its authenticity was vouched for Sultan himself because Dr. Hamilton had shown the manuscript of the book before publication to him for getting his clearance. In the Introduction she writes: "I have written *A Vizier's Daughter,* every character in which is drawn from a model, and should, therefore, as far as it goes, give an accurate description of one phase, at any rate, of Afghan life."[1] About Faiz's father she added those who knew him in his post-Afghanistan period would think that the author was 'unduly severe.' She made it plain that she did not flatter him. She, in fact, made a sincere attempt to present an accurate picture of him as he was in Kabul.

She stated that she tried to portray Ali Muhammad Khan (the name given to the persona of Sultan Muhammad Khan in the novel) as the complacent court favourite who was much in demand because of his proximity to the monarch and the heir apparent to the throne. He was also extremely overburdened with official work and because of his position of power was the target of his enemies who would frequently complain against him for committing all kinds of conceivable and outrageous crimes. She also informed her readers that she would not have published the book without his permission. So she gave the manuscript, to him when he was in London. Having gone through the manuscript he had only commented: "I think it is very like what I was." She did not overstate when she said in the novel that the Chief Secretary was so overworked that he was doing the work of twenty men. Besides being Chief Secretary he was the head of the Intelligence Department.

The Chief Secretary was a disciplined person because of which his house was also a 'well-ordered one.' He was faithful to the sole wife. Though as per the social norms of Afghan society of the nineteenth century slavery was rampant and the Chief Secretary himself had quite a few female slaves (that included the charming and extremely handsome fictional protagonist Gul Begum, daughter of a Hazara Vizier who ended up as a slave in the house of the Chief Secretary because of the conquest of Hazara territory by the King of Kabul. Faiz had mentioned in one of his interviews that when his father went to Afghanistan he had taken along with him a servant, Imam Baksh, from his village. He remained loyal to Sultan all the way through. Ms. Hamilton rolled her own character and that of Imam Baksh in the fictional persona of Gul Begum. Like Dr. Hamilton, Gul Begum would advise Ali Muhammad Khan to set eyes on the conspiracies and flee from the country. Again, like Imam Baksh, it was Gul Begum who accompanied him when he finally escaped in disguise from Afghanistan) he never slept with any slave girl. In that respect he always remained an outsider despite being one of the most powerful men in Afghanistan. When an old acquaintance once jeered at him because of his dark skin, the Chief Secretary was not annoyed. He knew that he was a Rajput and not an Afghan to inherit a fair skin. He was very proud of his lineage.

The Chief Secretary was a large-hearted person and would shower his friends, visitors, slaves and deprived people with expensive gifts. As Dr. Hamilton mentioned that it required least urging on the part of those who knew of his generosity to make him part with expensive fur, a brand new coat or a *posteen* (fur cloak). At the same time, he was also presented frequently with expensive gifts because of his position of tremendous power and influence in the Afghan Court. The religious isual that Sultan had acquired while living in the Cheeniyonwali Masjid remained intact in Afghanistan as well. Dr. Hamilton found him to be "a most religious man according to the ordinarily accepted standard." He would not only say the mandatory prayers five times a day but also say regularly an optional prayer (*tahajjud*) by waking up in the middle of the night. He believed that saying this optional prayer every night brought "certain special blessing and favours." When his wife fell ill his religiosity became very intense. He would spend all his free time night and day in praying. The night before she died she saw a dream that she narrated to her husband in the morning. She saw herself dead in the vision and that her husband crying dejectedly by her dead body. Then appeared a saint and whispered in the ear of her husband that she should be buried beside his tomb. The Chief Secretary was naturally in great discomfort on hearing what his wife just told him, yet he managed to ask her whether she could see the face of the saint. She said she did and asked for the completion of the saint's wish. She tried to comfort him by saying that he would recover from the blow of her demise but by burying her beside the tomb of the saint, he could keep visiting her grave every time he would go to meet an Indian friend or each time he would go to India to meet his relatives. The tomb was obviously on the road to India. She added that by visiting her grave frequently would please his soul and even if he took another wife, her memory would not be forgotten altogether.

The Chief Secretary was dumbstruck. He had never thought of a life without his wife. Every night he would beseech for her recovery after the midnight prayer and was self-assured that God would accede to his supplications. Her vision, however, contradicted all his hopes. He himself was a devotee of the saint who had appeared in the vision of his wife and signalled her about her death and the place of her burial. After a long pause of silence, he made an attempt to cheer her up by saying that it was after all a dream and she would certainly be restored to her health and that he would himself go to the saint's tomb that very day and implore for her speedy recovery. He said that God would not let him down. A weak smile appeared on her face while she laboriously turned on her side. She was at peace with herself because she was convinced that her husband would bury her beside the tomb of the saint. Next morning she was dead and the Chief Secretary, as per her wish, buried her beside the tomb of the saint on the hillock, the serene place that was known as Budh Khak.

Ali (Sultan) Muhammad Khan was devastated with distress because he could not visualise his home without her. Though he was not passionately in love with her, he would always feel at home when she was alive. This realization dawned upon him only after her demise. His routine life got totally disoriented with her passing. He was not certain how he could carry on in her absence. He had been extremely busy in his official duties that left almost no time for him to spend some quality moments with his wife. Now, when she was no more, he felt pangs of guilt that he had neglected her. His mental state was such that he would have relinquished all his possessions and also his position of power and prestige in exchange of his lost wife. The ever busy Chief Secretary was so much in grief that he did not attend the office for a month. However, he would not miss his daily trip to his wife's grave.

When he resumed work he, as a matter of course, got busy in completing the official work that had amassed manifold because of his long absence. He was still very efficient at work but the zest was gone. He would regularly attend the Durbar but would keep himself aloof from all the things that did not concern him. Having finished the day's official business he would go back home. The king noticed the change in the Chief Secretary's behaviour and asked him whether he was not keeping well. Chief Secretary acknowledged that he was somewhat listless since the death of his wife and he needed a break. He asked for the permission to go to India to meet his mother. The king promptly shot down the idea for he did not want his Chief Secretary to go back to the land of his birth. Instead the king suggested that he should start taking an expensive tonic that the royal *hakim* had prepared for the monarch and that was supposed to rejuvenate the energy and passion in a queasy person. The Chief Secretary could hardly do anything except thank the monarch for his consideration.

A courtier then informed the king that there was nothing wrong with the health of the Chief Secretary but it was his heart that made him sick since the death of his wife. The monarch was also informed about the Chief Secretary's weekly visits to the grave of his wife. The king recalled that the Chief Secretary's wife had died three months ago and inferred that he was missing the company of a woman. The king advised his secretary not to aggravate his grief by keeping the memory of the dead woman alive. That, according to the king, was the cause of the Chief Secretary's lassitude. The monarch reminded him that it was not merely for the performance of his official duties that the Chief Secretary was required to be present in the *Durbar*, but of late the monarch was badly missing his company during the evenings. Though the king, in that meeting, did not directly suggest that the Chief Secretary should get married again but he gave him a hint to make the necessary efforts to get back to his normal self. Thereafter, the Chief Secretary adopted a routine of staying in the company of the monarch and other members of the royal family until midnight. He, however, did not abandon his weekly visits to his wife's grave. The king was informed about it in due course. Accordingly, the king started proposing repeatedly that the Chief Secretary should take another wife. It was an extremely difficult task to turn down the continuous suggestions of the monarch but the Chief Secretary somehow managed to wriggle out of the difficult situation.

Then the Chief Secretary became aware of his enemies who were vigorously engaged in plotting against him. They were jealous of his competence that brought him closer to the king and as a result made him a very powerful man in Afghanistan. On various occasions the conspirators tried to entrap the Chief Secretary by spreading rumours about his disloyalty to the king or about his secret plans to flee the country to join the British service in India. The rumours did reach the ears of the king but he always refused to believe such canards for he had always found the Chief Secretary a very competent and absolutely loyal official of his kingdom. Next, the conspirators got a stroke of luck when they got to know that the Chief Secretary had been constantly turning down the king's proposal about marriage. They quietly hinted to the monarch that the Chief Secretary was not taking an Afghan woman as his wife only because he intended to leave the country permanently. Though, the king reprimanded the conspirators for spreading unfounded stories about a trustworthy member of his Court, he too got perplexed about the Chief Secretary's obstinate attitude in the matter of taking another wife.

The king was aware that the Chief Secretary was not like any other courtier, interested only in pleasures, extravagance, money and power. He was a very competent member of his Court having an unrivalled command over Persian and English and a methodical style of implementing his commands. Many of the Chief Secretary's proposals concerning education and welfare of the common people did improve the condition of a sizable section of the masses and consequently enhanced the reputation of the king. It was for these reasons the king detested the idea of allowing the Chief Secretary to go to India to meet his mother and other relatives. He did not want to lose him. The king, nevertheless, could not understand the precise reason of the unremitting restiveness and anxiety of the Chief Secretary. Apparently the Chief Secretary was among the richest men of Afghanistan; he enjoyed the confidence of the king, though he had lost his wife recently, he was young and could easily marry one of the most eligible Afghani girls. He, however, turned down all the proposals. This was a cause of concern and as the conspirators expected, a faint suspicion cropped up in the king's mind about the real intention of his secretary. Was he really planning to go to India and join the British administration? Was it the real reason for his persistent refusal to get married so that there should be no strings attached? These posers troubled the king's mind.

The monarch was in such a state of mind when the conspirators made another treacherous move against the Chief Secretary. A confidential document that was given to the Chief Secretary by the king himself found its way to the police department. The high ranking police officers, who were obviously hand in glove with the enemies of the Chief Secretary, presented the document to the monarch as a proof of the Chief Secretary's incompetence or rather evil intentions. The police claimed that they got hold of the document through their secret agent who was an infiltrator in the British administration. The conspirators accused the Chief Secretary of working for the British, of duplicity, treachery and disloyalty to the king who had always treated him like his son. The charges were extremely grave and the proof of the Chief Secretary's complicity was in the hands of the king. He obviously demanded an explanation. The Chief Secretary was perplexed about the confidential document which he had himself kept in the safe at his residence. Then by what means did the police get hold of that document? He doubted the authenticity of the paper and requested the king that he should be allowed to go to his residence and check whether the document was still there or missing. The king granted him permission and the Chief Secretary rushed to his residence. He was, however, now under surveillance.

The Chief Secretary was extremely relieved to find the document where he had kept it. He picked it up and started towards the Durbar to face his detractors. He was, however, apprehensive of the extent of hatred against him. His enemies hatched a perilous conspiracy that could have landed him in the dreadful jail of Kabul or even cost him his life. On his way to the Durbar he made up his mind that he would confront the enemies headlong and expose their crafty tricks before the king. He was thinking about the document that the king showed him. It almost looked like the original one. Who had made such a meticulous copy and how? It made him realise that the enemies might have implanted a mole at his residence. It could be anybody. He had many servants and slaves but the needle of suspicion was pointing towards a clerk whom he had appointed to reduce the burden of work without informing the king. Could he be the mole? Whoever it might be the fact remained that his enemies had infiltrated the Chief Secretary's household and for that reason he was in grave danger. He thought that he would have to do something about it. However, it would come later. Presently he had the task to unmask his enemies in the *Durbar*.

On entering the Court he straightaway approached the king and presented the original document to him. The king was stunned on seeing it. He compared it with the one that was earlier given to him by the police and realised that the accusers had presented him a forged document. Then, the Chief Secretary faced his accusers calling them 'pariahs' who thought he would be an easy target to be attacked on account of his foreign roots. He also told them that it was below his dignity to answer their accusations for his answer to prove his incorruptibility was the original document that he had handed over to his majesty. The king too saw through the dangerous scheme the accusers had devised to put his secretary in trouble. He verbally abused them and warned them that they would face the gallows if they came up with such scandalous plans next time. Later he advised the Chief Secretary to go home and rest. He had also promised that the accusers would be severely punished.

Once back at home the Chief Secretary pondered over the serious danger he was in. He could fortunately frustrate their evil plan this time but they might succeed next time. At this point, the storyline of the novel informs the readers that it was Gul Begum, the protagonist of the novel, who advised him to take flight to India. It was she again who accompanied him in disguise from Kabul. In the novel, however, she was shot dead by an acquaintance who had reasons to be disgruntled with her. The Chief Secretary, thereafter, had to flee alone towards the border of India. In reality it was Dr. Hamilton who had advised Sultan Muhammad Khan to escape from Afghanistan and it was Imam Baksh, the loyal servant whom Sultan had brought from India, who accompanied him in his clandestine journey to India. They travelled only during the night on horses disguised as pilgrims. In this manner Sultan returned to his motherland after spending thirteen years in Afghanistan. Sultan Khan, before leaving Kabul, had handed over his entire wealth to Dr. Hamilton who had previously left for England.

Now, Sultan Muhammad Khan was not an ordinary man whose sudden arrival in Lahore would have gone unnoticed. He was the Chief Secretary to the king and most importantly he was head of the Intelligence Department of the kingdom of Afghanistan. The British Government was naturally alarmed by the unexpected appearance of such a high ranking official of a neighbouring country with whom it had always had a love-hate relationship. The British administrators thought that Sultan was on an espionage mission and, therefore, they promptly arrested him. When the King of Afghanistan, Abdur Rehman Khan got to know that his Chief Secretary had actually fled from Kabul and was in jail in Lahore he had mixed feeling of surprise and annoyance. He informed the British authorities that he wanted his Chief Secretary back in Kabul. Sultan Muhammad Khan, nevertheless, had no inclination to go back to Afghanistan. He somehow established contact with Dr. Lillias Hamilton and asked her to help him get out of the British prison. According to a statement of Faiz, she was the niece of Queen Victoria and for that reason had much influence in official circles in England. She drummed up support for the release of Sultan Khan without delay that led to his release from prison. Subsequently, she wrote a letter to Sultan Khan wherein she advised him to come over to London. Sultan Khan liked the idea and sailed for England.

In London the considerate Dr. Hamilton returned all the riches of Sultan Khan which he had handed over to her for depositing in her account. He was a rich man again but he did not splurge the wealth on pleasures but decided to seek higher education. He got admitted to Cambridge University and was subsequently elected Fellow of the Royal Geographical Society. Sultan Muhammad Khan was one of the richest students at the University. He started circulating among the elite of London. The Prince of Wales who later ascended the throne of England as King Edward VII was among the friends of Sultan with whom he would often play polo. His intellect, suave manners and wit made him a well-liked member of British high society. In the intervening time the monarch of Afghanistan got to know that his favourite Chief Secretary was pursuing higher education in London. He sent him the message that if he did not wish to go back to Kabul, he should, instead accept the post of Ambassador of Afghanistan to Britain. By this arrangement he could continue his education as well as serve the interests of Afghanistan by becoming its representative in London. Sultan Khan accepted the offer that further enhanced his financial position and prestige.

Having finished his education at Cambridge, Sultan Khan made up his mind to become a barrister which was a very sought after discipline in those days. He enrolled himself for the law course. During this time certain students from Punjab who later achieved prominence in their respective fields such as Muhammad Iqbal, Muhammad Shafi, Fazl-e-Hasan and Abdul Qadir were among his contemporaries in London. Later, these four were honoured with knighthood. All the same, they were just students confined only to the circle of students having limited resources in a foreign country while Sultan Khan was a very wealthy person, a member of the British high society and the Ambassador of Afghanistan to Britain. His socio-economic status in London was higher than most of the students. Yet, the common bond of ethnicity and culture of Punjab brought them closer and they became friends. Sultan Khan completed the law course and was called to the bar as a barrister from Lincoln's Inn.

On completion of his education, Sultan Khan was in a dilemma about the future course of action. He had before him two options. He could have continued to be the Ambassador of Afghanistan to Britain or he could go back to India and start practising law. He opted for the latter, selecting the town of Jhelum for permanent stay and legal practice. In those days Jhelum was a small town and despite its historical significance (a few miles from the town is the site where the Battle of Hydaspes was fought in 326 BC between the armies of Alexander the Great and Rajah Porus), the town could not develop because it had always faced the wrath of the invaders from the north-west. During the British rule the town and the surrounding areas provided soldiers to the army in large numbers. So it was in this impoverished town that Sultan Muhammad Khan had set up his legal practice. His aristocratic lifestyle was in complete contradiction of even the well-heeled residents of the town. He would go to the court in a luxurious phaeton drawn by four horses. The economy of the town was not such that it could provide the kind of income required for the sustainment of Sultan Khan's grandiose lifestyle. Soon enough he saw the futility of continuing his legal profession in Jhelum and shifted to Sialkot.

It was a much bigger place compared to Jhelum and it was here that Sultan Khan became a very successful lawyer.

Now, the British Government had adopted an altogether different attitude with regard to Sultan Khan whom they had put behind bars once. His British education and particularly his connections with many British nobles including King Edward VII made him an important personality in the eyes of the colonial masters. He was still in Jhelum when the British administration solicited his goodwill by allotting him lands in Sargodha and Montgomery. Sultan Khan had built farm houses there. The British also conferred the title of Khan Bahadur on him. It took him barely two years to establish a money-spinning legal practice in Sialkot. So therefore, he decided to marry again. The bride, Sultan Fatima, was the daughter of Choudhary Adalat Khan who was a landlord of village Jastar in the *Tehsil* of Narowal. The village Jastar was quite close to Sultan Khan's village Kala Qadir. Faiz had said in an interview that it was the fifth marriage of his father and there was no record available about the three wives (the first one as we have noted was the niece of the king of Afghanistan) that he took before. Sultan Fatima bore him three sons. Faiz was the second one. His elder brother Tufail Ahmed Khan was three years older than him. The name of the younger one was Inayat Ahmed Khan.

According to Faiz's account his father had now become one of the most prominent residents of Sialkot. He was practically the president of almost all the charitable organisations of the town. He was a member of the Court of Aligarh Muslim University, the President of Anjuman-e-Islamia, Sialkot and a very important member of the Managing Committee of Anjuman-e-Himayat-ul-Islam. His philanthropic enthusiasm was phenomenal. He had funded quite a few schools and contributed substantially to the upkeep of various mosques. He had also built a mosque in Kala Qadir, his ancestral village. He owned vast properties in Sialkot and also in the Mochi Darwaza locality of Lahore. He had been the friend of Sir Muhammad Iqbal and Sir Muhammad Shafi while studying law in London. Now they were living in Lahore and tried on quite a few occasions to convince Sultan Khan to shift to Lahore.

Nonetheless, he refused to move away from his own district and its people. In Sialkot his position was that of paramount dignitary and he loved it.

Faiz has provided some noteworthy information about some of Sultan Khan's friends in Sialkot. One was Mammun, the gambler. Though his real name was Muhammad Baksh, he was widely known by his assumed name. He was quite an interesting character. He would not mind being called a gambler; in fact he liked it. He was, as Faiz had put it, "a sort of local Robin Hood." He was running gambling dens and was also deeply involved in smuggling. He was acknowledged the king of the underworld in that part of undivided Punjab. Faiz remembered him by the sobriquet of 'Robin Hood' because he would distribute money among the needy and poorer residents of the town. He would also donate money generously to the charitable causes. He was obviously fairly popular among people that helped him become a member of the Municipal Committee. Another friend of Sultan Khan was a *pesh imam* (one who leads prayers) of a mosque, a teacher and a reasonably wealthy man, Maulavi Ibrahim. He also taught Faiz the Urdu primer. Remembering his style of teaching, Faiz had said his classes were out of the ordinary because he would teach not only students of all primary standards simultaneously but the students of theology would also sit in the same class learning *ahadith* and *fiqhe* from him. Faiz also learned the Quran from him with translations over a period of seven years. Another teacher whom Faiz had mentioned with fondness was Maulana Mir Hasan who was famous as the teacher of Sir Muhammad Iqbal. Though his *madrassa* was quite a distance away from Sultan Khan's *haveli,* he insisted that Faiz should learn Persian and Arabic from him.

Another well-known friend of Sultan Khan was the famous leader of the Sikhs, Baba Kharak Singh. He was the originator of the Akali Movement in undivided Punjab. He started the Movement precisely against the British policy of keeping gurudwaras under government control. The priests of the gurudwaras were also appointed by the government. This was unreasonable interference in the religious affairs of the Sikhs. Through the Akali Movement,

Kharak Singh wanted to force the British government to give up the policy of controlling the religious places of the Sikhs. He wanted the community's control over gurudwaras. There was, of course, an anti-imperialism slant attached to the Akali Movement and for that reason the police had often opened firing to disrupt the meetings and processions of the Akalis. Under the leadership of Kharak Singh, the Akalis also lent support to the Khilafat Movement that not only ensured Muslim-Sikh unity but also created myriad problems for the government to keep the agitation under control. Baba Kharak Singh is a much revered name in the Akali Movement. He strived for religious freedom and restoration of dignity and respect of the Sikh community.

The foregoing events of the life of Sultan Muhammad Khan are testimony to the fact that he was without doubt an exceptional man who literally rose from rags to riches. It must also be added that he had an impressive physique. Faiz spoke highly of his impressive personality. Faiz cautioned those who might venture to visualise his father on the basis of his physical features. Faiz said: "Don't try to imagine him from my height and features, for I seem to have acquired my looks from my mother's family." Sultan Muhammad Khan, on the other hand was a tall and very handsome man. He also possessed a commanding voice which he would often raise to have the desired impact on the addressees. Faiz recalled an anecdote to underline the point. On the occasion of *Eid-ul-Ad'ha*, a servant was assigned the job of bringing the goats for sacrifice. For some reason he could not reach on time. When he finally arrived, Sultan Khan shouted at him in such a manner that the poor servant, "was so overawed by his loud and peremptory manner that he fell backward against a wall and fainted with fear." In deference of the Ameer Abdur Rehman Khan, the king of Afghanistan who had taken care of him like his son, Sultan Khan wrote his biography. He was also the author of the Constitution of Afghanistan.

When Faiz was in the fourth year of the undergraduate course in Government College Lahore, the wedding of his younger sister was fixed. Everyone related to the family of Sultan Muhammad Khan reached Sialkot to attend the event. The eldest daughter of Sultan Khan was settled in Dharamshala (now in Himachal Pradesh, India) after marriage. He wrote to her: "If you wish to see me alive then attend the wedding of your sister or else you won't have the chance to see me alive." She naturally obliged. Sultan Khan got himself involved in making arrangements for his daughter's marriage. He personally supervised every chore so that there should remain no failing. The entire town of Sialkot looked forward to the wedding which according to everyone's expectations was going to be a magnificent event. All of a sudden, Sultan Khan complained of discomfort. He was rushed to a doctor but died before reaching the destination. It was probably a massive cardiac arrest. All the guests who had assembled to attend a superb wedding full of joy and elation turned into mourners. The death of Sultan Muhammad Khan was as dramatic as his life. He had started as a destitute shepherd and through his intellect, diligence and ingenuity reached such an exalted position which very few could even imagine to reach. The story of his life had already been made known through Dr. Lillias Anna Hamilton's novel before his son, Faiz, became a celebrity.

# Chapter 2

# Faiz: The Man

> The man who is truly good and wise will bear with dignity whatever fortune sends, and will always make the best of his circumstances.
>
> **—Aristotle**

> As far as men go, it is not that what they are that interests me, but what they become.
>
> **—Jean-Paul Sartre**

## (I)

Faiz was born with a silver spoon in the mouth. He was raised in great comfort and pomp. He had the best education that was available in Sialkot and Lahore. Nonetheless, before he could complete his graduation his luxurious world with its opulent lifestyle came crashing down. Immediately after the burial of his father, quite a few *sahukars* and *mahajans* (moneylenders) started making rounds of Sultan Khan's haveli demanding the repayment of loans that the deceased had borrowed from them. At that point of time, Faiz realised that his father owed Rs. 80,000 to the moneylenders. His magnanimous way of life, overindulgence and openhanded philanthropy was sustained on borrowed money. Many friends and well-wishers advised Faiz and his brothers to refuse payment of loans as they were not aware of the transactions and therefore, not legally a party to them. Tufail Ahmed Khan, Faiz's elder brother, however, refused to take such a position. To him the dignity and reputation of the family of Sultan Muhammad Khan was more important than the riches. He assured the moneylenders that he would repay all the loans. He began selling properties located in Sialkot, Lahore, Sargodha and Montgomery and finally repaid the entire loan. Now, the family was left with the agricultural properties of Kala Qadir which were under the effective control of the peasants who were mostly the poor relatives of Sultan Ahmad Khan. Those properties neither fetched any monetary gains to Faiz's family nor was it an easy task to get rid of the peasants. Tufail Ahmad Khan, the new head of the family set out on long-drawn-out litigations against the peasants of the ancestral village, Kala Qadir where, besides his father, he and his younger brother Faiz Ahmed Khan were also born.

The exact date of Faiz's birth was a matter of controversy. The school records were also conflict-ridden as one document suggested January 7, 1911, whereas another file mentioned January 7, 1912. In those days there was hardly any reliable system of recording dates of births and deaths even in the urban areas. In villages, such as Kala Qadir where Faiz was born, it was much more untrustworthy. Much later, when Faiz had become a celebrity and many writers approached him to record his life-story, he asked a friend to make a thorough check of the municipal records to find the correct date of birth and consequently it was found that the date was February 13, 1911. At birth he was a very healthy and fair baby. The mother, Begum Sultan Fatima, was naturally delighted and so was the father for he was born three years after the birth of the first son. In keeping with the tradition, the *azaan* (call for prayer) was pronounced in the ears of the infant. Sultan Muhammad Khan christened him Faiz Ahmed Khan. A sumptuous party was arranged for the entire village and the musicians were kept busy for the whole night.

Faiz's mother was an extraordinary person in the sense that she was an educated Muslim woman in those days. Faiz described her as short but an extremely fair lady. She was intelligent too. Her Urdu prose had its own appeal and Faiz had put on record that she would write genuinely fascinating letters. She was also extremely religious and would never miss offering the midnight prayer. Among her three sons she loved Faiz the most.

When he was barely five years old, his initiation in education commenced with the learning of the Quran with meaning. He showed remarkable progress in recitation of the Quranic verses. His father was the President of Anjuman-e-Islamia, Sialkot. The Anjuman would invite prominent Muslim leaders and intellectuals on the occasions of its annual meetings. Once, Muhammad Iqbal was invited as the chief guest at one such meeting. The first item of the meeting would always be the recitation of the verses from Quran. Faiz had started learning the Quran barely a few months ago. Nonetheless, the secretary of the Anjuman, Sheikh Manzoor Ilahi lifted him and made him stand on a table. Then, little Faiz recited the Quranic verses so sweetly and perfectly that Iqbal was much impressed. He patted Faiz on the back and praised his intonation and pronunciation of Arabic words. This was the first public function that the five-year-old Faiz addressed and was admired.

Faiz had often mentioned that during his childhood there would always be a crowd of women in the house who loved him so much that they would not leave him alone. As a result, he never got the chance to go out in the street and play with the urchins of the neighbourhood. Faiz thought it was a sort of plan to make him lead a virtuous life in future. The trait of bashfulness that had remained with Faiz till the last was supposed to be a throwback of the early formative years which he mostly spent in the company of doting women. It was not surprising, therefore, that despite being a Punjabi (Punjabis, particularly men, are famous in the Indian subcontinent for their excessive use of vulgar swear words) the worst word of verbal abuse that Faiz ever used against someone he disliked was '*paji*' (roughly unscrupulous or crooked). Much later, however, he remarked regretfully that during his childhood he could not enjoy the kind of freedom and bumpiness that the children of his age had. He could observe from the secure confines of his home that some child would be enjoying kite flying; another one would be busy playing marbles and yet another would be having great fun just scampering around. Despite craving, Faiz could not join the fun and frolic that would go on daily in the street because he was given to understand, of course by the doting women of the house, that 'good' and 'dutiful' children did not play such 'wicked' games. Thus, his early childhood remained bereft of hullabaloo, wrestling matches and vulgar swear lingo that were common pursuits for most children of his age.

Persian was the language that was mainly spoken in Faiz's home. His nanny, strangely called Nana Jan, was an Afghan woman and was sent as a servant with Bibi Gul by the king of Afghanistan. Bibi Gul was the first child of Sultan Khan born to Sair Jan, his first wife who was the niece of the king. When he escaped from Afghanistan incognito, naturally he could not bring his daughter along with him. It was many years later when he had settled in Jhelum that the king sent his daughter along with Nana Jan and other servants. A teacher, Master Ata Ahmed, was appointed to teach Faiz Urdu and Persian. When Faiz was about eight years old, he was admitted to the Anjuman-e-Islamia school in the fourth standard. The particular school was chosen mainly because Sultan Khan was the president of the Anjuman. On the very first day, little Faiz reached the school in a two-horses-drawn carriage wearing a velvet suit. When he entered the classroom, he got the first shock of his life. Almost all the children in tattered and filthy clothes were seated on jute flooring that was as unclean as their clothes. The students were equally shocked on seeing a child of their age in a velvet suit with slicked hair and wearing smart footwear. They looked at him in bewilderment. Faiz was confused and did not know how to react. He slowly sat on the floor. Though, at the time he was too young to recognise that most children of his country were in a similar condition as he saw on the first day of school. One thing, nonetheless, was surprising. Faiz, even at that young age did not resent the children who were in rags. On the contrary he felt uncomfortable wearing a velvet suit. From the second day he wore cotton clothes. Yet, the other students could not treat him as one of them because he was still not wearing filthy, torn clothes like them. They would continuously make fun of him that would make Faiz nervous. He also felt uncomfortable because of the behaviour of the teachers. Since he was the son of the President of the school, every teacher would greet him with respect on entering the class. All this was too embarrassing for the eight-year-old Faiz. When he could not take it any more he told his father that he would not attend that school. He was immediately shifted to the Scotch Mission School.

Though there were many good teachers in the Scotch Mission School, Faiz particularly remembered two of them. The first one was Maulavi Ibrahim Mir Sialkoti who taught him the Quran, *ahadith* and theology. He was not only a competent teacher but was also a kind-hearted person. Faiz would always mention his name with reverence. The second teacher was Shams-ul-Ulema Maulavi Mir Hasan who had also taught Muhammad Iqbal. He taught Faiz Arabic grammar. Faiz had an exciting time at Scotch Mission. He was good at academics as well as sports. In a little while, students started treating him as their leader though Faiz observed years later that "I did not possess leadership qualities. One should either be a bully to force others to obey him or he should be a brilliant student. I was reasonably good at studies. I was also a standard sportsman. Nonetheless, I had not excelled in studies to such an extent that other students should take notice of me."[1] Humility had always been a prominent trait of Faiz's character.

Faiz was a favourite son of his father as well. Sultan Khan would wake him up early in the morning and take him along to the mosque for morning prayer. After the prayer Faiz, for an hour or so, would learn the Quran from Maulavi Ibrahim. Subsequently, he would go together with his father for a morning walk. At nightfall, Sultan Khan would ask him to read out newspapers for him. His father would often assign him the task of taking dictation of letters in both Urdu and English. In a way at that early age, Faiz worked as his father's secretary. This routine ultimately helped Faiz improve proficiency in Urdu as well as English. Faiz was also exposed to Sufism by his father though at that time he was too young to comprehend the humanitarian mode of Islam. Sultan Khan would often take Faiz along on trips to meet a darvesh, Sahabzada Faiz-ul-Hasan, who had his abode outside the town of Sialkot. The darvesh was, Faiz recalled, a poet and a quaint character. There was also the abode of another darvesh in Alu Mahar, a tiny hamlet in the suburbs of Sialkot. Faiz had gone to meet the Darvesh of Alu Mahar often with his father. Faiz himself believed that these visits to dervishes at an early age did help him develop a fascination for the humanistic core of Sufism.

The period between 1917 and 1920 was momentous both for national and international politics. Faiz was in school during the period. Obviously, on account of his youth, he could not figure out the significance of those events but his young mind could register that the happenings that the adults around him were discussing were out of the ordinary. In later years, Faiz said that he had in his mind some hazy images of the politically surcharged atmosphere of Sialkot. He could recall the newspaper hawkers shouting, "Czar overthrown in Russia/Lenin sets up workers' government," and "the Red revolution has arrived." When the First World War ended the British rulers and their lackeys decorated the buildings and streets of Sialkot with multicoloured buntings and victory processions were taken out with bands playing and soldiers marching with faultless synchronization. The monstrous incident of Jallianwala Bagh too happened during this period. It was a crime against humanity wherein a malevolent British officer massacred hundreds of Indians including women and children in cold blood. People were out in the streets of Sialkot protesting against the diabolic crime. The freedom fighters would also take out processions against the British and slogans such as *Jo bole so nihal, sat sri akal/ Allah-o-akbar* and *Vande Mataram* would rent the town's atmosphere. Faiz had also brought to mind the commotions the visits of the prominent nationalist leaders like Motilal Nehru, Maulana Azad, the Ali Brothers, Baba Kharak Singh and Dr. Saifuddin Kitchlew would cause in Sialkot. The political events would also be hotly debated in the drawing room of Sultan Khan and the young Faiz would be a silent listener.

Then there were "knowledgeable" and "expert political commentators" of the neighbourhood such as Allah Diya, the wrestler, Charagh Din, the oilman, Allah Rakha, the butcher and Khushia, the barber who would invariably gather on the platform adjacent to Faiz's house the moment after Faiz's father left for the court. There were benches and stools placed on the platform meant for Sultan Khan's clients, which these petty shopkeepers would occupy and get engaged in political gossip for hours. "Have you heard," someone would say, "Mahatma Gandhi and the Ali Brothers have announced that within a year all British governors, commissioners and district collectors will be expelled and their place taken by our own people." To this piece of 'glad tiding' another would add, "They say the Turkish army is coming through Afghanistan after defeating the British." Such an 'exhilarating news' would be lapped up by someone else who would put in another elating dimension to it, "Yes, and the Russian forces have joined the Turks and overthrown their king. They have a new leader called Lenin who has set up an army of workers, made the king flee and distributed all the wealth among the people. They have a workers' government now." The notion of a workers' government would excite a listener so much that he shouted, "Buck up! You son of a lion! I say, let us ask our Agha Safdar to do something similar." (Agha Safdar was a locally popular leader.) "What a great thing it would be," he toted up further, "if this could happen here. Imagine the wealth of Lala Harjan Rai, the moneylender, being distributed among us all." The young Faiz would constantly overhear this kind of political gossip and many years later he recollected that it was through the gossip sessions of local shopkeepers, he for the first time heard of the Russian Revolution and the name of Lenin. He was, nonetheless, not sure what effect these words had on his young mind then.

Faiz got addicted to reading literature when he was in the seventh standard. In the vicinity of his house there was a bookstore where one could borrow any book by paying a rent of two paise per day. Faiz, by using this facility, had read many Urdu fables and novels that were popular in those days. Then he turned to poetry. He read the collections of Mir, Ghalib and Dagh. He admitted later that in those days he could not figure out Ghalib at all; he could barely comprehend the poetry of other poets. Poetry, as he owned up, would however, stir up his heart in a strange way. Sultan Khan's clerk was practically the manager of his household. Once he got annoyed with Faiz for some reason and informed Sultan Khan about Faiz's 'foible' of reading novels instead of school textbooks. Sultan Khan advised his son that if he was so addicted to reading novels then he should read English ones. "You can borrow English novels from the Fort Library,"[2] Faiz's father recommended. It was a stroke of luck for Faiz. He read almost all the major novels that he could lay his hands on. Thus, English fiction and Urdu poetry became Faiz's preferred areas of literature.

Tufail Ahmed Khan, Faiz's elder brother was also a student of the Scotch Mission. When Fiaz's reading habit became the talk of the school, Nazir Ahmed, a friend of Tufail, ran into Faiz and asked, "You read a lot of poetry books. Have you ever taken a crack at composing poetry yourself?" Faiz obviously replied in the negative. Nazir spoke about a boy Chhajju Ram who was his classmate and asked Faiz to make an effort to write a *hajva* (derisive poem) about him. It was a demand of a close friend of his elder brother which Faiz could not ignore. Faiz wrote a scornful piece scoffing at, in the established tradition of *hajva*, the physical features of Chhajju Ram. Nazir liked the poem immensely and read it out among his friends. Next day, the poem and Chhajju Ram, were the rage in the school. Everyone praised Faiz's talent as a poet. Faiz did not know Chhajju Ram personally but when every student would come up to him and congratulate him for writing a thoroughly abusive poem about the boy, Faiz felt guilty about attacking the dignity of someone whom he did not even know. He looked for Chhajju Ram and he finally met him and tendered his apology for writing the poem. Chhajju laughed heartily and said, "Apology for what? In fact, I'm thankful to you that your poem has made me popular in the entire school." On hearing this, Faiz's feeling of guilt subsided. Faiz was thirteen years old then and it was his first attempt at writing poetry.

When the fifteen-year-old Faiz was in the tenth standard, he became conscious of the enticement of early youth. He started thinking and appreciating the beauty of the opposite sex. Everything around him appeared charming. He suddenly developed an immense liking for nature–flowers, trees, rivers, mountains, birds and of course human beings. He would often feel that the sky had changed its colour, certain things had gone afar, the colour of sunshine had swiftly turned crimson, the things that were familiar had changed their appearance and the world around him had got converted into a fascinating movie. In a nutshell, he was passing through a dreamy phase with its romantic overtones. At this time the principal of the school announced a competition of poetry writing. One of the teachers, Master Bihari Lal, proposed a poetic line to fix the meter and rhyming (*misra'e tarah*) that each participant was required to adhere to. The judge was Shams-ul-Ulema Syed Mir Hasan. Faiz was already in the proper romantic mindset that helped him compose a fine *ghazal* that fetched the first position. He was awarded a medal and Re. 1. Faiz was on cloud nine. For him the award was a testimony to the fact that he could write poetry. That medal had always remained with Faiz. He was sentimental about it. Subsequently, Faiz composed many poems, mostly romantic, and like any other fresh poet, would always be in search of an audience. It was also the time when Faiz fell in love with a young girl. Though, he never spoke about who she was and what happened to his first love, he had acknowledged this much that at that age he thought he was in love with her. This further gave impetus to his fascination for composing poems.

Adjacent to Faiz's haveli, there was a bigger haveli where *mushairas* (poetry recitation gatherings) would be held on a regular basis. An established Urdu poet, Munshi Raj Narain Dehlavi lived in Sialkot and he was the one who arranged these poetic meets. A resident of Kashmir, Munshi Sirajuddin was also stationed at Sialkot. He would usually preside over the poetry recitation sessions. The ghazals were to be composed on the proposed poetic line (*misra'e tarah*). The young and quite bashful Faiz did not have the nerve to participate in these meets because Sirajuddin's scathing comments would be a dampener even for well-known poets. Having faced the mental dilemma to participate in the poetic meets or not for quite a while, Faiz finally could gather enough courage to recite a ghazal at one of the meets. He was expecting that Sirajuddin would tear apart his every couplet. Nonetheless, he was pleasantly surprised when Sirajuddin praised his composition by saying that he took meticulous care while selecting content and diction but also added that Faiz was too young to take on a pursuit like composing poems. He wanted Faiz to finish his education first and only after attaining maturity he could think of composing poetry. Faiz later related, "And I gave up composing poems."[3]

Faiz passed the matriculation in the first division and got admitted to Murray College, Sialkot. There, Prof. Salim Chishti was the Urdu teacher. He would also arrange mushairas for college students. He invited Faiz to write a ghazal on a proposed poetic line. Faiz composed a few couplets and recited them at the poetic meet. Everyone praised Faiz for his first-rate ghazal. Prof. Chishti gave him advice that was exactly the opposite of the one given by Munshi Sirajuddin. Prof. Chishti counselled: "Pay attention to writing poetry without delay. Perhaps, one day, you may become a poet." Thus, Faiz had always been appreciated as a poet even during the early days when he was making efforts to versify on the appeal of his friends or teachers. Nonetheless, in those days he never gave a thought to become a full-time poet. He was more interested in sports. He was fond of playing cricket and was an above average player of the game. As he related years later: "In those days I wanted to become a cricketer." He regretted not becoming one.

Faiz passed the FA (First Year Arts) examination in the first division and got admitted, in 1929, to the third year BA course in Government College, Lahore. He was now on his own in a big city. Leaving behind the comfort of the home was not as agonising as the disconnection with his sweetheart who was in Sialkot. Though Faiz never expressed his love to her, he could not forget her charming face and enticing smile. The loneliness that he experienced for the first time in Lahore further worsened his state of mind. In those days, lovers could not even exchange letters. They had to quietly suffer the pangs of separation. In Faiz's case, he could not even discuss the condition of his heart with a friend because he was not certain whether the girl would reciprocate his love. They never talked to each other; their 'love affair' did not go beyond bashfully gazing at each other's faces and smiling. He was a loner and would always be lost in his thoughts. He would often be seen standing alone in the gallery of his hostel room staring at the sky. Once, a student who stayed in the same hostel came up to Faiz and asked, "Excuse me! Who are you and what do you constantly stare at in the sky?" Faiz was as usual lost in his thoughts. He was surprised by the intrusion of a fellow student but replied, "My name is Faiz. I did an FA from Sialkot's Murray College and got admission in the third year. I don't know anyone here." The student introduced himself, "I'm Nabi Ahmed. I'm also a student of the third year." Then he introduced two of his friends, Rafiq Sher Muhammad Hameed and Aga Hameed to Faiz. The four of them became very dear friends. There was another student, Khwaja Khurseed Anwar, who was pursing the science course in the college. He also became an intimate friend of Faiz.

The thought of the sweetheart left behind in Sialkot, nonetheless, kept him restless and gloomy. In this state of mind Faiz was attracted to the romantic poems of Akhtar Shirani which were hugely popular in those days. Akhtar Shirani was notable for addressing the beloved directly by her name, a tradition of the old Dakhani ghazals which Shirani had revived. What is more, his romantic compositions, written in simple lyrical style, were interlaced with a tinge of nostalgia. These poems had an alluring appeal for a teenager Faiz who was also nostalgic about Sialkot. He composed many romantic poems and ghazals during this period, a few of them were later included in the first part of his first anthology, *Naqsh-e-Faryadi*. Now, he had started writing poetry quite regularly.

The *mushaira* of Government College had a very high reputation as reputed poets would usually be invited to present their compositions. In one such *mushaira*, presided over by the renowned Urdu humourist-satirist, Patras Bukhari, who was also the professor of English in the College, Faiz's name, who was sitting among his student friends, was called out. He went up to the stage with bated breath, took out a piece of paper and read out the ghazal. It was highly praised even by the veteran poets. In the second round of poetry recitation, Faiz's name was again called for everyone wanted to hear more from this young poet. Now, he was in a fix for at that time he had only one ghazal with him that he had already recited. Another piece of poetry that he had with him at that time was a letter written in poetry on the insistence of a close friend, Brij Mohan. He read out the letter with freshly acquired self-assurance. It was also much-admired. After the *mushaira*, much respected poets like Charagh Hasan Hasrat, Sufi Ghulam Mustafa Tabassum and Abdul Majeed Salik came up to Faiz and one of them commented, "it seems you are broken-hearted." Faiz admitted that he was. Then, all three of them showed appreciation of his poetic talent and advised him to keep writing poetry. Faiz was obviously very thrilled on hearing the words of praise from the acclaimed poets. He observed later: "I thought I had arrived as a poet because the prominent poets were applauding my poetic talent." Thereafter, he got totally devoted to poetry writing.

Government College Lahore had a constellation of extremely gifted teachers. Prof. Patras Bukhari and Prof. Lang Hornforth had a very high reputation as teachers of English. A close friend of Faiz, Sher Muhammad Hameed, mentioned in an article that Prof. Lang Hornforth was the Head of the Department of English and when he assessed third years' answer-papers, he gave Faiz 165 marks. When a student asked Prof. Hornfurth, "How could Faiz get 165 marks out of 150?" The professor commented, "Because I could not give more." Prof. Chatterjee of the Department of Philosophy, Dr. Sadruddin of Arabic and Qazi Fazl-e-Haq of Persian too were erudite scholars and competent teachers of their respective disciplines. Sufi Ghulam Mustafa Tabassum was a notable poet and also a famed teacher of Urdu. Besides, these learned members of the faculty the presence of eminent poets and writers such as Dr. Muhammad Iqbal, Imtiyaz Ali Taj, Charagh Hasan Hasrat, Hafeez Jalandhari, Muhammad Din Taseer and Akhtar Shirani in the city had made Lahore one of the leading literary centres of India. All these academics and litterateurs were very friendly in exchanging ideas and opinions with younger writers and students. Faiz got himself actively involved in the literary circles of Lahore. As he related, "I have not learnt much in college classrooms but the proximity with these elderly poets and writers and their affection and guidance helped me learn a lot. They would fondly express kindness to me in their meetings and more often than not, I would gain knowledge in them."[4]

The anti-British activities of Bhagat Singh and his revolutionary colleagues motivated quite a few students to join the underground militant groups. Faiz's close friend Khursheed Anwar was one of them. He had perfected the art of assembling a bomb in the college laboratory and had supplied a few bombs to his militant friends. He was arrested and jailed. It was only because of the influence of his well-connected family that his conviction was revoked. The intelligence personnel had also questioned Faiz in this connection. Though Anwar was his dear friend, Faiz was completely in the dark about his militant activities. He was also not aware that Anwar was an expert 'bomb maker'. The authorities were convinced of Faiz's innocence in the matter and he was left alone. Subsequently, Khursheed Anwar said goodbye to militancy and got hooked to music. Now Faiz started spending his evenings in Anwar's drawing room where his father Khwaja Firozuddin would invite leading masters of classical music to exhibit their talent. At these concerts Faiz got the opportunity to listen to great artistes such as Ustad Tawakkal Husain Khan, Ustad Abdul Waheed Khan, Ustad Aashiq Ali Khan and Chhote Ghulam Ali. These music sessions helped to fashion his silky poetic style in a more musical vein.

Faiz would spend summer vacations in the company of his elder brother or his friend Khursheed Anwar at different hill stations. Sometimes it would be Srinagar, at other times, Dharamshala where her eldest stepsister Bibi Gul was living. Her husband, barrister Shujauddin was a major in the British army. On some occasions, Faiz would also go to Lyallpur, where the residence of another sister was located. It was in Lyallpur that Faiz met Bari (Alig) and some other like-minded people. At hill stations Faiz would spend most of his time wandering in the wooded area appreciating the beauty of nature. He and his friend Khursheed Anwar were also passionate about listening to music on the gramophone. Bibi Gul had recalled, "They would play records on the gramophone. If Anwar did not like any record he would break it. They liked classical songs the most." Faiz and Anwar had also appeared for the ICS examination. Faiz could not take the entire examination because he suffered from a bout of cholera. Anwar, however, topped the merit list. Nevertheless, he declined to join the British service. When Faiz was in the fourth year of graduation, his father died. Faiz wrote to Sher Muhammad from Sialkot, "Your Faiz is now an orphan."

The significant feature of the second *mushaira* that was held in the college, when Faiz was a student there, was that instead of the *misra'e tarah* theme, Muhammad Iqbal, was given to the young poets. Faiz wrote a poem and bagged the first prize. Faiz was an active member of the Students' Federation when Iqbal returned home after participating at the Round Table Conference. Faiz and his friends arranged a reception for Iqbal. Sufi Tabassum asked Faiz to recite his award-winning poem on Iqbal on the occasion. Faiz was hesitant because of the presence of the famous poet. On the insistence of his teacher, however, he recited the poem, which Iqbal appreciated. The poem is included in Faiz's first anthology.

Having completed graduation, Faiz got enrolled for Masters in English. He, however, became quite irregular in attending lectures. Rather than concentrating on the prescribed text books, he would pay particular attention to reading other books. His teachers were aware of his proficiency and erudition in English language and literature. Prof. Dickens was supposed to teach English Literature of the Nineteenth Century. He did not have his heart in the assigned paper. He would often ask Faiz to deliver the lecture in his place, which Faiz did quite competently. Another professor, Harish Chand Katapalia would also ask Faiz frequently to engage his classes. Prof. Bukhari, nevertheless, was a very strict disciplinarian. He would always be present for his lectures. Though Faiz could not achieve anything exceptional in the Masters examination, he was a more accomplished scholar of English language and literature than those who found themselves in the merit list. Soon after, Faiz also took a Masters in Arabic literature from Oriental College, Lahore.

Faiz eagerly searched for a job as the death of his father had brought about deterioration in the financial condition of his family. Having struggled for about a year, he got the lectureship in English in the Muhammadan Anglo-Oriental College, Amritsar. This proved a defining moment for Faiz and his poetry. Sahabzada Mahmood-uz-Zafar was the Principal of the College. He had studied in England where he got involved in the Progressive Movement that had its sway across Europe. Ideologically, the Movement had Left leanings. The other significant man of letters on the staff of the college was Muhammad Din Taseer who, very soon, was destined to be Faiz's brother-in-law. Nevertheless, most of his colleagues noted that the young poet was given to brooding in silence. It was the romantic phase of Faiz's poetry. He was still nursing the memory of his first sweetheart from Sialkot. He would spend his spare time wandering aimlessly in the bazaars of Amritsar. At this point in time, Mahmood-uz-Zafar's wife, Rashid Jehan (her real name was Rashida, the feminine form but she was popularly called Rashid) had reached Amritsar. She was a medical doctor by profession and had studied in England and Russia. She was also a committed Marxist. When she got to know that Faiz was a poet, she asked him to recite some of his poems. Having listened to his poems, she realised that the young poet was intensely in love with someone who either did not reciprocate his love or the two lovers were separated for some other reason. She made Faiz realise, "Be free from this snare of love. What mess you got yourself involved into? This is a worthless venture. The kinds of sufferings people undergo the world over are much more severe. This love affair of yours is an insignificant issue." Faiz was thunderstruck. A new viewpoint to look at the affairs of life is visible before him. As he related later that she "taught me that one's personal grief is of no consequence. She made me broaden my vision and look at the miseries of the people of the world, the sufferings of our own people, and the deprivations of the people of our country. She counselled me to think about the misfortunes of impoverished people. Reflecting only about one's own being is mere selfishness."

Dr. Rashid Jehan gave Faiz the *Communist Manifesto* and asked him to read it attentively. Having read the *Manifesto*, Faiz did not remain the same person as he was before its reading. He underwent an intellectual revolution and started looking at life and its phenomena with a new point of view which was more realistic and humane. The focus of his poetry shifted from romantic to the realistic, from his sweetheart to the afflictions of the world.

## (II)

The history of the Progressive Writers Movement (PWM) in the Indian subcontinent is officially traced from its inaugural meeting in Lucknow held on April 9-10, 1936 in which a Progressive Writers Association (PWA) was established. Nevertheless, there were quite a few events and movements both in India and Europe that had come about prior to the Lucknow meet and prepared the ground for Indian writers to establish an organ for promoting progressive ideas in literature. In Europe, the spread of progressive ideas corresponded with the Age of Reason and Industrial Revolution in the seventeenth century. The orthodox elements in collaboration with the agents of the Church, however, posed stiff opposition to rational and scientific forces for quite a while. With the collapse of the Holy Roman Empire, the peddlers of organised religion were marginalised in many European countries. The French Revolution put the values such as liberty, equality and fraternity on the political agenda of responsible governments. The rise of nationalist states and democracy as the preferred form of government dealt a heavy blow to the theory of divine right and theocracy. The movement of secularism with its emphasis on separation of political and religious spheres, agnosticism and atheism formed the core of a modern progressive culture with Man being the standard of everything–social, political and economic. The ascendancy of socialist ideas during the nineteenth century, in particular, the publication of the *Communist Manifesto* in 1848, provided the real fillip to the progressive ideas. The Bolshevik Revolution in Russia was a momentous event that had brought into focus the power of the working class. Nonetheless, the rise of fascist forces in Italy, Germany and in Spain threatened all that was progressive and humane. The victory of the Allied Powers in the First World War, instead of curbing the reactionary and militant forces, led to the rise of Nazism in Germany. It was an alarming development and it was with the intention of countering the ideas of Nazism and Fascism, that the intelligentsia in Europe settled on organising the progressive writers and artists. Sajjad Zaheer states in his memoirs, *Roshnai*, that Left leaning intellectual and writer Ralph Fox was the guiding force in the establishment of an organisation of the progressive writers in London.

One need not be apologetic about the linkages between Marxism and the PWM. The Marxist literary theory has been one of the most outstanding theoretical models that has influenced the leading litterateurs the world over. Literature, the Marxists believe, largely reflects the social realities of its environs. It mirrors the socio-political, economic and cultural institutions that help create the literary works in the first place. The Marxist literary critics also believe that literature itself is a social institution and in that respect it has a definite ideological function to play. The nature of the ideology is, of course, determined by the worldview of the litterateur. In the opinion of Terry Eagleton, the Marxist literary critic and cultural theorist: "Marxist criticism is not merely a 'sociology of literature', concerned with how novels get published and whether they mention the working class. Its aim is to explain the literary work more fully; and this means a sensitive attention to its forms, styles and meanings. But it also means grasping those forms, styles and meanings as the product of a particular history."[5]

One of the issues that had been of considerable significance in the classical Marxist literary criticism was the evaluation of the 'political leaning' of a literary work that determined whether the essential values intertwined in the work were progressive or retrograde and conservative. Another aspect that came under scrutiny was the class constructs that got illustrated in the piece of literature. The truly progressive literature was the one that depicted socialist realism which according to the classical Marxist literary theory was the highest kind of literature. Socialist realism essentially underscored the struggles of the working classes towards social change, exemplified by a classless, egalitarian social order. These were the ideas that dominated Marxist literary criticism in the late nineteenth century and were respected even at the beginning of the twentieth century in Russia. Later, the Marxist literary critics all over Europe altered these ideas by recognising that literature reflects both personal insights and external influences of a writer's social setting. Consequently, the Marxist aesthetics converges the application of Marxist dialectics to literary and cultural spheres, in particular those aspects that concern talent, beauty and exhilarating style of expression. In brief, the Marxist aesthetics upholds the primacy of economic and social conditions that have an effect on almost all areas of the life of a writer or artist. Literature or art, therefore, should not only portray the social conditions honestly but should also ask for a change for the better.

In India, the spread of scientific, rational, secular, democratic and progressive ideas was ironically an offshoot of British imperialism. The social reform and educational movements, both among Hindus and Muslims were started by those who were directly or indirectly exposed to the Western ideas of democracy and rationalism. Later, the rise of nationalism and struggle for freedom of the country were also by-products of colonial rule. Most historians in India make readers believe that the freedom struggle was solely kept going by the Indian National Congress. Similarly, the historians of Pakistan give the entire credit of the anti-British movement to the Muslim League. These are dishonest assessments of the freedom movement of the Indian subcontinent. In the post-1917 period, many young Indians were deeply attracted and drawn to socialist ideas and revolutionary zeal. The inception of the Communist Party of India in 1925 and thereafter a robust trade union movement under the leadership of the communists were significant landmarks in the history of anti-colonialism. The Left movement was not only tremendously anti-British, it also contributed substantially to promote, nurture and spread the enlightened ideas among Indians. The PWM was a logical corollary of the emergence of socialist ideas in India.

The first tangible suggestion, that literature should be the vehicle to disseminate anti-feudal, anti-orthodox and anti-patriarchal ideas, was the publication of *Angarey* (Burning Coals), an anthology of Urdu short stories in 1932. Sajjad Zaheer, besides contributing a story also edited the collection while Ahmed Ali, Mahmood-uz-Zafar and Dr. Rashid Jehan were the other contributors. *Angarey* generated intense heat as the orthodox Indians assailed it for its bold and spirited ideas. The British rulers in due course banned it "for hurting the religious susceptibilities of a section of the community," and also for its political radicalism and alleged obscenity. All the contributors were educated in Europe where they were drawn towards radical ideas and the literary avant-garde movements that had their impact in Britain, France and other European countries. The ban of *Angarey* did not perturb those behind the book. Ahmed Ali and Mahmood-uz-Zafar established the League of Progressive Authors in Allahabad in April 1933, which was the precursor of the Progressive Writers Association. The Association was first established in London where Indians studying in British Universities and inspired by the leftist progressive ideas came together to create an association of Indian Writers. So, Sajjad Zaheer, Mulk Raj Anand and Jyotimaya Ghosh drafted a manifesto which inter alia stated: "Radical changes are taking place in Indian society...We believe that the new literature of India must deal with the basic problems of our existence today—the problems of hunger and poverty, social backwardness, and political subjection. All that drags us down to passivity, inaction and un-reason we reject as reactionary. All that arouses in us the critical spirit, which examines institutions and customs in the light of reason, which helps us to act, to organise ourselves, to transform, we accept as progressive." Subsequently, Sajjad Zaheer and Mulk Raj Anand attended the International Congress for the Defence of Culture that was held in Paris on June 26, 1935. The major thrust of the Congress was to uphold freedom of expression and to draw attention to the interrelationship between art and society. On returning to India, Sajjad Zaheer visited Zafar and Rashid Jehan in Amritsar a few months before the Lucknow

Conference. The duo introduced him to Faiz. It was the first meeting between the two.

Zaheer had the intention of meeting the litterateurs of Punjab and explore the possibility of establishing the PWA. Lahore was the hub of literary activities and Faiz personally knew almost all the notable poets and writers of the city. On his suggestion, the four of them reached Lahore. Mian Iftikharuddin, a well-heeled and enlightened friend of Faiz, made arrangements for their stay at his residence. The next evening, twenty prominent litterateurs came together to consider the role of the writers and poets in the rapidly changing socio-political conditions of India and insist on disseminating progressive ideas through literature. The prominent among those who participated were Mian Bashir, Maulana Charagh Hasan Hasrat, Vaqar Anbalavi, Maulana Abdul Majeed Salik, Sufi Ghulam Mustafa Tabassum and Firozuddin Mansur. Faiz, Rashid Jehan and Sajjad Zaheer emphasised the need for an organisation of the truly progressive writers. Subsequent to a keenly debated prolonged session, the participants arrived at the decision to establish the PWA that would have the following aims and objectives:

1. Literature should reflect social realities. Realism has to be the underpinning of literature.
2. To oppose British imperialism and struggle for independence should also be the aim of writers and intellectuals.
3. The language of literature should be such that the common people can understand it. Simple language should be preferred even at the cost of artistic sophistication.
4. Society should be freed from superstitions. Common people should be unchained from blind faith and irrational notions.

Sufi Ghulam Mustafa Tabassum was elected the Secretary of the PWA while Faiz was chosen as the Secretary of its Punjab branch. Thereafter, the first all India conference of the PWA was held in Lucknow on April 9-10, 1936. Premchand presided over it. Faiz attended it. In his remarkable presidential address Premchand observed:

There have been quite a few definitions of literature. In my opinion, however, its best definition is "criticism of life", be it in the form of articles, short stories or poetry. It must do appraisal of our life...

I have no hesitation to state that I, like other things, weigh art on the scale of utility. No doubt, the purpose of art is to reinforce discernment of beauty and it serves as the key to our spiritual contentment. Nonetheless, there is no discerning connotative or spiritual contentment that does not have a utilitarian dimension. Contentment in itself is a thing of utility and from the same thing, from the point of view of utility, we get contentment as well as grief. The redness of the sky at twilight is, without doubt, a lovely spectacle, however, if the redness covers the sky during the months of June-July, it cannot be reason of joy for it announces the impending drought.

We have to alter the criterion of beauty. Till now, its criterion has been pro-rich and debauch. Our artiste would prefer to be in the company of the rich. His existence hinged on their patronage and, therefore, the purpose of art was to explicate and explain their pleasures and pains, their melancholies and desires, their conflicts and enmities. His eyesight would turn towards seraglios and bungalows. Huts and ruins were not fit for his attention. He would believe that these were outside the extent of humanity. Art was the name of a limited view worshipping of beauty, the constructions of words, the fastening of thoughts. There was no ideal of life, no sublime purpose of living...

If we read the reports of international conferences of writers then we will realise that there is no educational, economic, historical and psychological issue which has not been deliberated upon in those forums. On the contrary, if we look at our stash of knowledge then we feel ashamed of our lack of knowledge. We believe that an alert disposition and a swift writing prowess alone are enough for creating literature. The reason for the low standard of our literature is this perception. We have to raise the standard of our knowledge so that it can better serve our community. It must procure that position in the community that it deserves. It should deliberate upon every walk of life. We should not be complacent on partaking the leftovers of other

> languages and literatures but we must ourselves contribute to them. We must select our area of interest as per our natural inclination and then attain mastery in that area.
>
> Our aim is to create such an environment in the country wherein the desired literature can be created and flourished. We want that our associations get established in the centres of literature where there should take place proper discussions on the trends of literature, articles should be read out, there should be seminars and criticisms. Then alone the kind of environment would emerge in which the renaissance of literature could happen. We intend to establish such associations in every state and of every language so that our message gets disseminated in every language.
>
> This will be a mistake to think that it is our invention. The collective emotions do rage in the hearts of the litterateurs of the country. Natural surroundings and the prevalent conditions have already sowed the seeds of such ideas in each language of India. Their sprouts appear here and there. To irrigate them and to make their ideal stronger is our goal.[6]

The PWM was certainly the most dominant movement in Urdu literature. Under its auspices, the poets, fiction writers and literary critics contributed to Urdu literature and quite a few excellent works of poetry and fiction. Most litterateurs associated with the PWA were committed to put an end to British imperialism and ideologically they were inspired by the ideals of Marxism. It was through the works of the progressive writers that the slogan *Inquilab Zindabad* (long live revolution) became the legendary catch phrase of the Indian freedom struggle. Though the PWM was supposed to be brought about in all Indian languages, the Urdu poets and writers were far more unswerving in keeping it going than their counterparts in other languages. The progressive poets and fiction writers broke free from the classical mould and its conformist feudal values. They also questioned the soundness of conventional wisdom particularly the one deeply embedded in religiosity. They did not abandon the indubitable aesthetic values, as many critics of the movement have alleged. They only insisted that the aesthetic values were not necessarily the ones cherished and promoted by the feudal aristocracy. The beauty, serenity and enthralment could also be situated among the workers, peasants, the have-nots and their dingy dwellings. When the PWM was launched, India was largely feudal but a small class of the Indian capitalists was also emerging with its odious tendency to reduce everything, including art and culture, to a commodity. The progressive writers, therefore, had also to preserve the aesthetic values that were seriously threatened by the rising commercial order. In this respect, the progressives had to wage a four-fold fight–first, the political struggle against British imperialism, second, the battle against the feudal aristocracy, third, the crusade against religious obscurantism and fourth, the tussle against the emerging commercialism.

The progressive writers also brought about striking changes in form, style and diction of Urdu literature. Though, the primacy of ghazal was challenged earlier by the litterateurs associated with Sir Syed's Aligarh Movement, notably Altaf Husain Hali, the progressive writers consolidated it further by laying emphasis on the genre of *nazm*. They made creative experiments in the rhyming pattern with wonderful results, introduced new forms of poetry such as free verse, allegorical poems, long-thematic poems and sonnets. They also unfettered Urdu poetry from traditional chains of meters it was confined to by the preceding poets. Their contribution to enrich Urdu vocabulary by adding to its lexicon countless ordinary words, which were an essential part of the common people's speech, was mammoth. They also assigned new connotations to the traditional words, terms and set-phrases that were excessively used in the traditional poetry. In the case of Faiz, the archetypal darling or sweetheart of traditional Urdu poetry who never appeared within the reach of the poet/lover and his love, almost as a rule, had to remain unrequited, gets transformed into socio-political revolution that the revolutionary/poet looks forward to meet with the enthusiasm of a lover. Similarly, night does not mean really a dark spell of separation in which the lover forlornly remembers the beloved; in progressive poetry as well as fiction it epitomises the period of oppression/colonialism and injustice. For that reason dawn, morning and sunshine mean the arrival of revolution with its indispensable features of justice, egalitarianism and prosperity of all. There are many more illustrations that can be cited. The significant point is that the progressive poets and fiction writers have endowed exquisite aesthetic standing to the words of common speech. Thus, the literature they have produced, though born out of political turmoil and social vicissitude, has a fresh appeal not only for the so-called upper echelons of society but also for the common men.

The PWM attracted some of the finest poets and fiction writers that the Urdu language produced. Besides Faiz and Sajjad Zaheer, Makhdoom Mohiuddin, Majaz Lakhnavi, Sardar Jafri, Sahir Ludhianvi, Majrooh Sultanpuri, Kaifi Azmi, Jan Nisar Akhtar, Ahmed Nadeem Qasmi, Moin Ahsan Jazbi, Wamiq Jaunpuri, Habib Jalib and Ahmed Faraz were the leading poets associated with the Movement. Though, Raghupati Sahay Firaq Gorakhpuri and Josh Malihabadi were rather senior and well-established names in Urdu poetry, they felt proud to be a part of the PWA. So far as the domain of fiction was concerned, the PWM produced the finest fiction writers in the history of Urdu fiction. Premchand, who presided over the first annual conference of the PWA had been a Gandhian all his life but, as Carlo Cupola pointed out, in the last years of his life he was rather disillusioned with Gandhism as regard to fighting British imperialism, eradication of poverty, caste and community prejudices and the overall plight of Indians. It was for this reason he whole-heartedly welcomed the ideas of the PWM and agreed to preside over the first annual session of the PWA. The other short story writers and novelists that the PWM brought into being included Ismat Chughtai, Krishan Chander, Rajinder Singh Bedi, Sa'adat Hasan Manto, Khwaja Ahmed Abbas, Ahmed Nadeem Qasmi et al. Urdu fiction, because of the creative contributions of these stalwarts could achieve a reasonable degree of respectability that enabled it to be placed together with the best fiction works of other languages. Equally outstanding were the works of the literary critics that helped elucidate the ideals of the PWM and lent a hand to the common reader to appreciate interrelationships between life and literature. In this category the names such as Majnu Gorakhpuri,

Akhtar Husain Raipuri, Ehtesham Husain, Muhammad Hasan, Zoe Ansari, Dr. Abdul Alim, Sibte Hasan, Mumtaz Husain and Qamar Rais have been the most prominent.

Commenting on the progressive movement Faiz observed: "In this school (progressive movement) the first lesson we learnt was that to think of separating oneself from the world is, in the first place, useless. This is so because the experiences around us necessarily affected us. The self of a human being, despite all its loves, troubles, joys and pains, is a tiny, limited and humble thing. The measure of the vastness of life is the whole universe. Thus the agony of love and the agony of time are two aspects of one experience." In the post-1935 period, Faiz's poetry presents a fine fusion of romantic lyricism and social commitment. The outstanding feature of Faiz's poetry is the kind of diction he employs to convey his socio-political message. The words are beautiful and charming and the pitch is soft and mellifluous. In this respect he has achieved a unique status among all his progressive contemporaries who, more often than not, seem to be struggling to maintain a creative balance between the demands of poetry and significance of the message. This quality has been one of the major reasons for Faiz's unprecedented popularity.

Looking at the relationship between ideology and literature Faiz said: "Various questions have been raised about poetry and literature at various points of time." The critics of the progressive movement would frequently ask should literature have any correlation with any ideology? For them there should not be. For Faiz, "Every poet is committed to some kind of ideology. It actually means from what perspective he looks at the world and how does he find it. I am also committed to an ideology; however, the question of writing poetry keeping in mind your ideology does not arise. When a thought stirs the heart and gets absorbed in the self of the poet then alone it takes the shape of poetry." For Faiz progressivism meant that a poet or a fiction writer should have a clear awareness about the environs he was located in. "Facing up to the grave problems (of life) is the indication of progressivism," asserted Faiz. He pointed out that everyone had to live in two worlds. One world represented the environs, the external realities and the second world comprised one's inner self, his mind. The two worlds were filled with many beautiful things and realities; the ugly and repulsive things were also present in the two worlds. Progressivism, according to Faiz, demanded that a writer should candidly bring forth the realities of the two worlds. He believed that the discussion of beauty was necessary; however, ugliness of life should also be expressed. He believed, 'Life is a complex phenomenon. Its simplification is not correct."

Faiz pointed out that the PWM was born at a time when the freedom struggle was underway in the subcontinent because of which the objective, i.e. the independence from the British rule was clear and everyone believed in that. Then there were the destitute, the poor, the suppressed and deprived masses who had been the victims of the exploitation at the hands of the privileged classes for centuries. They were hardly represented in the fine arts and literature of the country. Many were in agreement that the lives and realities of the poor and marginalised people should also be reflected in our literary works. It was hoped that the independence of the country would also herald the end of the economic exploitation of labour. The PWM was also about liberating literature from the sway of fantasy, fairy tales, myths and supernatural phenomena. It insisted on reflection of the realities of life in the works of literature.

Faiz lamented that the political independence of the subcontinent gave rise to a horde of other problems. True democracy and social justice remained distant ideals. The lot of the poor and deprived masses in both countries could not gain anything out of political independence. In fact, their condition deteriorated further. Then, there appeared bitter differences on the issue of linkages between realism and literature. A few litterateurs who were associated with the PWM changed their point of view in the changed political realities of the subcontinent. They completely shunned the illustration of social realities in their poetry and fiction; instead they insisted on exploring the inner self and gave currency to terms such as unconsciousness and sub-consciousness. Their argument was that a creative writer was compelled to write as per the dictates of his unconsciousness or subconsciousness, so there could not be a difference between something that was perceived to be good and another thing that was believed to be bad. This led to a kind of intellectual anarchy in the literary world. Making a distinction between progressive writer and a non-progressive write, Faiz observed that the former would be committed to perceive his society, its history and its future course from a specific viewpoint while the latter would have a complete disconnect with these issues; for him the exploration of his inner self was enough. Faiz, nevertheless, pointed out that it was a false propaganda that a progressive poet would not write romantic poetry. His own poetry in the initial phase was purely romantic and even after he embraced progressivism the romantic tone and tenor remained intact particularly in all his ghazals. A progressive poet would write truthfully about the realities of life that might include romance, beauty, ugliness, moonlight, scorching heat, the earth, the skies, hunger, poverty and so on.

Appraising the reasons for the decline of PWA in Pakistan, Faiz referred to the birth of the Communist Party of Pakistan. The CPP was born in Calcutta during the Second Party Congress of the CPI in 1948. Sajjad Zaheer was elected the General Secretary of the CPP and when he, along with a few comrades like Sibte Hasan and Mirza Ashfaq Ali Beg arrived in Pakistan, they were seen as intruders. Zaheer was one of the most active founders of the PWA and when he was also elected to be the General Secretary of the CPP, the PWA came to be viewed as the literary front of the Communists. Though it was not the reality, many writers who were not Communists distanced themselves from it. In 1948, when Sajjad Zaheer was in hiding and Faiz was the editor of *The Pakistan Times*, a mammoth meeting was held to celebrate Labour Day on May 1. Besides workers and trade union leaders, many poets, writers, journalists and intellectuals were present at the meeting. The exterior and interior of the hall was decorated with red flags of the CPP. Faiz presided over the meeting. An Urdu newspaper, *Ehsan* was resentfully opposed to PWA and progressivism. Attacking the Labour Day meeting it emphasised that a) Islam was ridiculed; b)

Lenin was depicted as a bigger leader than Quaid-e-Azam and c) a group of apostates had emerged. This was a dirty ploy to exploit the unsuspecting masses emotionally. In fact, the anti-people and anti-left religious extremists panicked because of the huge crowd that was present at the meeting and they got engaged in launching quite a few cunning and hideous onslaughts on the PWM.

The same year, a mullah, Wazir Khan, who had been a stooge of the British during the colonial rule, issued a *fatwa* (religious edict) against Faiz. Thereafter, the mullahs of Lahore read out sermons against the members of the PWM in about forty mosques and goaded people to take violent action against the progressive writers and their sympathisers. After a short while, the annual conference of the PWA was held in Lahore. Ahmed Nadeem Qasmi was the Secretary of the Association at that time. Hundreds of people were present in all the sessions and many of them passionately expressed their solidarity with the PWA. Faiz recited his famous qawwali, *Sar-e-Maqtal*, for the first time at the conference. It instantly became a sensation. Though the conference was a great success, a few problems arose within the PWA.

Some of the staunch communists who happened to be associated with PWA became rigid in their ideological position. They would judge every work of literature with a yardstick of socialist realism and if any work was found wanting its creator would be right away declared a reactionary litterateur. Sardar Jafri had adopted a similar practice in the Indian chapter of the PWA when he became its Secretary after Sajjad Zaheer left for Pakistan. Consequently quite a few writers became hostile to the PWA. In 1949, Muhammad Din Taseer a founding member of the PWA and brother-in-law of Faiz revolted against the so-called official line of the Association. N.M. Rashid was ostracised. When Sa'adat Hasan Manto migrated to Pakistan, he too became the victim of hardliners because, as per their estimation, most of his short-stories belonged to the category of soft pornographic writing. Though Manto was only a year younger than Faiz, he was his student at MAO College, Amritsar. Faiz had a great regard for him and for his brilliant stories. He, therefore, expressed his unhappiness over the unjust criticism of

Manto's fiction. Then the hardliners targeted Muhammad Iqbal for his Islamic poetry. At a meeting presided over by Safdar Mir, the Secretary of the PWA, Ahmed Nadeem Qasmi, read out an article against Iqbal's poetry. Faiz objected because he was of the opinion that Iqbal also wrote quite a few poems against imperialism, feudal lords and autocrats. However, he found himself in the minority that dampened his spirits immensely and thereafter he stopped attending the meetings of the PWA. He, however, never left the Association.

Nonetheless, the creation of Pakistan as an Islamic state was the greatest setback to the PWM in the subcontinent but its ill effects were noticed more in Pakistan. The left-leaning intellectuals and litterateurs in that country were rendered vulnerable to the machinations of and at times open violent attacks by the right-wing religious fanatics. The extremists belonging to the Muslim League and Jamat-e-Islami launched a vitriolic hate campaign against those who had links with the PWA. The most deplorable development was the opportunist strategy adopted by some of the poets and writers who were opposed to the PWM right from its inception on ideological grounds. One of its major adversaries was Muhammad Hasan Askari, an emigrant of Indian origin who had pretentions of a connoisseur of the finest literary values, announcing himself an ardent fan of Firaq Gorakhpuri in undivided India. In Islamic Pakistan he showed his true colours by raising the bogey of 'Islamic literature' with the ulterior motive of attacking the members of the PWA for their ideological links with Marxism. His protégé, Salim Ahmed, had taken upon himself the task of deriding the entire literary output of the progressive poets and writers. Faiz, being the most prominent name associated with the PWA was obviously the prime target of these literary fanatics. His renowned poem, *Subh-e-Azadi*: *August 1947,* penned on the eve of partition of the country and that questioned the worth of an independence that caused the massacre of hundreds of thousands of people in the name of religion and had no promise for the millions of miserable masses, would often be cited to prove that Faiz and other progressive poets and writers, had never accepted the movement for Pakistan and the ideology behind it. The arrest of Faiz, Sajjad Zaheer and some other progressive writers in the Rawalpindi Conspiracy Case further weakened the position of the members of the PWA and consequently the attacks on them became more planned and grubby. This point will be addressed later in the context of the Rawalpindi case but the fact remains that the partition of India and the creation of Pakistan as an Islamic state had dealt a heavy blow to the secular, rational and progressive forces from which they have not recovered. The greatness of Faiz was that he suffered humiliation, mental agony, the tribulation of imprisonment but refused to compromise on his ideological commitment.

## (III)

Alys Catherine George was a young, beautiful woman. She arrived in Lahore in 1938 to meet her sister Christobel who was the wife of a famous Urdu poet, Muhammad Din Taseer. Alys had joined the British Communist Party at the age of 16 and thereafter actively participated in left-wing programmes and radical endeavours. She was a familiar face among the circle of leftist intellectuals and was involved in political agitations and protest marches even when she was a teenager. She had also worked in collaboration with the well-known Indian leftists such as Krishna Menon, Iqbal Singh, Mulk Raj Anand and other members of the India League. Though her entire family was ideologically committed to the British Conservative politics, she was a dedicated communist.

Faiz met Alys at Taseer's residence and got to know her radical views. In her words: "Taseer's home was a meeting place for scholars, writers, poets, journalists, teachers and political workers who gathered during weekends, coming from Lahore, Jullunder and even farther. They stayed the night and beddings were spread in the large, airy drawing-room and talk continued till the early hours on literature, politics and all the subjects near the intellectuals' hearts of those exciting days...And there was Faiz, a teacher at the MAO College, who came regularly, was so silent, reciting poetry when called upon and claiming my early attention."[7]

Faiz was surprised by her extremely mature political attitude when she discussed the iniquities of unbridled capitalism with him. She said that the capitalist economic order was abominable because it thrived on exploitation of the working classes and that she hated all forms of exploitation. Faiz was, of course, impressed. On the issue of his marriage to Alys, Faiz pointed out that it was not 'love at first sight' kind of incident. The two kept meeting and exchanging ideas for almost two years before they decided to tie the knot. This sort of prolonged courtship, in those days, was unheard of even among the most Westernised sections of Indians. Faiz's mother and sisters had earlier suggested the names of quite a few eligible girls but Faiz had turned them down. When he finally made it known that he wanted to marry Alys it was shocking for the members of his family. Nevertheless, his sisters and brothers gave in after a while and ultimately the mother had to accept the choice of her son. Faiz later commented that it was a 'love marriage' in the sense that he had selected his bride against the wishes of his family members.

Alys had agreed to take on all the healthy practices of an eastern family except the veil. On the issue she was rightfully adamant because she believed it was a symbol of woman's repression. The members of Faiz's family had to respect her opposition to the veil. A decision was made that they should get married in Srinagar. The Maharaja of Jammu and Kashmir had offered his summer palace for the wedding ceremony. Faiz at the time was merely a college lecturer and his financial position was not commensurate with the ensuing expenditure of marriage. Alys was well aware of his meagre salary. Yet, she went ahead with the decision of marrying a comrade-poet. Owing to financial constraints, Faiz could not invite all his friends and family members to Srinagar. From the side of the bridegroom only two people were present at the wedding–"Inayat, a younger brother whom I grew to love; Naeem, a communist worker; and the groom. The first thing Faiz did was to show me the wedding ring. I slipped it on. A perfect fit. 'How did you know?' I asked. He slipped it onto his own finger. Another perfect fit. 'The eternity ring', I said. Faiz laughed."[8]

Thus, on October 28, 1941, Sheikh Muhammad Abdullah acted as the *qazi* of the wedding ceremony and signed in that capacity on their marriage certificate. Incidentally, Dr. Muhammad Iqbal had acted as *qazi* when Alys's elder sister Christobel got married to Taseer. Iqbal had added two conditions to the marriage certificate that Taseer would not take another wife in the presence of his first wife and that Christobel would also have the right to seek a divorce from her husband. When the news of such conditions was made known widely the orthodox mullahs and their henchmen had attacked Iqbal for inserting 'un-Islamic' conditions in the marriage certificate. Nevertheless, many years later, when the personal laws were formulated during Ayub Khan's regime, they had, more or less, similar clauses. Alys observes: "The contract made our marriage monogamous and Faiz had delegated his right of divorce to me."[9] Faiz willingly agreed to incorporate those conditions in his marriage certificate. In the evening a *mushaira* was arranged as part of the celebration in which Josh and Majaz also participated.

Three days later the newly-wedded couple was back in Lahore. Alys had donned the traditional wedding dress of a bride for the imperative meeting with Faiz's mother and other female relatives. When her mother-in-law saw her in the guise of an eastern bride she enthusiastically blessed her and suggested Kulsum as her Islamic name. Salima, the eldest daughter of Alys and Faiz, reminisced: "But there's a story behind how my mother came to be named Kulsum. When the *nikah* was to take place she was informed she had to assume a Muslim name. She had already selected a couple of fashionable names. She wanted to be called Rehana or Suraiya or Shehnaz, but when it came to brass tacks my Dadi, whom we used to call Bebejee, had already selected Kulsum which my mother was not very happy about. But for a smooth passage to the signing of the *nikah* she agreed to be called Kulsum; she never used the name after that till *Dast-i-Saba* appeared." In this context Alys states: "The Quran was put into my hands, and my venerable mother-in-law blessed me after her own fashion and named me Kulsum."[10] The second anthology of Faiz's poems, *Dast-e-Saba,* is dedicated to Kulsum. Salima was born in Delhi in 1943 and the second daughter, Moneeza, in 1945 in Shimla. Salima is an artiste and had also served as the Principal of the National College of Arts, Lahore. Moneeza is a senior producer with Pakistan Television.

As the later events would prove, Alys turned out to be an extremely devoted wife, a courteous daughter-in-law and an affectionate mother. Bibi Gul, Faiz's eldest sister, recalled that Alys succeeded in winning over the hearts of everyone in the family in a short while. It was her love and kindness for everyone that helped her become an endearing member of her husband's family. Comparing both parents, Salima observed that they were as different as 'chalk and cheese.' Alys would be vociferous having a binary approach. For her everything would be either black or white. On the contrary for Faiz things appeared in shades of grey. According to Salima, "She (Alys) was always the life and soul of a party and had tremendous energy, while with Abba it was very sedate and the highs and lows were well kept under covers. I also think that he enjoyed the fact that she would do and say things that were very audacious and from which he got a lot of vicarious pleasure." The younger daughter Moneeza's earliest memories about her mother belong to the period when she was five years old and Faiz was taken to prison. She recollected: "I can hear the doors clanging and the shouts and my mother screaming when he was arrested. I can hear it, I can't see it. And I remember her crying. I think I was five. And I remember the long train rides to Hyderabad (jail) and back. I remember the cell, sometimes. Of going inside and coming out. I remember sitting outside. I remember waiting, I remember coming home alone... Mama was always upfront, a nice version of blunt. I can't for the life of me think of another word. That's probably what I have imbibed from her. I do not regret it though many people tell me I should. I'll be damned if I do. I am upfront. Say whatever you want to say and get it over with. She would not mince her words. 'This is not the time for this, do this, don't do this'. And she would mother him (Faiz), to some extent, and bully him." Alys withstood all sorts of problems and tribulations particularly during the period when Faiz was in jail. The remarkable fortitude and endurance that she had displayed for the major part of her married life appear far more appreciable considering the fact that she was a foreigner and had to bring up two small daughters all alone when her husband was in jail and the religious fanatics would torment her by shouting degrading slogans against her husband outside her house and would also attack her dignity by calling her 'daughter of Clive.'

## (IV)

A year before getting married, Faiz had shifted base from Amritsar to Lahore where he joined Hailey College as lecturer in English. The Second World War was well under way. Hitler and his racist ideology, Nazism, had threatened the very foundation of humanity. Though the players in the war were the Western powers, it had put tremendous pressure on the Afro-Asian countries as most of these nations were the colonies of the major European powers and for that reason the point of view of the enslaved population of the colonised countries vis-à-vis the war did not count. India was the most prized possession (the jewel in the Crown) of the British. The vast resources of India as well as its huge population were blatantly exploited by the British to counter the challenge of the Axis Powers. The colonial masters had started a major drive to recruit Indian youths in the British army and deploy them in various theatres of war. There was a 'no-war-pact' in place between Germany and the USSR in the initial years of the war. This had put the communists and leftist intellectuals of India in a quandary.

Despite the fact that the Communist Party was banned in India, its members had always been active against British imperialism. Their underground activities were, to a great extent, directed against the imperialistic interests of the foreign rulers. The position of the USSR, in those days was that of an ideological guide and inspirer of the communists of the world and under the instructions of the Communist Party of the Soviet Union, the members of the CPI and the fellow-travellers had declared that the Second World War was an imperialistic war and the Indian comrades should oppose the British of deploying Indian soldiers on the war fronts and exploiting Indian resources to pay for the war measures. The PWM too took a stand to oppose the British in its war efforts. It was at this point of time that Makhdoom Mohiuddin had penned his famous poem—*janey waley sipahi se poochho wo kahan ja raha hai*— (ask the departing soldier where is he headed to) that was later used by Bimal Roy in a film. Whether the Indian communists and the intellectuals associated with PWM were justified in taking an anti-British stance in the initial phase of the Second World War or not is a matter of heated controversy that falls outside the purview of this book. On their part, the supporters of the PWM, however, maintained that achieving freedom from the enslavement of the British was a more pressing objective than helping the foreign rulers fight fascism. The British rulers had arrested thousands of communists, fellow-travellers and their sympathisers and put them behind bars.

Nevertheless, the nature of the war abruptly changed for the CPI, the fellow-travellers and the PWM when Hitler, suddenly attacked Russia on June 22, 1941. Consequently, a month later the Anglo-Russian Alliance was formed with the objectives of mutual military aid and action against Germany. Now, for the communists of the world 'the imperialist war' all of a sudden had turned into a 'people's war' against fascism. The Indian communists too made up their minds to cooperate with the British rulers in their war enterprise against the Axis Powers. By extending a helping hand to the British they were, in a roundabout way, helping the Soviet Union. In the changed circumstances, the British rulers released all the communists and their sympathisers from jails who in turn threw themselves into the British preparations for the war. Many communists and fellow-travellers had made themselves available for the military service and other allied positions.

This is another issue of controversy whether the communists and their sympathisers were guilty of betraying the cause of national independence by cooperating with the foreign masters during the Second World War or were they rightly justified in doing so. In India, the so-called nationalist historians belonging to the Hindu Right and the ideologically-muddled Congress members never lose any opportunity in disparaging the communists for their cooperation with the British during the Second World War. The Hindu Right or for that matter the Muslim communalists associated with the Muslim League, do not deserve any response for their claptrap because they had always been stooges of the foreign masters during the national struggle. So far as the Congress members are concerned they must be reminded that Mr. M.K. Gandhi, who later came to be known as the Mahatma, too had cooperated with the British during the First World War on the logic that the Central Powers led by Germany were a greater threat to humanity than the Allied Powers whose command was in the hands of the British. When the First World War broke out, Gandhi was in England where he immediately called a meeting of Indian friends to raise an ambulance unit to help the British. Soon after, he returned to India. When the British Viceroy invited Gandhi during the course of the war in April 1918, to elicit his support for the British against the Central Powers, he unreservedly agreed not only to cooperate but actively recruit Indians to fight for the British. In a leaflet, *Appeal for Enlistment,* Gandhi stated: "To bring about such a state of things we should have the ability to defend ourselves, that is, the ability to bear arms and to use them...If we want to learn the use of arms with the greatest possible dispatch, it is our duty to enlist ourselves in the army."[11] The statement reveals that the tallest leader of the Congress had not only supported the colonial masters passionately in their war efforts but also compromised on his much-trumpeted principle of non-violence.

The Communists were at least justified in extending co-operation to the British during the Second World War because, a) opposing Hitler's Nazism and Mussolini's Fascism, the most monstrous ideologies the 'human' mind could ever produce' was an obligation of all reasonable people of the world and b) unlike Gandhi, the communists never declared non-violence an article of faith. This bit about the Second World War has been necessary to be referred to here because Faiz's detractors often cite his service in the British army as a confirmation of his betrayal to the cause of the Indian freedom struggle. Faiz made it plain that he joined the army because he loathed fascism and had always been restive to counter the menace. The Anglo-Russian front against the fascist forces made available the opportunity and he seized it. In 1942, he said adieu to the lectureship of Hailey College and went to Delhi to appear before the army selection panel. First he was interviewed by Brigadier Ivor Jehu, who was less than impressed by Faiz's credentials and had reservations about allowing him to join the army. Subsequently, Faiz presented himself before Colonel Frank Messervy (nicknamed the Bearded Man) who revealed the real reason for Brigadier Jehu's reluctance. The Colonel informed Faiz that in the secret file there was a noting which said, "You are an advanced communist." Faiz quipped, "Are there retarded communists too?" Colonel Messervy did not react to the jibe. He kept his cool and asked, "Are you an advanced communist?" Faiz stated the fact, "I'm not a member." It clinched the issue and Faiz was selected as Captain to serve in the army's department for public relations.

Why did Faiz opt for the British military service when India was still a colony? It is worthwhile to make an allowance for one of his letters that sheds some light on the issue:

> "Prior to the Second World War, when the Nazi and Fascist movements had their sway in Europe under Hitler and Mussolini, the enlightened intellectuals of the world including Indian progressive writers, made up their minds to face up to this global menace. However, the imperialist powers like Britain and the USA, instead of pinning down this storm, kept egging on Hitler and Mussolini. As a result of it, the demon of fascism embarked on gobbling up one weaker nation after another. When countries like Ethiopia, Spain, Austria and Czechoslovakia were finished, the imperialist and capitalist countries thought that the hurricane would head towards the Soviet Union and thus the real rival of their (politico-economic) system would be wiped out from the face of the earth. The strategy boomeranged and their houses got ignited by their own lamp. In the beginning this war was between two imperialistic powers and we were not directly involved in it. Nevertheless, the fascist armies having destroyed Europe in the West turned their aggressive march towards Africa

reaching the borders of Egypt and on the other side having destroyed large parts of Soviet Russia reached the Caucasus. Also, the Japanese fascists joined the war and after conquering Burma reached the gate of India. Then, the war for us did not remain any more a war between two distant adversaries but its flames reached our home. At that point of time, I felt that having a neutral stand would be an impossibility and for the defence of our land as well as for the continued existence of human civilisation one must, to the best of his abilities, fight against fascism. I, therefore, like many like-minded friends, joined the army. In those days, many short-sighted Asian nationalists that included Congress leaders too, were stuck in a pipe-dream that the Japanese army would free them from the British control and, therefore, instead of supporting the Allied Powers, the British rule should be opposed. In India, this wave was very strong. Its reason was that in the aftermath of the British army in Burma, the Japanese caught hold of many Indian prisoners of war. The majority of these prisoners, under the patronage of the Japanese, joined the Indian National Army and because its command was in the hands of the famous Congress leader, Subhas Chandra Bose, the Congress had proclaimed him as the harbinger of national independence. On the other hand, some Indian fugitives were constantly propagating through German and Japanese radio broadcasts that rebellion against the British and extending support to the Japanese armies was the national duty of every patriotic Indian. In these circumstances, Gandhiji launched the Quit India Movement that added to the mental unrest of the nation. At this point of time the army gave a call, which I accepted. (My responsibilities included providing information and news to the Indian soldiers–in other words publication of military newspapers and journals, planning military programmes for radio etc. Advising the officers of the Indian British High Command on political issues was also part of my duties.)

Faiz had got married barely four months ago. His posting was at the army headquarters in Delhi. He and Alys settled in a house in Karol Bagh. Faiz's job did not stipulate him to go to the war front and actually fight against the enemy. He was entrusted with the responsibility of maintaining public relations with the Indian soldiers deployed on various fronts of the war. As is evident from the letter cited above it was, in essence, the job of keeping the soldiers informed about relevant developments. It involved publication of newspapers and magazines for the army and providing the written material for radio broadcasts. The most significant part of the duties was to give political advice to the High Command of the British Indian Army. In this context, Faiz mentioned that the British officers belonged to the old school and were not open to any new suggestions. They wanted that to keep the morale of the Indian soldiers high they should be motivated by appealing to them to be loyal, to be true to the salt and to keep the reputation of the regiment intact. Faiz was of the opinion that such appeals would not work. He suggested that the emphasis should be on defending the motherland from the German and Japanese tyrants. In this connection, he recommended that some sort of study circle should be established in each unit of the army and the leader of the study circle should be thoroughly informed about political realities. It led to a much prolonged debate among the officers of the High Command. The Commander-in-Chief, Field Marshall Claude Auchinleck accepted the suggestion, however, the Viceroy, Lord Linlithgow did not approve of it. So the suggestion was finally forwarded to London where the British Government gave its consent. Accordingly, a study circle called 'Josh Group' was set up in each unit and the leaders of all these groups were trained suitably. This experiment proved successful and Faiz was honoured with Member of the British Empire (MBE) for it. Faiz argued that the experiment had at least made the Indian soldiers conscious of being loyal to their motherland rather than being loyal to the British.

With the conclusion of the war, the Indian soldiers had rebelled against their British commanders at a few places. First the Air Force units stationed at Jabalpur rebelled and later there was a major revolt in the Indian Navy in Bombay. This frightened the British masters because they had been ruling over India primarily with the support of Indian soldiers of the British Indian Armed

Forces. In order to contain the unrest, the British established a new department, Inter-Services Morale Directorate, within the army. At the time, Faiz was stationed at Rawalpindi that was the Headquarters of the Northern Command. He was summoned to Delhi and was appointed the adviser attached to the newly created department. The Commander-in-Chief was heading the department while Colonel Haq Nawaz was appointed its Deputy Chief. Faiz and Haq Nawaz were entrusted the job of inquiring into the revolt of the naval forces in Bombay. During its trial, Colonel Haq Nawaz who appeared before the court as a representative of the Morale Directorate emphatically justified the grievances of the Indian naval soldiers and officers and affirmed that they did not deserve any punishment. The defence pleader was the famous Congress leader, Pandit Hriday Nath Kunzru. Later, Nawaz found fault with Kunzru's line of argument as he told Faiz that instead of appreciating his pro-Indian stand, Kunzru vehemently attacked him probably because he represented the Armed Forces and was a Muslim.

When the British Government announced the Cabinet Mission Plan, Faiz was asked to address the army officers about the political scenario in India emphasising particularly the mutual distrust between the two major political outfits, the Congress and the Muslim League. When Faiz dictated his lecture to his steno, an Anglo-Indian lady, she naively remarked, "Sir, Mr. Gandhi and Mr. Jinnah don't seem to get on with each other at all." Faiz gently agreed, "No, they don't." Faiz made his presentation before the army officer eliciting the political scenario of the country. He informed the audiences about the Muslim League and its arguments for Pakistan as well as the Congress and its reasoning to oppose the partition of the country. At the end of the lecture, a British Brigadier rose and asked: "Well Mr. Faiz, tell me, what the attitude of the Muslim League towards Pakistan is?" Faiz almost fainted on hearing the query and later wondered "such people had been the masters of our fate."

When Faiz was stationed at Rawalpindi, he met comrade V.D. Chopra who was a prominent communist and had close connections with comrades of foreign origin who had been serving in the army. Once, Chopra told Faiz that he was looking for a safer place for the meetings with other comrades because his own house was constantly under surveillance by the intelligence personnel. He pointed out that Faiz's house could be an ideal rendezvous. Faiz allowed him to use his house for the meetings of the comrades with a rider that personally he would not attend the meetings. Thereafter, quite a few meetings were held at Faiz's house in which Indian, British and American comrades participated. The secret service department reported the meetings to the Deputy Commissioner who was British. He, on some pretext, arrested comrade Chopra and ordered an inquiry into the whole affair. Faiz, even before the inquiry could commence, approached the Brigadier and raised a pandemonium about the high handed behaviour of the Deputy Commissioner. He argued that in the capacity of an army officer, he was within his rights to meet any leader whether he happened to be a member of the Congress, Muslim League or Communist Party. The British Brigadier picked up the phone and reprimanded the Deputy Commissioner severely. Thus, the proposed inquiry died down but Faiz on his part, thereafter never let the comrades use his official residence for their meetings.

The issue of the soldiers and officers of the Indian National Army, who were taken into custody after the end of the war, was also referred to the Inter-Services Morale Directorate when Faiz was attached with it as advisor. For both the Congress and the Muslim League they were heroes. A few top INA officers such as Shahnawaz, Sehgal and Dhillon had become household names in India. Faiz's position on the three INA officers was that they were neither criminals nor heroes. Prior to joining the INA they were absolutely apolitical people. The British stand in the matter was: a) among the prisoners of war belonging to the INA, the ones who had political linkages should be court-martialled and severely punished; b) those who had no political linkages but fought against the British should be punished and c) the ones who did not have any political ambition and who were forced to be part of the INA should be acquitted. Faiz was opposed to this policy. He suggested leniency in dealing with all the members of the INA.

The end of the war also marked the end of the honeymoon between the USSR and the Western powers. Faiz realised this when he was attached to the Northern Command Headquarters at Rawalpindi. The provinces of the North Western Frontier, Sind and Baluchistan were included in the jurisdiction of the Northern Command. Faiz would be occasionally asked to join the secret meetings of the senior army officers. Thus he became privy to the secret future plans of the British to strike at the Soviet Union that they were to execute in collaboration with the USA. The Viceroy, Lord Wavell, reached Rawalpindi in April 1946, to have consultations with the top military officers. After the meeting, the Viceroy went to attend the dinner party at the residence of General Officer of Command, General Thomas Rees. Faiz was also invited to the party. Lord Wavell, commenting on the political situation of India, argued that if Pakistan were to become a reality it would be extremely vulnerable to the northern threat, i.e. aggressive push from the Soviet Union because it would not have any ground depth. It would pose a problem for the British army (the British seriously believed that even after the partition of the subcontinent, they would retain their control over the army) of forming the defence line against the Soviet Union. If the defence line were to be formed somewhere else it would be disastrous from the military point of view. Faiz could easily discern the real intention of the British—to attack the Soviet Union in the name of securing India's northern boundaries. The existence of a socialist state was unacceptable to the Western powers that were committed to capitalism. Their ultimate objective had always been the decimation of the USSR.

The revelation was a rude shock to Faiz. For him it was a case of unabashed treachery because hardly a few months ago the British and the American forces were fighting along with the Soviet forces against the fascists and immediately after the war they were planning to demolish the socialist state. It was quite apparent for Faiz that the British Indian Army would soon adopt a new policy of aggression with which he could not obviously reconcile. He made up his mind to leave the military service and find ways and means to expose the wicked designs of the British and the

Americans against the USSR. He could not be disloyal to the cause of socialism and that made him decide to quit the army. At that time he was Lieutenant Colonel.

## (V)

During the period he was in the army, he could not write much poetry. He had joined the army to fight against fascism but, on account of his busy military schedule, could not express disapproval of the gruesome ideology by way of poetic output except a beautiful poem, *Ae Dil-e-Betab Thaher*, wherein the rise of fascist forces is metaphorically referred to as dense darkness. The first two lines are:

*Teergi hai ke umadti hi chali aati hai*
*Shab ki rug rug se lahoo phoot raha ho jaise*

The darkness keeps pressing on
As if blood is oozing from the veins of night

Besides this poem, during the army service, he did write a few poems and ghazals that included a poem addressed to Gandhi, *Siyasi Leader ke Naam*. He contended that when a poet was personally fighting a war then the inspiration for writing poetry would become a rarity. When he mentally prepared himself to leave the army, he did not inform Alys about it. It was a thorny issue considering that by now he was the father of two little daughters who, at the time, were living in Delhi with their mother. The most pressing problem was that of money. He was not certain what kind of a job he would get after quitting the army or would he get a job at all. Personally, he wanted to rejoin the teaching profession and to explore the possibility he had discussed the issue with the Director of Education, Prof. Chatterjee who was his teacher in Government College, Lahore. Although, Faiz was drawing a monthly salary of Rs. 2500 in the army, he was looking for a job that could give him a minimum of Rs. 500. The college lectureship could not fetch him even that much.

India was about to become independent. However, it was also certain that the country would be partitioned and Pakistan would become a reality. Faiz would naturally find himself in the newly created nation. In these circumstances, Faiz's progressive friend, Mian Iftikharuddin informed him that he had planned to bring out an English daily, *The Pakistan Times*, from Lahore and that Faiz would have to take up its editorship. Faiz got panicky on hearing the proposal. He was reluctant to take upon himself the responsibility of running a daily newspaper because he did not possess even basic knowledge of journalism. He declined to accept the offer. Nevertheless, Mian Iftikharuddin won through as he refused to listen to any of Faiz's arguments. Having failed to convince his friend about his incompetence to run a daily, Faiz left the army to become the founding editor of *The Pakistan Times*. Additionally he was made head of the editorial board of its sister publications, *Imroz*, the Urdu daily and *Lail-o-Nihar*, a political and literary weekly. The first issue of the daily appeared on February 4, 1947. It has been reported that Faiz wrote many of his editorials minutes before the deadline. The main points of a few of his more significant pieces can be cited. Commenting on his editorial competence one of his admirers I.A. Rehman says: "As the editor of *The Pakistan Times*, Faiz often gave his reporters tips about news stories ripe for reporting instead of the reporters informing him of developments worth noting. He also demonstrated an ability to unobtrusively inspire members of his staff to deliver to the best of their abilities."

Faiz, being a fellow-traveller was obviously not in agreement with quite a few ideas that had been in circulation as Gandhism. In his poem addressed to Gandhi (*To a Political Leader*) he had criticised the principle of non-violence that was as dear to the 'political leader' as his religion. Nevertheless, Faiz was not blind to Gandhi's mammoth contribution to the freedom struggle and particularly his endeavours in the last days of his life to save the Muslims from the marauding gangs of Hindu fanatics. Writing on the assassination of Gandhi, Faiz entitled the editorial as "Long Live Gandhiji" and wrote:

"Nearly 25 years ago, Mahatama Gandhi writing a moving editorial on the late C.R. Das in his exquisite English captioned it as "Deshbandhu is dead, long live Deshbandhu!" If we have chosen such a title for our humble tribute to Gandhiji, it is because we are convinced, more than ever before that very few indeed have lived in this degenerate century who could lay greater claim to immortality than this true servant of humanity and champion of the downtrodden. ..The first impact of the shock is slowly spending itself out, and through the murky mist of the mourning and grief a faint light of optimistic expectation that Gandhiji has not died in vain, is glowing. ..At least we can claim at the top of our voice suspicious friends in India that the passing away of Gandhiji is as grievous a blow to Pakistan as it is to India. We have observed distressed looks, seen moistened eyes and heard faltering voices in this vast sprawling city of Lahore to a degree to be seen to be believed. ..The Government of India too seems to have at long last realised that they are sitting on top of a volcano. ..a small incident in Bombay in which a Hindu mob broke open the office of the Anti-Pakistan Front on Saturday and reduced its furnishings to smithereens is, we believe, realisation–though tragically belated–of the fact that Muslims are, after all, not the sinners–not to say the enemies of India. ..Not long ago, at Lucknow India's Deputy Prime Minister, Sardar Patel, while hauling nationalist Muslims, who had assembled there a few days earlier, over the coals, sang a paean of praise for the RSS and the Hindu Mahasabha–the organisation which, alas, produced that worst criminal in history, Nathuram Vinayak Godse. Sardar Patel pandered to their jingoistic vanity by asking the Congress to flirt with them. Paradoxical though it may seem, his chief, Pandit Nehru, while at Amritsar two days prior to the tragedy pricked the RSS and Sabha bubbles in no uncertain manner by describing their politics as doing the greatest harm to the country...If the Government of India would have tried to take some of the conceit and "fire" out of these rabidly communal and militant leaders, maybe Gandhiji would have lived to be 125...We would be less than human if we were to make even the least attempt to exploit Gandhiji's death in furtherance of our co-religionists' interests in India. But we are

> gratefully conscious of the fact that nothing would give greater pleasure to the soul of the illustrious dead than dispensation of justice and fair play to Indian Muslims, which he so passionately preached and for which he laid down his life."[12]

When the rights of the people were denied to them in the name of law and order and national security by the implementation of the notorious Public Safety Act that gave the state vast powers, Faiz criticised the move in an editorial, *What Price Liberty?* :

> There are no halfway houses between liberty and thraldom. The public have to choose and decide whether they are going to permit this and similar inroads on their hard-won freedom or whether they are content to live in daily fear for their freedom and honour. The weapon of the Safety Act that they have placed into the hands of their government is a dangerous weapon and is not a fit thing for children or sadists to play with. It should either be taken back or the people entrusted with it should be taught its proper use. It must be realised that a weapon like this cannot be used properly either by men who are cursed with the vindictiveness of an elephant and the ferocity of a wolf or by men who lack the guts of a rat and the courage of a sparrow.[13]

The secular and nationalist people were naturally opposed to the movement for Pakistan that was being carried on purely communal lines. Nevertheless, the Communists in undivided India, for the reasons best known to them, did not disagree with the Muslim League's bid for the division of the country. Regrettably, Faiz like many comrades did not resist the partition of India. It is hard to swallow how could a party believing in Marxism, for which religious and cultural identities merely constitute the *superstructure*, went along with a campaign that had no other justification except *religious identity* of a section of the Indian population. Although, Faiz lamented the lack of true independence in the 'independence' that turned up for Indians and Pakistanis in mid-August 1947, in his famous poem, *The Dawn of Independence–August 1947,* he, as such, did not take a stand against the division of the country. Commenting on the partition of the subcontinent on religious lines in an editorial (*Progress of a Dream*), Faiz stated that it was a means

"...to end the vertical division that separated the two major peoples of the sub-continent ... by a horizontal division so that the divided halves could each develop an internal harmony that the undivided whole lacked." He added, "The dream is as yet unfulfilled. The division has come but neither half is as yet completely at peace, either with itself or with its neighbour."[14]

He, however, missed the point that the horizontal division of the two major peoples of the subcontinent did not really take place because more Muslims stayed back in India than the population of Pakistan. It was perhaps because the patriotism of a Pakistani editor overpowered the conscience of a sensitive and humanitarian poet. During his first spell of chief editorship from February 4, 1947 to March 1951, Faiz was not the only one to write editorials. There were others too who wrote on the all-consuming issues of this momentous period of the Indian subcontinent. Among the editorials that have been identified as the write-ups of Faiz, his insightful comments deeply ingrained in humanistic values and nationalist fervour are worthy of note. While welcoming the creation of Pakistan on August 15, 1947, he expresses grief over the indiscriminate and barbaric killings of men, women and children in the name of religion. He calls it "a cruel contradiction that the day of joyous thanksgiving is also the day of mourning." In another editorial on the issue of the small Christian minority he confidently envisages that it will enjoy more freedoms in Pakistan than they had in united India. Had he been alive today he would have got a rude shock on knowing the brutal and awfully inhuman manner with which the religious minorities are treated in today's Pakistan.

There exists the so-called 'blasphemy law' in Pakistan which is, more often than not, invoked to eliminate poor and hapless Christians who are first cunningly dragged into some made-up controversy and then sentenced to death for being guilty of irreverence shown to the Prophet of Islam. The inhuman 'blasphemy law' was introduced by the dim-witted and appallingly fanatic dictator, Zia-ul-Haq. Since then, the civil society in Pakistan has been relentlessly campaigning for its abrogation but the mullah-zamindar-military nexus that has been controlling the affairs of Pakistan for long would not allow any government to repeal or alter the draconian law. In recent times, Sherry Rehman, a prominent member of the Pakistan People's Party and one of the few enlightened and secular leaders of the Islamic Republic, had moved a resolution in the national legislature to repeal the blasphemy law. She was particularly moved by the tribulation of a Christian lady, Aasia Bibi, who was, as usual, falsely implicated in a blasphemy case and was summarily sentenced to death. Although, quite a few reasonable politicians mostly belonging to the PPP, had supported the move, the resistance to the resolution both within and outside the national legislature, which was orchestrated by the fanatic mullahs, the members of the Jamat-e-Islami and the goons who go by the name of Pakistani Taliban, was extreme and ugly. If he were alive, Faiz would have supported Sherry Rehman's move. Nevertheless, Faiz's nephew did what he would have done. Salman Taseer (Salman was the son of Christobel George and Muhammad Din Taseer) who was the governor of Punjab had valiantly condemned the atrocious blasphemy law and approved of Ms. Rehman's move. On January 4, 2011, he was shot dead in Islamabad by his own security guard who was a religious fanatic. Thus, one of his relations proved Faiz wrong!

The gruesome communal riots that had engulfed Punjab, Bengal and many other parts of the country had started out. Though Faiz was promised all the perks appropriate to the status of chief editor of a national daily newspaper, the residence and the official car could not be made available straight away. In the communally charged atmosphere of Lahore, Faiz had to go back to his hotel walking in the dead of night. It was the new-found passion for making *The Pakistan Times* a true organ of democracy and freedom that made possible for him to hold out against all sorts of troubles. Without delay, he got engaged in establishing trade unions of journalists of Pakistan. First, he formed a Committee of Editors. The Government of Punjab introduced press censorship by which no newspaper or magazine could carry news of communal riots or reports of violent incidents. Faiz vehemently opposed this undemocratic policy. There was another journalist, Hameed Nizami, who made a common cause with Faiz in defying the despotic policies of the government. Then there was the furious controversy over Faiz's poem, *The Dawn of Independence–August 1947*, which was feverishly condemned by the members of the Muslim League, the religious fanatics and reactionaries precisely because it mirrored the embittered realities after the independence and creation of Pakistan. The rabid communalists accused Faiz that he had always been opposed to the creation of Pakistan and that was what he expressed in the poem.

In fact, the poem reflects the pitiable conditions of the common people, the refugees, the survivors of the ghastly communal riots that the Indian subcontinent had ever witnessed. For these people independence did not bring any solace. They had no reason to rejoice as for them independence was just a mirage. Faiz's poem had given expression to the feelings of the destitute, the oppressed, suppressed and exploited masses of the subcontinent. Though, it was written more than 70 years earlier, the basic assertion of the poem seems to be valid even today both in India and Pakistan.

In spite of the fact that his job of running a daily did not give him much time to pay attention to other pursuits that were dear to him, Faiz got involved in trade union activities. He was already a passionate member of the journalists' trade union. Later he joined the industrial workers' trade union. Prior to the creation of Pakistan, Mirza Muhammad Ibrahim, a member of the Communist Party, was active on the trade union front. After 1947, he became the President of the Railway Union while Faiz got elected as Vice-President. In 1948, Faiz became the Vice-President of the Pakistan Trade Union Federation. When Mirza was arrested, Faiz became the President of the Railway Employees' Trade Union. Additionally Faiz was also the President of the Postmen's Union. He would regularly attend the meetings of the trade unions, often address public meetings and occasionally lead protest marches. Faiz represented the workers of Pakistan in the ILO's meeting held in 1949 at San Francisco. In those days there were no labour laws in Pakistan and in their absence the Pakistani workers could not enjoy the protection that the ILO could provide them. On his return, Faiz ceaselessly worked for creating a national federation for all the trade unions of Pakistan. His efforts bore fruits in the form of the inception of the Pakistan Federation of Labour. ..In 1949 Faiz led Pakistan's delegation to the annual conference of the International Labour Organisation at Geneva and also became an active member of the World Peace Council. With the growing involvement in trade union and human rights movements, Faiz practically became a representative of the destitute and oppressed people of the world and lent them the voice in his poems, editorials and articles.

The roots of democracy and its essential values could never get a firm hold in the soil of Pakistan. Although Jinnah misused religion by converting it into a political weapon and creating a separate state for the Muslims in the subcontinent, personally he was not a religious fanatic and he also had a different vision of Pakistan. In fact, at the beginning of his political career, Jinnah was a supporter of Hindu-Muslim unity and a forceful crusader of India's freedom from the British. It was the proverbial paradox of history that a truly secular son of India ultimately ended up dividing India in the name of religion. Nevertheless, once he achieved his political aim he underlined the need and significance of a set of secular and democratic principles to run the newly carved-out state. In his famous Presidential Address to the Constituent Assembly of Pakistan, Jinnah, *inter alia,* stated: "If you change your past and work together in a spirit that every one of you, no matter to what community he belongs, no matter what relation he had with you in the past, no matter what is his colour, caste or creed, is first, second and last a citizen of this state with equal rights, privileges and obligations...and you will find that in course of time *Hindus would cease to be Hindus and Muslims would cease to be Muslims, not in the religious sense, because that is the personal faith of each individual,* but in the political sense as citizens of the state." (Emphasis added)[15]. What noble words and how brazenly they were invalidated by the political successors of Jinnah! The democratic freedoms, in particular freedom of expression and freedom to fight for the rights of the poor people, were never made available to the people in Pakistan. No wonder *zamindari* with all its evil characteristics still thrives there. How can a democratic polity that presupposes the political and social equality of all the citizens flourish in a country that is still trapped in feudalism of the medieval ages?

After the creation of Pakistan, the Second Congress of the CPI was held in Calcutta in 1948. It was a huge gathering in which a few delegates from Pakistan such as Prof. Eric Spreen, Muhammad Husain Ata and Bukhari too participated. It was decided at the meeting that a separate Communist Party of Pakistan (CPP) would be established that would have its presence in the Eastern and Western wings of the country. It was unanimously decided to appoint Sajjad Zaheer the General Secretary of the proposed CPP and a few comrades were also advised to emigrate to Pakistan. Consequently, Sajjad Zaheer and Sibte Hasan moved to Pakistan where the local comrades collectively elected Zaheer the General Secretary of the CPP. In retrospect, it seems that the CPI's decision to send a sophisticated, Urdu-speaking comrade like Sajjad Zaheer to establish and strengthen the Communist Party in Pakistan was a mistake. He could not speak Punjabi or any other regional language of Pakistan and despite his efforts to declass himself, his aristocratic background was revealed in his speech and mannerisms. As a result, the CPP, right from its inception, suffered from factionalism and squabbling. Some of the local prominent comrades left the CPP to form independent peasants and workers' organisations.

Prime Minister Liaquat Ali Khan, Jinnah's political heir, badly trampled all the democratic principles that were so dear to his political mentor. When the Communist Revolution was brought about by Mao Tse Tung in China in 1949, the capitalist world, in particular, the USA got a rude shock. In American reckoning, the poor countries of Asia would, sooner or later, grab hold of the Communist form of government. The US launched its 'policy of containment' and for its effective implementation devised the strategy of formation of military alliances. NATO was the first such alliance. The newly decolonised countries of Asia and Africa were also lured to join the anti-Communist military pacts led by the US. India had the fortune of having a politically sagacious Prime

Minister in Nehru who refused to be entrapped in the American military alliances. He made India one of the founding members of the Non-Aligned Nations. The US policy makers, however, succeeded in ensnaring Pakistan in their imperialistic web. Liaquat Ali Khan was invited to the USA where he was thoroughly coached in anti-Communism. Consequently, a few years later, Pakistan joined the South East Asia Treaty Organisation (SEATO) and Central Treaty Organisation (CENTO). On returning to Pakistan, Liaquat Ali Khan appointed Ayub Khan the Commander-in-Chief of the Pakistan Armed Forces in place of the outgoing British General Douglas David Gracey and put severe restrictions on the activities of the Communist Party of Pakistan, though the Party continued to be active in East Pakistan. Although Faiz was not a card-holding member of the CPP, he had been busy promoting the cause of communism in Pakistan. As the editor of the *The Pakistan Times*, he frequently lent editorial support to the party. With the government's latest hostile attitude towards the CPP and its sympathisers Faiz became a marked man.

# CHAPTER 3

# Faiz: The Accused

Under a government which imprisons any unjustly, the true place for a just man is also a prison.

**—Henry David Thoreau**

I would like you to understand completely, also emotionally, that I'm a political detainee and will be a political prisoner, that I have nothing now or in the future to be ashamed of in this situation. That, at bottom, I myself have in a certain sense asked for this detention and this sentence, because I've always refused to change my opinion, for which I would be willing to give my life and not just remain in prison. That therefore I can only be tranquil and content with myself.

**—Antonio Gramsci**

A large group of policemen surrounded a modest bungalow in Lahore in the early hours of March 9, 1951. The hubbub they created made the British lady of the house wake up. She crossed the verandah, went to the gallery of the first floor and looked down into the garden below. She saw many armed policemen who had surrounded her house. The lady was Alys Faiz and the large posse of the armed policeman had arrived to arrest her husband, Faiz Ahmed Faiz. But why? What crime had he committed? The officer in charge himself was not aware of the exact charges against the man he was about to arrest. Faiz, who was editing *The Pakistan*

*Times* at the time, deduced that the intent of the government could be to keep him under detention during the elections for the Punjab Assembly that were scheduled for the next day. Of late, Faiz had been very critical of the rampant corruption and appalling incompetence that were the hallmarks of the federal government led by the Prime Minister Liaquat Ali Khan. So, he thought, the government's objective could be to keep him silent so long as the elections were over.

The armed policemen barged into the bedroom and asked Faiz to go with them. He refused to leave unless he was allowed to talk to Mazhar Ali Khan, one of his senior colleagues at *The Pakistan Times*. The word was sent to Khan. He arrived after a while. In the intervening time the police had procured a warrant under a defunct law of the colonial past that was designed by the foreign masters to keep the Bengali revolutionaries under detention indefinitely without trial. It was outrageous, so thought Faiz and his colleague Khan, objected to invoke an obsolete law to detain the most prominent living poet of the country who was also the editor of one of the respected daily newspapers. However, they could not resist the arrest. Faiz was allowed to take with him a few items of personal use and then ordered to get into the waiting jeep. At that time no one, except the top officials of the government, was aware where he was taken. Later, it was revealed that he was taken to the Lyallpur (now Faisalabad) jail and was kept there in solitary confinement for three months. It was an unlawful action because as per the law an accused or even a convicted person could not be kept in solitary confinement for more than a week or two.

In the evening, the Prime Minister of Pakistan who also held the charge of the Defence Ministry, broadcast a message to the nation on Radio Pakistan. He said:

> A conspiracy hatched by the enemies of Pakistan has only just come to light. The objective of the conspiracy was to create chaos in the country by violent means and in order to achieve this objective the loyalty of the defence forces was to be forfeited. The government got to know about the conspiracy on time. Consequently, today, the key players in the conspiracy have

been arrested that include Major General Akbar Khan, Chief of the General Staff, Brigadier M.A. Lateef, Mr. Faiz Ahmed Faiz, Editor of *The Pakistan Times* and Begum Akbar Khan, wife of Major General Akbar Khan.

The two army officers involved in the conspiracy have been immediately dismissed from the service. It is our good fortune that the conspiracy came to light before it could firm up. Certainly, like me, the people of Pakistan must be dejected on hearing this news of the conspiracy. However, I am confident that people will very well understand that, for the sake of national security, it is not possible for me to reveal the details of the conspirators' scheme. On this occasion I can only say that if God forbid, their scheme would have been successful, then it would have dealt a heavy blow to the foundation of our national life and the stability of Pakistan would have been devastated. This conspiracy has been caused to be a fiasco because of the (exertion of) people who are responsible for the security of the Pakistani military. The collapse of this conspiracy is, without doubt, a great compliment to the unswerving loyalty of Pakistani armed forces, which were not influenced at all by the wickedness of a few depraved, treacherous conspirators and they have rebutted all the desecrated efforts of these enemies of Pakistan. We must all thank God for their vigilance.

"With deep regret I have to say that I have taken action against two very highly placed army officers. However, in these conditions when there is a threat to the security of Pakistan, my duties, in the capacity of Prime Minister and Defence Minister, are obvious. I have full confidence that I have the backing of the entire nation, in particular, the defence forces of Pakistan for the unpleasant duty that I have performed in this regard. I have been, therefore, in touch personally with the soldiers and officers of every department of the defence forces and I have not seen any person whose loyalty (to the nation) is more intense than those who are associated with the military or who has a deeper passion to nurture his country with his blood than the military. The defence forces have proved that no damaging action can shift them an inch from their unwavering loyalty. I admire the deed of those who have opposed the exploit of these

> enemies. At the same time, I congratulate the armed forces who have expressed their total loyalty with Pakistan and refused to be influenced by the elements who intended to create chaos. Certainly, because of such attributes of them, the conspiracy of the enemies has been rendered a failure. For this, the entire nation is thankful to the armed forces. I know for certain that the entire nation is with me in paying this tribute.[1]

The common people obviously believed whatever was being told to them by the government. However, most writers and journalists, in particular, those who knew Faiz were in a state of confusion. They were aware that Faiz had left-leanings and was also very critical of the clique that came to rule over Pakistan since its creation but they had never imagined that a soft-spoken person and ultra sensitive poet like him would join hands with some 'treacherous' officers of the armed forces and hatch a conspiracy to overthrow the civilian rule by force and install in its place a military dictatorship. They also knew that though Faiz would prefer a socialist economy, he was a person who had a great regard for democratic processes, constitutionalism and human rights. In his editorials and articles he attacked the government precisely because it had systematically stifled these ideals. He was, of course, critical of the government's hostile policy towards the CPP and merely demanded that it should be allowed to continue with its activities just like any other political party. This was not an anti-national or undemocratic demand. Marxism as an ideology was close to his heart but he never showed any inclination to join the Communist Party. He was not an arm chair intellectual though; he was actively involved in trade union activities and on a few occasion led Pakistani workers' delegations to international meets. He never thought of keeping secret his contacts with some top military officers. He had himself served in the British Indian army and some of his relatives were also army officers. However, it was difficult for Faiz's acquaintances to think that he could actually be a party to a military coup.

One could easily imagine the state of despair Alys was in after the rifle-wielding policemen took away her husband. She had to make crucial decisions as she observed: 'Arrest of the breadwinner meant a great deal of readjustment in the family circle. I became the sole breadwinner, but I also took on the breadwinner's many other duties, and at the same time set out to understand legal procedures, how lawyers were to be paid, by whom and how much!"[2] She had two little daughters to take care of. They were too young to comprehend the severity of the situation. Alys told them that their father had gone away somewhere for a few months. She counselled them not to be petrified as people might say anything to scare them. They should not pay attention to people's gossip. However, she herself was worried about how she would handle the unexpected situation singlehandedly. The foremost issue of concern was of money. Though, Mian Iftikharuddin had promised some help, she could not fathom how their existing lifestyle would be maintained. The two girls, Salima (fondly called Chhemi) and Moneeza had to put up with the first effect of the austerity measures that Alys had devised to deal with the financial constraint. They were the students of an expensive school. Alys, in the changed circumstances, enrolled them in an affordable one. Though Faiz's relatives did extend a helping hand, Alys had taken up a job to meet the expenses.

Neither Alys nor any other relative or friend knew where Faiz was taken and what condition he was in after the arrest. The right-wing newspapers started a vicious campaign against all the 'traitors' by demanding that they should be immediately hanged. Faiz, in particular, was the target of their malicious propaganda. The very next day of his arrest, the *London Times* had labelled him as one of 'the most dangerous and influential leftist figures in Pakistan." The religious fanatics too, with an objective of demoralising Alys and Faiz's friends, joined in spreading horrifying rumours against him such as that all the five fingers of Faiz's right hand were amputated, he was thrashed so severely that he could not even walk, his eyes were wheedled out from their sockets or all his nails were pulled out. The spiteful rumour-mongers would see to it that such ghastly rumours reached the ears of Alys and Faiz's daughters. Alys's condition would obviously become disconsolate and sometimes she would even curse the hoodlums who would keep announcing the torturous treatment meted out to Faiz. The little girls, unable to do anything, would naturally start crying. Alys would have to console them for long before sending them to school.

On one occasion, a girl who was the classmate of Salima invited her for the birthday party. It was a pleasant surprise for Salima as well as Alys because since Faiz's arrest almost everyone except their relatives and a few friends had shunned them. Alys was as much delighted as her daughter. She helped her select the best clothes for the occasion and sent her to the party. When Salima reached her classmate's home she was taken to a room where six men were seated around a table. She was made to sit on a chair. For the next three hours the six men interrogated the eight-year-old girl very harshly to extract the information about Faiz's close confidants and their whereabouts. The innocent little girl did not know anything. She had gone there to attend a party but had to face a terrible cross-examination. Salima, nevertheless, faced the arduous situation with remarkable poise and self-respect that was not anticipated from a little girl. She refused to answer most of the questions and also did not give her interrogators the opportunity to draw vicarious pleasure by not wailing at all. She remained quite dignified throughout the three-hour long ordeal. When she reached home she hugged her mother closely and cried inconsolably. What else could Alys do except comfort her daughter?

The Pakistani press had, by and large, adopted the pro-establishment line. Most journalists believed whatever was fed to them by government agencies. They had already arrived at the conclusion that all the arrested persons were deeply involved in an anti-national conspiracy. No one seemed to be interested in listening to clarification of the conspirators. In such depressing circumstances a close friend of Faiz, Hameed Nizami, who was the Chief Editor of an Urdu daily, *Nawa-e-Waqt,* took a forthright stand. Showing exceptional courage, he demanded that, for the sake of upholding justice, the conspirators should be tried. He asserted that without a fair trial no person involved in the conspiracy should be punished. Commenting on Faiz, the editor wrote: "Whether he is guilty or not should be decided by the court but whatever he has done cannot be so vicious."

In the radio announcement the Prime Minister had informed the nation about the arrest of only five persons. Subsequently more conspirators were arrested at different times and from different places. They included, Air Commodore M.K. Janjua, Maj. Gen. Nazir Ahmed, Brigadier Sadiq Khan, Lt. Col. Ziauddin, Lt. Col. Niyaz Muhammad Arbab, Lt. Col. Siddique Raja, Major Muhammad Yusuf Sethi, Captain Khizar Hayat, Major Hasan Khan, Major Ishaq Muhammad, Captain Zafarullah Poshni and Syed Sajjad Zaheer. One more 'conniver', Muhammad Hussain Ata had dodged the police and fled to East Pakistan. He could only be arrested a month after the commencement of the trial. Lt. Col. Raja and Major Sethi, later turned approvers and obtained state pardon. It was also revealed afterwards how the government got to know about the plot. Major General Akbar Khan who was the 'kingpin of the plan' had one more confidant, Askar Ali Shah, a police officer who was not present at the last meeting of February 23, 1951, though he knew about it. Initially he was in agreement with Akbar Khan's risky scheme but later he got frightened and divulged all that he knew about the conspiracy to the Inspector General of Police who, without delay, informed I.I. Chundrigar, the Governor of NWFP. The Governor instantaneously passed on the information to the Prime Minister who, at the time, was on election tour. He sent for Iskandar Mirza, the Defence Secretary and Ayub Khan, the Commander-in-Chief instructed them to take action against the conspirators right away.

The Rawalpindi Conspiracy was the first among the series of military coups that were brought about against the democratically elected civilian governments in the history of Pakistan. It was a plot to overthrow the Muslim League government led by Liaquat Ali Khan. The mastermind behind the coup Major General Akbar Khan had a few grouses against the Prime Minister. The partition of the subcontinent was, in principle, executed on the basis of the faith of the people. The areas that had Muslim majority were allotted to Pakistan. The fate of Kashmir, where the Muslims constituted the majority, was left unresolved because it was an Indian native state ruled by a Hindu Maharaja. Therefore, within months after the division of India, warfare began in Kashmir when the Pathan tribesmen, under the command of 'General Tariq', having seized a sizable area of the valley, advanced towards the capital city Srinagar. It was at this point, the Maharaja appealed to the Indian Prime Minister for help and subsequently after procuring an Instrument of Accession from the ruler of Kashmir, the Indian forces stopped the further advance of Pakistani aggressors. At that point of time north-western Kashmir had been occupied by Pakistan and the rest was controlled by India. The position continues to be the same even now though Pakistan handed over a part of Kashmir that it had occupied in 1948, viz. Aksai Chin to China in the early 1960s. The commander of the Pakistani regulars and irregulars, 'General Tariq' was actually the codename of Akbar Khan who was at that time a Brigadier. When the Pakistani government agreed to ceasefire it was extremely despised by the military and more so by 'General Tariq' who thought that the civilian government committed a blunder that helped India consolidate its military position in the region and took away from Pakistan the prospect of occupying entire Kashmir.

Another reason that disconcerted Akbar Khan with the government led by Liaquat Ali Khan was that he was denied the post of Commander-in-Chief of the Armed Forces of Pakistan. At the time of superannuation of the British General Douglas David Gracey who continued to be the C-in-C even after the creation of Pakistan, Liaquat Ali Khan had made up his mind to appoint General Iftikhar in place of the outgoing British General. However, even before the announcement of his name, he died in a plane crash near Karachi. At that time Akbar Khan was among the senior most army officers and as a consequence of his exceptional track record, he was expecting to be appointed the C-in-C. Nonetheless, because of the lobbying done by Sardar Bahadur Khan, who was a cabinet minister and also a member of the Constituent Assembly of Pakistan, his younger brother Ayub Khan, despite being junior to Akbar Khan, was appointed the Commander-in-Chief of the

Armed Forces of Pakistan. Ayub had always been wary of Akbar Khan and for that reason, as he admitted in his memoirs, *Friends, Not Masters*, he posted Akbar Khan in the GHQ so that he was deprived of having direct command over troops as well as he could be kept under watch by the C-in-C personally.[3]

Akbar Khan was obviously discontented and on occasions shared his displeasure with fellow army officers. His frustration made him think about a coup d'état and he started consultations with some of the like-minded military officers to explore the possibility of overthrowing the government of Liaquat Ali Khan. Akbar Khan's wife, Begum Nasim Khan was incautious while chitchatting with friends, many of them were the wives of military officers. She would often criticise the policies of the government without realising that her indiscretion might put her husband in trouble. In fact, it was because of Begum Nasim Khan's bragging that the government became suspicious and the couple came under the surveillance of the intelligence agencies.

Having secured the allegiance of a few military officers, Akbar Khan then thought of enlisting some influential civilians who could extend their support to the military immediately after the coup. Working on the principle of 'enemy's enemy is your friend', he decided to get in touch with the leaders of the Communist Party of Pakistan (CPP). Though not officially banned, it was passing through a very difficult phase. It was not allowed to operate openly as a political party. Almost all the top leaders had gone underground because arrest warrants had been issued against them. The situation of the ordinary members and fellow-travellers was precarious. They would often be arrested and tortured mercilessly. The Secretay General of the Party, Sajjad Zaheer was also underground and would keep moving from place to place in disguise. Akbar Khan thought that the Communist leaders would willingly agree to cooperate with him because they had so many complaints against the government of Liaquat Ali Khan. Begum Nasim Khan knew Faiz very well. Thus, through Faiz, Begum Nasim Khan and her husband planned to get in touch with the leadership of the Communist Party.

Akbar Khan's intention was to seek the support of the CPP and its affiliated organisations such as the trade unions and peasants' groups after the coup. He wanted them to react favourably to the transitory military government that would come to power after the coup. Faiz, being the editor of a very influential newspaper, *The Pakistan Times*, was expected to write approvingly about the coup and ensuing military rule in his group of newspapers and magazines. On his part, Akbar Khan had promised that after establishment of the military government, the pestering of the Communists and their sympathisers would be completely stopped. The Communist Party of Pakistan would be given complete freedom to carry on its activities like any other political party. He also assured that the military rule would last for a brief period to ensure normalcy and that the election would be announced soon in which the CPP could participate without any restriction.

The CPP was so insignificant in the political scenario of Pakistan that it could hardly do anything of significance for Akbar Khan and his plan. Nevertheless, it inadvertently got involved in the conspiracy. The CPP did discuss the proposal and Sajjad Zaheer authorised to plan the future course of action. Consequently, Sajjad Zaheer met Akbar Khan at a cocktail party where the General briefed the Communist leader about the details of the plan and sought his assistance in the preparation of a manifesto and the draft of the action plan. Though, Zaheer was not in agreement on quite a few issues he did not dissociate himself from the Party immediately. For two months the consultations between the CPP and the military officers concerned continued. The Party leadership was divided on the issue. In an interview, Sibte Hasan, a senior member of the Politburo, said: "Sajjad Zaheer and other leading members of the CPP who intended to support the conspiracy lost by a solitary vote against the leaders who were opposed to the Party's involvement in the coup." As per Sibte Hasan's statement, the CPP thus informed the military officers that it did not intend to be a part of the coup.

Afterwards, as per the particulars of the conspiracy that were revealed during the course of trial by the two approvers,

Lt. Col. Raja and Major Sethi, the conspirators held four meetings to put together a fail-safe plan. The first meeting was held at Attak on December 14, 1949. The major issue that came up for discussion was the upcoming tours of the Governor General and the Prime Minister of Punjab. It was concluded that the plan should be executed when the Governor General would be in Lahore and the Prime Minister in Peshawar. It would make it easier to arrest both of them simultaneously. The persons who participated in the meeting were: 1) Major General Akbar Khan; 2) Major General Nazir Ahmed; 3) Brigadier Sadiq Khan; 4) Brigadier M.A. Lateef Khan and 6) Lt. Col. Siddique Raja. It was also decided that the entire action should be taken during the night and in the morning the Governor General would be forced to make an announcement on the radio that the Government of Pakistan was dismissed and the administration of the country was assigned to a military council that included 1) Akbar Khan; 2) M.A. Lateef Khan; 3) Brigadier Habibullah; 4) Sadiq Khan and 5) Siddique Raja. Major General Nazir Ahmed was to be appointed the Commander-in-Chief.

The second meeting was held near Rawalpindi on December 21, 1949, in which only four officers participated. They were: 1) Akbar Khan; 2) M.A. Lateef Khan; 3) Sadiq Khan and 4) Siddique Raja. Akbar Khan updated the other officers that Brigadier Habibullah had reservations about the success of the coup because the conspirators were not in control of sufficient number of troops. He also revealed that the government had decided, despite his refusal, to ask him to enrol for a course in the Inter-Services Staff College. He also informed that since the two very senior officers, Major General Iftikhar and Major General Sher Ali had died in a plane crash some of the officers associated with the coup plan would be promoted to higher positions. This would help them to have under their command a larger number of troops.

The third meeting was held after a gap of ten months on October 14, 1950, at Sialkot. Three officers were present who included Akbar Khan, Sadiq Khan and Siddique Raja. Begum Nasim Khan was the first civilian who was present at this meeting. The meeting was scheduled before the upcoming visit of Akbar Khan to the UK.

He wanted to explain to those present the necessary groundwork that was already done and what remained to be carried out. Begum Nasim Khan gave a lecture on Communism and the need for a pro-USSR policy in order to protect the national interests of Pakistan.

The fourth and the last meeting was held at the official residence of Major General Akbar Khan in Rawalpindi on February 23, 1951. Eight military officers and three civilians were present. They included: 1) Akbar Khan; 2) Siddique Raja; 3) Lt. Col. Niyaz Muhammad Arbab; 4) Lt. Col. Ziauddin; 5) Major Khwaja Muhammad Yusuf Sethi; 6) Major Hasan Gulgati; 7) Captain Zafarullah Poshni; 8) Captain Khizar Hayat; 9) Syed Sajjad Zaheer; 10) Faiz Ahmed Faiz and 11) Muhammad Husain Ata. Akbar Khan revealed the plan that the Governor-General, Khwaja Nazimuddin and the Prime Minister, Liaquat Ali Khan would be arrested on April 31, 1951, when they would be on a tour of Rawalpindi. Akbar Khan would control the entire operation from the GHQ. A posse of troops would be dispatched to arrest the Prime Minister and at the same time the C-in-C would also be taken into custody. Some necessary action would also be taken in Karachi, the capital of the country (at that time Karachi was the capital of Pakistan while Rawalpindi was the military headquarters) under the command of Air Commodore M.K. Janjua. Muhammad Husain Ata, a member of the CPP, was to receive 500 rifles to establish a centre of a people's army. The apprehended Governor General would be asked to address the nation on the radio informing people that an emergency was clamped in the country and the government of Pakistan led by Liaquat Ali Khan was dismissed. The administration of the nation was handed over to Akbar Khan, C-in-C (Army), M.K. Janjua, C-in-C (Air Force) and Chaudhary, C-in-C (Navy).

It was the only occasion when Faiz and Sajjad Zaheer attended the meeting of the conspirators. Faiz expressed his discontent about the entire plan and urged that the plan should be shelved. Sajjad Zaheer backed Faiz's point of view and also made it clear that the CPP was not in a position to raise a people's army to help sustain the coup. Then followed a lengthy discussion in which almost everyone expressed his opinion. Finally, it was decided to shelve the plan of the coup. Ironically, the only voice of dissent was that of Siddique Raja, who later turned into an approver. The next day Akbar Khan left for Karachi where he had a clandestine meeting with Janjua and Lateef Khan. On March 3, Janjua called Akbar Khan to inform him that the coup plan was exposed. Ayub Khan, the C-in-C, without delay, issued orders for the encirclement of the army headquarters from where Akbar Khan had planned to execute the coup. The government troops moved rapidly to arrest Akbar Khan. Later, he described in a write-up the drama that was enacted in the early hours of the morning of March 9, 1951 in these words: "Then Major-General Mian Hayatuddin knocked at my bedroom window and said that he had to see me about something most urgent. I had gone at once, without even putting on my shoes, through the study door to meet him. But as I emerged, men with bayonets and sten guns had rushed at me from three sides–the front and both flanks. I had been rushed at before, during the war, by the Japanese in fighting–but never by 20 to one and not when I was unarmed. I had only a split second to think and I had let them come on. I think it had been the complete failure of this melodrama to impress me at all that had stopped the men mid-stride. No bayonet or sten-gun had reached my body–and the few hands that had been laid at me had been quickly withdrawn. A mere telephone call would have sufficed to tell me that I was under arrest. But instead all the troops had been alerted and these men had apparently expected to be gunned down by some sort of desperado." Thereafter, other conspirators were picked up from different places.

The right-wing press and the government that toed the American line, launched a wilful campaign that it was a Communist conspiracy for the 'traitors' who had hatched it had planned to establish a Communist government after overthrowing the civilian rule. Subsequently, followed the emotional exploitation of the common people's religious susceptibilities through spreading outrageous stories about Communists and their 'intense hatred' for religion, in particular, Islam. The reality was that most persons implicated in connection with the Rawalpindi Conspiracy had nothing to do with Communism. As Faiz informed Alys in a letter of August 7, 1951, that those implicated in the coup comprised an assorted group of people hailing from different regions and committed to various ideologies.[4] During the course of the secret trial the diverse backgrounds were made known to the tribunal. For instance, Nazir Ahmed was a Qadyani, Muhammad Khan Janjua was a Sunni, Hasan Khan was a Shia, M.A. Lateef Khan was a Deobandi, Sadiq Khan, Ziauddin and Khizar Hayat were adherents of Sufism. Thus, only four of the accused, viz. Sajjad Zaheer, Faiz Ahmed Faiz, Muhammad Husain Ata and Major Ishaq Muhammad were either Communists or sympathisers of Communism.

## (II)

Initially, most of the conspirators were lodged in different jails of Punjab but nobody except the top government officials were aware of the details of the detention plan. After about three months when the government ultimately decided to try the accused they were shifted to Hyderabad (Sind) jail by a special train under heavy security. A part of the jail premises was converted into the court and a special tribunal was constituted to try the accused. The tribunal comprised Justice Sir Abdur Rehman, who was on the bench of the Federal Court of Pakistan, Justice Muhammad Sharif of the Punjab High Court and Justice Amiruddin of the Dacca High Court.

There was no law in Pakistan to be applied on the kind of conspiracy that came to light and frame charges against implicated persons. The Constituent Assembly that was engaged in framing a constitution for the newly carved out state of Pakistan was assigned to make an appropriate law to deal with the Rawalpindi Conspiracy Case. Accordingly, the Constituent Assembly, on April 16, 1951, enacted an Act to provide for setting up of a Special Tribunal to try the case and other related matters. The democratic-liberal members of the Assembly had opposed the enactment of the statute because, in their opinion, it was damaging to the very concept of justice. However, they did not have the backing of enough members to defeat the proposed law. After the passage, the Act was published in the Gazette on April 28, 1951. The Act *inter alia* described the composition of the Special Tribunal and provided that for framing charges against the accused persons Section 271 of the Code of Criminal Procedure of 1898 would be applied. It was this particular feature of the Act that was objected to by the liberals because by invoking a colonial law that was designed by the foreign masters to deal with the 'terrorists' of undivided Bengal in the late nineteenth century, the Constituent Assembly of an independent state of Pakistan was treating its own citizens as potential criminals and terrorists. Furthermore, the Act provided that the proceedings of the Tribunal would not be open to the public. Most of all, there was no provision for appeal for revision of the verdict of the Special Tribunal in any court of Pakistan.

After three months Alys got to know that Faiz was in Lyallpur jail and that she could go there to meet him. She gave the children the good tidings and taking them along with her reached the jail. When three of them were waiting in the visitors' room, the elder girl, Salima, looked through the solitary and a very small window that had a view over the courtyard of the jail, she saw a man wearing black glasses staggering towards the visitors' room. As he came closer, Salima recognised him and bellowed in excitement, "Abbu!" Alys did not move from her place but asked what he looked like. Salima said that his hands and feet were perfectly intact but he wore dark glasses. Suddenly, the three of them were thunderstruck with fear. The stories that Faiz's eyes were taken out of their sockets recurred back tormenting their hearts. They waited with bated breath till Faiz entered the room and removed the dark glasses. Finding his eyes in perfect condition, the three of them went berserk with joy. Faiz hugged the three of them tightly for more than once. When the time of the visit came to an end, Salima asked: "Abbu! What have you done?" Faiz said: "It is a lie...it is a fraud... Don't be scared of these things...everything will be fine."

The trial commenced more than three months after the arrest of Faiz, and as Alys reported: "It appeared that Faiz had been charged with almost every heinous crime possible except rape, (as later he smilingly comforted me), each carrying a death sentence or life imprisonment."[5] In the newly constructed structure that was designated as the venue of the Special Tribunal, the three judges took up their lofty positions and ordered the prosecution to open its case. The main lawyer of the prosecution team was A.K. Brohi who later became quite notorious for his legal services to military dictators and despotic rulers of Pakistan. The case per se was not a false one. However, the charges that were framed against the accused persons and the inferences drawn on account of some oral statements of the prosecution witnesses were blatantly false. The implicated persons had hired various lawyers not as a unit but different lawyers appeared on behalf of different individuals. Akbar Khan, M.A. Lateef and Z.H. Lari were represented by a reputed lawyer, Husain Shaheed Suhrawardy, Faiz, along with a few other accused, had hired the services of Manzoor Qadir and for sometime of Sahibzada Nawazish Ali. The other lawyers associated with the defence of the accused persons were Malik Faiz Muhammad, Khawaja Abdur Rahim and Qazi Aslam. Nevertheless, when the proceedings of the trial continued indefinitely, most defence lawyers stopped appearing for the defendants because their clients could not pay their fees. Suhrawardy was the only dedicated lawyer who fought the case on behalf of all the defendants with total commitment and passion till its conclusion even when his clients were not in a position to pay any remuneration. Faiz wrote a *Tribute,* in recognition of his selfless services at the end of the trial, which, on behalf of all the defendants, was presented to him as citations of gratitude. The poetic tribute is included in Faiz's sixth anthology, *Shaam-e-Shahr-e-Yaran.* In the third section of the poem, Faiz, following the tradition of classical panegyrics, writes a few couplets of supplication. Two of them are:

*Har kaam mein barkat ho, har ek qaul mein quawwat*
*Har gaam pe ho manzil-e-maqsood qadam geer*__
*Har lahza tera tal'a-e-iqbal siwa ho*
*Har lahza madadgar ho tadbeer ki taqdeer*

May every act (of yours) meet with vast reward, every speech be forceful

May every step seize the destination sought for__
May the lofty fate augment every moment
May the fate of the feat help every instant

Suhrawardy ultimately turned out to be the Prime Minister of Pakistan.

The main charge against all those implicated in the case was that of "Conspiracy to wage war against the King." Yes, it was a charge of conspiring against the realm of the *King* because the section applied to frame the charges was that of the Code of Criminal Procedure of 1898. In the judgement that was eventually delivered it was pronounced: "A careful scrutiny of the first charge shows that it relates to a conspiracy alleged by prosecution to have come into being for overthrowing the government established by law in Pakistan by means of criminal force or show of criminal force." There were some other accusations which were also punishable but they were "either the consequences of this conspiracy or merely means to achieve the object for which it was stated to have been entered into." The verdict of the case therefore, depended on the thorough scrutiny of the evidence produced by the prosecution and to determine thereof "(i) the existence of conspiracy; and if that is found established, (ii) who are proved to have been parties to it?" The evidence that the prosecution could got together comprised documentary support as well as oral proof. The latter kind of evidence was delivered by the "persons, who, without being either parties or willing parties to it, either deposed to the existence of the conspiracy or stated facts which might lead a court to draw a conclusion in favour of its existence; and (of) persons who were either, on their own statements, or on account of admissions of facts made by them, or due to existence of other reasonable grounds, held to be willing parties to the conspiracy." In this connection the prosecution built up its case mainly on the statements of the two approvers as well as some other witnesses who helped supply circumstantial evidence.

The two approvers, Siddique Raja and Sethi were in fact promised the state pardon only on the condition to give false evidence that at the end of an eight-hour discussion that took place in the meeting of February 23, 1951, all the persons present had arrived at the decision to carry out the plan of overthrowing the government of Pakistan. It was the most crucial evidence for the prosecution because in its absence they could not have established the accusation of conspiracy. According to the relevant penal code a conspiracy could only be established "when two or more persons agree to commit an illegal act or a legal act by illegal means." The plainly false evidence made available by the double dealing approvers caused the allegation of conspiracy stuck on the accused. Regrettably, the details of the arguments of the defence counsels are not in the public domain but the fact was that in the crucial meeting it was unanimously agreed to abandon the coup plan. Thus, the truth was negated by the falsehood of the perfidious.

The trial continued for one and a half years and in the verdict delivered in the first week of January 1953, with the exception of Begum Nasim Khan, all were sentenced to imprisonment. The lightest sentence was awarded to Nazir Ahmed who was dismissed from military service and confined to the premises till the rising of the court. The sentences for the others ranged from a minimum of four years to twelve years. Faiz and Sajjad Zaheer were in the former category while Akbar Khan was in the latter. However, he did not serve the full sentence because, in 1957, when Suhrawardy became the Prime Minister, he obtained a reprieve for all the convicted persons in the case. After getting out of jail, Akbar Khan kept a low profile during Ayub Khan's dictatorship but when Zulfikar Ali Bhutto came to power in 1971, he was appointed as the chief of national security. He died in 1993 at the age of 81 in Karachi.

Faiz was convicted on account of three evidences: a) Faiz's liaison with Akbar Khan and Janjua; b) his participation in the meeting of February 23, 1951 and c) the entry of Faiz's name in a document that was recovered from Akbar Khan's possession. The prosecution called upon a few witnesses who stated before the tribunal that Faiz had always been in touch with Akbar Khan and Janjua. About Faiz's presence in the meeting of February 23, there was no confusion. Faiz himself had admitted that he was present at the meeting. The significant point, however, was what he had said at the meeting. The tribunal refused to take cognisance of the fact that Faiz had expressed his reservations about the feasibility of the coup plan and advocated its abandonment. In his statement Faiz had also said that the Punjab police had a hostile attitude towards him and for that reason he was implicated wrongly in the conspiracy case.

In support of his contention, Faiz referred to a few events: i) Mr. Jenkins, the Director General of CID had written a 'top secret' letter to someone in the UK regarding the establishment of a secret service system in Pakistan. Faiz somehow got to read the contents of the letter in the capacity of the Chief Editor of *The Pakistan Times* and wrote a scathing editorial with the title, 'Spy Ring.'[6] On its publication, Mr. Jenkis had ordered an inquiry; ii) on the behest of Chaudhary Muhammad Husain, the Superintendent of CID, Faiz was arrested in April 1948, under the Public Safety Act for 'intentionally publishing a false report' in *The Pakistan Times*. When Faiz was acquitted by the court, the government of Punjab, in a notification, stated that it had nothing to do with Faiz's arrest and that it was because of the irresponsible action of the police. This might have infuriated Chaudhary as he had been harbouring ill will against Faiz; iii) Faiz had strongly condemned the attitude of the policemen when they had handcuffed a trade union leader, Mirza Muhammad Ibrahim, who was arrested for political reasons and, iv) Faiz, in a scoop, had made public, the exchange of infuriated letters between Qurban Ali Khan, the Inspector of Punjab Police and Khwaja Muhammad Husain, DIG, Rawalpindi Range. Accordingly, Faiz's argument was, the Punjab police, in order to settle the old scores, had implicated him in the case. The tribunal judges, nevertheless, were not swayed by his line of argument and on January 5, 1953, Faiz was sentenced to four-year imprisonment subject to deduction of the period he had already spent in jail. So, he was to spend an additional two and a half years in prison.

# CHAPTER 4

# Faiz: The Coolest Inmate

I know not whether laws be right,
Or whether laws be wrong;
All that we know who be in jail
Is that the wall is strong;
And that each day is like a year,
A year whose days are long.

**—Oscar Wilde**

Jails and prisons are designed to break human beings, to convert the population into specimens in a zoo—obedient to our keepers, but dangerous to each other.

**—Angela Davis**

It is obviously difficult for those who have never been incarcerated to visualise how the thought processes of an imprisoned person go through marked changes because of the forced separation from those he loves. The popular perception is that life in prison is, as Gresham Sykes puts it, "depriving or frustrating in the extreme." It is also true that the adaptation to the frustrations and deprivations that are commonly known as the 'pains of imprisonment' entails emotional turmoil and psychological disarray. The psychologists believe that adaptation to incarceration is usually a difficult process. Nevertheless, they also stress that the psychological impact of imprisonment may vary from individual to individual. In many cases, a long period of imprisonment may cause a visible change in the behaviour of an individual that can be called dysfunctional. Some people, however, come out of jail completely unchanged or unscathed by the experience that is supposed to be dreadful. Faiz was one such person. Going by the account that comes out of his letters, his poetic output and the statements of his friends who spent years with him in jail, it can be safely surmised that the 'pains of imprisonment' hardly bothered him. Of all the accused he was perhaps the coolest inmate. Though he hated to be separated from his much-loved ones, he did not experience wrenches of depression or cycles of self-pity. He faced deprivation and difficulties in a confined environ but like Antonio Gramsci he never thought, "I turn and turn in my cell like a fly that doesn't know where to die." It seems that, except for three months that he had to spend in solitary confinement in Sargodha and Lyallpur jails, Faiz was completely at peace during the years he spent in various jails of Pakistan.

Pandit Jawaharlal Nehru, in *Glimpses of World History* (also a collection of letters Nehru wrote to his daughter Indira from jail), quotes Benjamin Disraeli, the British Prime Minister: "Other men condemned to exile and captivity, if they survive, despair; the man of letters may reckon those days as the sweetest of his life." The man of letters Disraeli referred to was the seventeenth century Dutch jurist and philosopher, Hugo Grotius, who was arrested for accentuating a theological controversy and sentenced to life imprisonment. Besides writing several beautiful poems he produced some remarkable works on international law and philosophy during the two years he spent in prison. Later, he managed to escape with the help of his wife and maidservant. There are many such examples when the men of letters made the most of their time in prison by producing some excellent works despite the inhospitable conditions of prison. In the political category there are *Prison Notebooks* by Gramsci, *The Development of Capitalism in Russia* by Lenin, *Permanent Revolution* by Trotsky, *Long Walk to Freedom* by Mandela and so on. In India some of the finest works of Gandhi, Azad and Nehru came out of prison cells. Among the literary gems that were produced in prison we may cite *Don Quixote* by Miguel de Cervantes, *De Profundis* by Oscar Wilde, *Our Lady of Flowers* by Jean Genet, *Pisan Cantos* by Ezra Pound and many more.

Among the Urdu litterateurs, Mirza Ghalib was the first significant man of letters who, in 1847, was sentenced to six months' imprisonment by a British magistrate for gambling. In the prison, Ghalib somehow got hold of a copy of *Burhan-e-Quate*, a very popular Persian dictionary in those days. While leafing through it, Ghalib realised that it was full of errors. Though he did not have access to any reference book in the prison, he jotted down a critical assessment along with an exhaustive errata relying on his memory and later published it as *Quat-e-Burhan,* which created a fierce controversy. Ghalib's disciple, Saiyyah Aurangabadi was also interned in Surat jail for a long period of time for printing counterfeit currency notes where besides teaching Persian to the children of the jail warden, he wrote some wonderful ghazals in Urdu and Persian. Many poets and writers associated with the PWM were jailed during the British rule as well as after independence. In India, Makhdoom Mohiuddin, had to spend years as an underground fugitive and also in prison for his commitment to Marxism in the Nizam's state of Hyderabad and thereafter in independent India during the Telangana Movement. Most of his ghazals and poems that are included in his first two anthologies, *Surkh Savera* and *Gul-e-Tar*, were written in various prisons. The other progressive poets who were incarcerated for being Marxists were Sardar Jafri and Majrooh Sultanpuri. Though Majrooh's total poetic output is small and it is also not known how many ghazals he actually wrote in confinement, most of Sardar Jafri's poems contained in the first anthology, *Patthar ki Deewar* were written in prison. Sajjad Zaheer had spent two years in Lucknow jail during the colonial rule for his association with the CPI. The collection of letters that he wrote to his wife Razia was later published by the name, *Nuqush-e-Zindan*. After the verdict of the Rawalpindi Conspiracy Case, he was sent to Machh jail in Pakistan and during two and a half years of internment there he produced two remarkable books, *Roshnai* (the history of the PWM) and *Zikr-e-Hafiz* (critical appraisal of the ghazals of the famous Persian poet, Hafiz Shirazi).

Faiz believed that imprisonment, like love, in itself was a fundamental experience that helped open a new aperture of ideas and insight. It would apportion a much sharper edge to sensations, which would restore the feeling of amazement about the crack of dawn, end of the day, the azure sky, the stroke of wind, etc. that existed in adolescence. It would also render the time and space of the outside world false. The things that were closer would become distant and the remote entities get closer. He also observed that the difference between today and tomorrow would get erased in the sense that sometimes a moment would turn out to be excruciatingly too long and at other times the things that happened centuries ago appear as if they transpired yesterday. The most significant change that was particularly relevant in case of Faiz was that imprisonment offered him the much desired time for reading, contemplation and aesthetic adornment of poetry. He made the most creative use of the time in prison. He read many books, learnt a language and produced two collections of exquisite poetry.

In order to reconstruct Faiz's life in prison a few sources are of utmost importance. First is the collection of his letters, *Saleebein Merey Dareechey Mein*, which he wrote to his wife Alys. The second source comprises his two anthologies, *Dast-e-Saba* and *Zindan Nama*, wherein almost all the poems are the ones written in prison. In the third category fall a few articles written by some of his friends who were with him in various jails. The original letters that he wrote to his wife were in English. He was not aware that they would, in future, be in the public domain and in fact he was reluctant to give the go-ahead to their publication. When Alys wanted to know his view on the issue he, in a letter of March 11, 1953, wrote: "It is better if you do not ask my view about the publication of the letters. I am afraid that they would not make any sense in the form of a book. It is better if you ask someone non-partisan about it. I wish A.S.B. (Ahmed Shah Bukhari, the famous humorist whose nom de plume was Patras) were on hand to make decisions in such matters. Anyhow, if you decide to publish them, then they should be published in Urdu. If I do not write with extreme caution and care then my English writing appears to be too ornate and baffling."[1] Accordingly, both Faiz and Alys had shelved the plan of publication of letters in the 1950s. Almost two decades later when Faiz's sixtieth birthday was being celebrated then on the urging of an aficionado, Mirza Zafarul Hasan, both Alys and Faiz agreed to publish them in Urdu rendition. Faiz himself translated the letters and thus *Saleebein Merey Dreechey Mein* came out in June 1971. The citations, therefore, are English translations of the Urdu version of letters that were originally in English. Since the original English letters are not in the public domain,[2] or at least I do not have access to them, my English translations carry the contents of the Urdu letters as faithfully as possible though the words and phrases used in the original ones could be different.

In these letters Faiz appears to be an incurable optimist. He hoped that everything would ultimately turn out to be fine, be it the personal perilous situation he was in, the tight spot Alys and his two daughters found themselves at because of his incarceration or the never ending oppression and exploitation of the masses by the powerful and the rich; he believed that truth and happiness were bound to prevail. About his involvement in the Rawalpindi Conspiracy he had been very forthright from the beginning that he did nothing that could morally or legally be construed as improper. In the letters he asserted the point repeatedly. In the very first letter (June 7, 1951) from Hyderabad jail though he mentioned that the first three months spent in solitary confinement in Lyallpur jail were the most agonising, he also wrote: "There is no feeling of fear and peril in my mind...because I have not done anything that can morally be called sin or committed an act that can legally be taken to mean a crime."[3] Though he was deeply concerned about the problems and exertions that Alys had to confront, he was completely at ease in jail. In the letter of July 2, 1951, he noted: "I have never felt the serenity of heart that I do now...At the present it seems that I do not have any grievance against anyone in the world. In contrast, I am afraid that by the time the prison term gets over I might end up a Sufi because currently no remark, no object appears to be bad. All the lies, all the deceits, all the shams and all those accusations that would trouble the heart earlier, make me laugh if recalled now..."[4]

Considering, some of the charges that might attract the death penalty, his self-assurance and equanimity might appear naïve but it was genuine and unfeigned, not a façade. He remained contented and at peace with himself even when the special tribunal ultimately sentenced him to four years imprisonment. He wrote to Alys on January 5, 1953: "The event of yesterday (the verdict) appears absolutely worthless and far-flung from heart. The real and consequential point is that I have not committed any crime, not perpetrated any sin and that my heart is completely contented and serene. This morning, my companions were, in fact, aggrieved on this count. They said that when they left my cell at about 9 last night, I was fast asleep within ten minutes and began snoring that disturbed their sleep."[5] This peace of mind and serenity of heart were partly because he was absolutely convinced that he did no wrong and partly because of the gentleness of his personality.

The shadow of gentleness of his persona is conspicuous in his poetry as well. Although he was a revolutionary poet, he dealt with subjects of oppression, injustice, grief, poverty, exploitation, revolution and so on in a style that is soft and melodious. In this respect, his poetry disproves T.S. Eliot's observation that a poet or writer repudiates himself in his creations. Faiz's silky and melodious style is, in fact, the alter ego of his persona.

Imprisonment brings about quite a few mental changes quietly without the inmate becoming aware of it. The world of an incarcerated person is reduced to his cell, a few inmates, an open courtyard that might have a few, some stray animals like dogs and cats, some birds that either dwell on the trees or visit them daily to interrupt the stillness of the jail and that is all. This massive diminution in the external physical world on the one hand turns the inmate into a hypersensitive being and on the other hand, enhances his observation faculty. He becomes a sharp-edged observer of everything that exists or happens around him. The sense of transient time gets intense but instead of counting it in hours and minutes he computes it in days and weeks. What is more, he identifies himself strongly with nature and its vagaries. Despite his apparent composure all these changes came about in Faiz. In most letters written during the summer from Hyderabad Central Jail, he grumbles about the inconveniences caused by scorching heat and strong winds that carry with them flecks of the Sind desert.

In a letter of October 15, 1951, he wrote: "The past few days were very hot and the conditions were sizzling. Today it is somewhat agreeable and the wind is blowing again. It is a peculiar situation here. If you avoid dust airstreams, you have to bear the curse of the heat and if you feel like enjoying the spring wind, the mouth gets stuffed with sand."[5] On May 11, 1952, he noted, "(Here) the wind, unluckily, also means dust-streams. You believe it or not, I bathe four times a day and yet, save for a few minutes, the sense of cleanliness remains missing."[6] A similar complaint is expressed in the letter dated June 2, 1952, "Here, surprisingly a lot of sand and dust that the airstreams spread gets deposited in a minute. After bathing when I come out of the bathroom, my hair gets filled with dust by the time I reach my cell and it seems as if someone has scattered the crushed rock on the hands and feet. I feel like giving up the thought of bathing and like my Sindhi friends lolling in dust and sand. Yet, this does not happen. So, I bathe about ten times a day, change clothes four to five times and after spreading over sandal and scent, feel as if the kingdom of the world is mine. However, a few moments later the heat, dust and the walls of prison..."[7] Nonetheless, he had not always complained against the hostile climate of the Sind province. When the temperature would fall because of unanticipated rains or during winter he had admired the kindness of the climate in many letters.

The imprisonment provided Faiz the much looked-for respite for reading that he had missed during the military service and as editor of *The Pakistan Times*. He had started reading the books that he always wanted to and for that purpose in almost every fourth letter he would either ask for books or inform his wife about the book he was reading. It is amazing to note the wide range of his interest that included poetry, fiction, philosophy, history, literary criticism, drama and even culinary books. Besides Urdu and English he had asked for, Punjabi, Arabic and French books as well. In the fifth letter he wrote: "Add an Arabic book to the list of books that I've sent to you for I need it. If you find it send it along with the other books. The name of the book is *Diwan-ul-Hamasa* and the author's name is Abu Tamam. In addition, send as many Urdu poetry collections as you can find."[8] In the seventh letter he informed her about his initiation of learning French: "Now, there is no worry about magazines. Ifti (Mian Iftikharuddin) has brought a heap of them that would last for many days. However, send some primary books of French and dictionaries. Banney (Sajjad Zaheer) has promised that he will teach us French."[9] Thus, he kept asking for an array of books or informing about the books he was reading that included Chekov's play, *Three Sisters*, books written in simple French either by Maupassant or any other writer, Daudet's novels, James Aldridge and Bodley Head's novel *The Diplomat*, George Saintsbury's *A History of Criticism*, L.H. Myer's novel, *The Root and the Flower*, the three volumes of *Life During the East India Company*, I.A. Richards' *The Principles of Literary Criticism* and *Practical Criticism*, C.K. Ogden and I.A. Richards' *The Meaning of Meaning*, Nietzsche's *Thus Spake Zarathustra*, Sir George Sitwell's novel, *The Making of Italian Gardens*, Upton Sinclair's novel, *The Jungle*, Joyce Cary's novel *The Horse's Mouth*, Waris Shah's *Heer Ranjha*, James Boswell's *Life of Samuel Johnson*, Arnold Toynbee's *A Study of History*, Sean O'Casey's play *The Star Turns Red*, E.M. Foster's novel *Howards End*, Elia Ehrenberg's novel *The Storm*, Reynold A. Nicholson's *A Literary History of the Arabs*, Ernest Sackville Turner's *A History of Courting*, James George Frazer's *The Golden Bough*, S. Radhakrishnan's *Indian Philosophy*, the works of Confucius, Havelock Ellis and Richard Burton, love letters of Franz Kafka, Oscar Wilde's *A House of Pomegranates*, Nikolai Gogol's *Collected Tales and Plays*, Williamson, Henry's *Dandelion Days*, Shakhsiyat (Personalities) a number of the reputed Urdu magazine, *Naqoosh* and many others.

In jail he also translated Henrik Ibsen's play *Pillars of Society* into Urdu even as in a letter he mentioned that he was planning to write a book on aesthetics in Urdu. In the 90th letter dated May 29,

1953, he let Alys know that he had completed the course in French and started learning Spanish. In a letter dated September 15, 1952, he wrote: "I have just finished the novel for which the Nobel Prize was awarded last year. Its title is *Magister Ludi*." It is the German title (though the book was published in English with the German title too, the more popular edition was published with the English title, *The Glass Bead Game*) of the final novel by Hermann Hesse for which he won the Nobel in 1946 and not in 1951 as Faiz wanted to imply. The interesting point, however, is what Faiz has to say about the novel and the Nobel Prize. He added: "It is too long and a tiresome allegory, good only in patches. If this is the criterion of the Nobel Prize, then there is no reason why I cannot win it if I make an effort."[10] Though Faiz was shortlisted for the Prize a year before his death, he did not get it.

Faiz got the news of Sa'adat Hasan Manto's demise when he was in Montgomery jail. His reaction was recorded in the letter dated January 27, 1955: "The news of Manto's death pained me a lot. Despite all his weaknesses he was dear to me and I am somewhat proud of the fact that he was my student in Amritsar. His studentship was only in name because he hardly attended lectures. However, we would often meet at my place and fiercely discuss the works of Chekhov, Freud, Maupassant and many other subjects. Twenty years have passed but it feels as if it happened yesterday. The nobles of our society who are neither aware of an artist's emotional setback nor do they have any sympathy for him would most likely say that Manto died because of his own fault. He would drink too much; led an undisciplined life; had spoilt his health and so on. However, no one would bother to think why he did all that. Similarly, Keats had harmed himself, so did Bernz as well as Mozart. Some other names can also be cited in the context. The point is that when the social conditions force the art and life confronts each other, one of them has to be sacrificed. The second option is that of making a compromise thereby sacrificing some parts of both. In the third option, the two should be unified to embark on a struggle that can only be done by great artists. Manto was not great but he was very honest, extremely proficient and absolutely straightforward."[11] Though Manto was only a year younger than Faiz, he failed twice in the matriculation examination and thereafter spent a few years in Aligarh and when he eventually joined the MAO College in Amritsar, Faiz was a lecturer there. Commenting on the *Shaksiyat Number of Naqoosh*, Faiz wrote: "If an attempt is made to get an idea based on these sketches then we will have an impression that all our writers were saints and angels except poor Manto whose nephew Hamid Jalal has measured him with a lot more inflexibility."[12] Faiz's coolness in prison could be gauged by the substantial number of poems and ghazals he wrote in various jails. In the first three months of imprisonrment when he was kept in solitary confinement, he composed a few poems which he could not put on paper because the facility was not available. Later, in Hyderabad jail he could restore a few of those poems that he could store in his memory. A remarkable short poem (*Qata*) that reflected his condition of deprivation in solitary confinement was:

*Mata-e-loh-o-qalam chhin gayi to kya gham hai*
*Ke khoon-e-dil mein duboli hain ungliyan main ne*
*Zaban pe muhr lagi hai to kya ke rakh di hai*
*Har ek halqa-e-zanjeer mein zaban main ne*

Why feel sad if the asset of pen and tablet are seized
For, I've soaked the fingers in the heart's blood
If the lips are sealed, so what, for I've put by
My tongue in every link of the shackle

When he, along with other accused persons in the conspiracy, were shifted to Hyderabad Central Jail, most facilities meant for Class A prisoners, were restored to him and thereafter he could read and write in comfort. So, in the second letter written from Hyderabad dated July 14, he wrote: "After the arrest this is the sixth poem that I've just finished. (He could recall, in addition to the short poem cited above, three ghazals and one more *Qata* that were written in solitary confinement). It means that whatever I could write during the last three years I've written the twofold of it during the last three months."[13] For the other inmates, though some of them were very high ranking military officers, it was a matter of honour that they were lodged with Faiz. The good fortune of listening to his poems from the poet himself almost every week was a godsend for them. Among the inmates, besides Faiz, Sajjad Zaheer was the only one who was a poet himself. However, he was not as prolific a poet as Faiz was and secondly his nazms and ghazals would either be too obscure or too stylised and sophisticated for many of the inmates. Faiz, on the other hand, was one of the most popular poets of the Urdu world and his presence in their midst enthused his prison colleagues to take an interest in poetry in a big way. It was, of course, because of the woefully restricted means of recreation in the prison.

Most of the inmates had read all Faiz's published works. Some of them had even memorised many of his famous ghazals and nazms. They would, therefore, always implore Faiz to recite 'something new' in their weekly gatherings. Whenever Faiz composed a new *ghazal* or poem and if someone got wind of it, the *news* would spread in a jiffy and stir the surroundings of the prison. In reaction everyone would head towards his cell. Within minutes they would all gather around him as his loyal admirers ready to lap up every word that he recited. On most occasions Faiz acquiesced to their demand but there were some rare times when he might not feel like obliging. Then, one day, to the delight of all, he suggested that instead of he alone reciting poems all the inmates should make attempts to compose ghazals and recite them in a sort of *mushaira* that could become a monthly feature. He also proposed that in the tradition of the classical *mushairas*, a few lines of the famous couplets could be made available as (*misra-e-tarah*) guidelines for rhyme and meter. Having agreed to his suggestion, they unanimously elected Zafarullah Poshni as the *mushaira* secretary.[14]

With common consent each one was also assigned a funny nom de plume reflecting his physical appearance or natural proclivity. Poshni had written reports of two such *mushairas* wherein he mentioned the comical pseudonyms that were given to each poet. Faiz was *Kahil* (lazy), Sajjad Zaheer *Laghir* (enervated), Major General Akbar Khan *Fituri* (malevolent), Major Nazir

Ahmed *Saaras* (flamingo), Brigadier Sadiq Khan *Musaddiq* (named so because like the ex-Iranian Prime Minister, Dr. Mussadiq Khan would also spend most of his time in bed), Brigadier Lateef Khan *Khabti* (insane), Lieutenant Colonel Niyaz Muhammad Arbab *Khar* (ass), Lieutenant Colonel Ziauddin *Gadbad* (chaotic), Major Ishaq Muhammad *Danga* (crooked in Punjabi), Major Hasan Khan *Jahil* (illiterate), Captain Zafarullah Poshni *Khabis* (iniquitous) and so on.

Obviously, the entire exercise was just for fun and in good humour but many of Faiz's entrancing ghazals comprised in *Dast-e-Saba* and *Zindan Nama* were written for these crank *mushairas*. The first couplets of some of the more captivating ghazals that Faiz wrote for these *mushairas* and otherwise in prison are given below:

*Tum aaye ho na shab-e-intezar guzri hai*
*Talash mein hai sahar baar baar guzri hai*

[Neither have you come nor has the night of anticipation gone by
The morn is looking for (and) has, time and again, gone by]

*Tumhari yaad ke jab zakhm bharne lagte hain*
*Kisi bahane tumhein yaad karne lagte hain*

[When the gashes of your reminiscence get to heal
(I), on some excuse, get absorbed in your recall]

*Wahein hai dil ke qaraen tamam kahte hain*
*Wo ik khalish ke jise tera naam kahte hain*

[It is there itself; inform the gildings of the heart
That twinge that is known by your name]

*Rang pairahan ka, khushbu zulf lahrane ka naam*
*Mausam-e-gul hai tumhare baam par aane ke naam*

[Colour is the name of your attire, the fragrance is the flutter of your hair
The season of flowers connotes your appearance in the loggia]

*Yaad-e-ghazaal chashmaan, zikr-e-suman izaraan*
*Jab chaha kar liya hai kunj-e-qafas baharaan*

[Reminiscences of the ones with the eyes of gazelle, the natter of the ones with rosy cheeks

Whenever (I) feel like (I) can satiate the prison cell with the season of spring]

*Sitam ki rasmein bahut thhein lekin, na thhi teri anjuman se pahle*
*Saza, khatae-nazar se pahle, itaab jurm-e-sukhan se pahle*

[There were practices of oppression earlier but none like the one that reigns in your realm

Penalty, prior to the lapse of vision, reprisal prior to the offence of expression]

Additionally, he wrote some of the finest Urdu poems in the confines of various jails in Pakistan. They include *Tumhare Husn ke Naam* (*Salam likhta hai shaer tumhare husn ke naam*/ The poet salutes your exquisite beauty), *Tauq-o-Daar ka Mausam* (*Rawish rawish hai wohi intezar ka mausam*/ The spell of anticipation abounds row after row), *Do Ishq* (the last four lines of the poem: *Chhoda nahin ghairon ne koi nawak-e-dushnam/ Chhoti nahi apnon se koi tarz-e-malamat/ Is ishq na us ishq pe naadim hai magar dil/ Har daagh hai is dil mein bajuz daagh-e-nadaamat/* The strangers have spared no arrow of abuse/ The friends have left no mode of profanity/ The heart regrets neither this nor that love/ There exists every sort of blemish in the heart save the blemish of regret), *Irani Talaba ke Naam* (*Ye kaun sakhi hain/ Jin ke lahu ki/ Ashrafiyan chhan chhan, chhan chhan/ Dharti ke paiham pyase/kashkol mein dhalti jati hain/ Kashkol ko bharti jati hain/* Who are the generous donors/ Whose blood/ Drips clink clink, clink like gold coins/ In the forever thirsty begging-bowl of the earth/ Fills up the earth), *Zindan Ki Ek Shaam* (*Shaam ke pech-o-kham sitaron se/ Zeena zeena utar rahi hai raat/ Yon saba paas se guzarti hai/ Jaise kah di kisi ne pyar ki baat/* From the spiral of the stars/ The night descends step by step/ The zephyr wafts by in a way/ As someone whispers words of love), *Zindan Ki Ek Subh* (*Raat baqi thi abhi jab sar-e-baalein aa kar/ Chand ne mujh se kaha- "jag sahar aai hai*"/ A bit of night was yet to pass/ When the moon came by the bedside and whispered: "Wake up the dawn has arrived"), Yaad (*Dasht-e-tanhai mein ae jaan-e-jahan larzan hain/ Teri awaz ke saye, tere hoonton ke sarab*/ There sputter in the desert of solitude/ The shadows of your voice, the chimeras of your lips), *Mulaqat (Ye raat us dard ka shajar hai/ Jo mujh se tujh se azeem tar hai*/ This night is the tree of the anguish/ That is greater than you and me), and a few more.

While we discuss the poetry Faiz composed in jails, mention must be made of an article that one of the prison colleagues, Major Ishaq Muhammad, wrote as an introduction to *Zindan Nama*, the third anthology of the poet. Ishaq was not trained as a literary critic nor was he particularly addicted to poetry of any sort before meeting Faiz in jail. Though the companionship of four years with Faiz had refined Ishaq's literary taste, he was conscious of his lack of proper literary background to appraise the poetry of someone of Faiz's stature. At the beginning of the article he says: "For a simple soldier it could be bothersome to write about the poetry of Faiz. Furthermore, what sort of fostering the son of a peasant and that too the peasant of a colonised nation can have. The education acquired in village schools that too under the dark shadows of ignorance and superstition..."[15] Having familiarised readers about his personal and educational background, Ishaq admitted that the four years he spent in jails proved profitable from the point of view of acquiring knowledge. He spent most of the time reading books that he had missed as a student and military officer. Then he devoted considerable space writing about Faiz's life and what psychological transformation could take place in a person after he was confined within the four walls of a prison. About Faiz he wrote: "Among the people I knew prior to the life as a prisoner, Faiz was the only one who was apparently unaffected... Mercifully poetry was an adequate conduit through which he would purge the disquiet of his heart."[16] Since Ishaq had his cell adjacent to that of Faiz, he had observed all the moods of the poet from close quarters. He mentioned that Faiz would become absolutely quiet when he was about to compose a poem. Afterwards when the poet showed signs of restlessness, getting up, walking in circles within the cell, then suddenly sitting down and humming to himself all the time, Ishaq would get the signal that a new poem was composed. He would then spread the word among all the inmates, who in turn, to Faiz's astonishment, would gather around him and appeal for the recital of the latest creation. Faiz rarely disappointed them.

Faiz's prison poetry, in Ishaq's estimation, accentuated four shades indicative of the mental conditions and level of physical comforts in which the poet found himself in different jails at different times. For the first three months Faiz was kept in solitary confinement in the jails of Sargodha and Lyallpur. It was an extremely trying time for the poet. He did not have access to newspapers, books, pen, paper and letters. No visitor was allowed. Later, Faiz recalled that it was quite a prolific period as he could compose many poems but could write none of them. It was the phase that got reflected in his short poems—why feel sad if the asset of pen and tablet are seized—and a few other works which he could bring to mind such as *Daman-e-Yusuf* (a Qata or short poem), *Tera jamal nigahon mein le ke uttha hoon* (a Qata), *Tum aaye ho na shab-e-intezar guzri hai* (ghazal), *Tauq-o-daar ka Mausam* (first part of the poem), *Tumhari yaad ke jab zakhm bharne lagte hai*n (ghazal) and *Shafaq ki raakh mein jal bujh gaya sitara-e-shaam* (ghazal). All these are part of his second anthology.

In Hyderabad jail all the comforts and facilities were made available to him that were right and proper to a Class-A inmate. Nevertheless, the anxiety of getting the death penalty on account of certain serious charges dangled in the minds of Faiz and his colleagues like the proverbial Damocles' sword. In order to keep the fretfulness under wraps they had adopted as a strategy to create mayhem in the court premises and be aggressively vociferous about their innocence. Ishaq pointed out that though Faiz could not personally join in the pandemonium that others would create before the tribunal, rather he would give expression to his passion and eagerness in his poems. His works of this phase comprised *Phir hashr ke saaman huye aiwan-e-hawas mein* (qata), the second part of *Tauq-o-daar ka Mausam* (poem), *Tum aaye ho na shab-e-intezar guzri hai* (ghazal), *Hamarey dum se hai koye junoon mein ab bhi khijal* (qata), *Ijz-e-ahl-e-sitam ki baat karo* (ghazal) and a revolutionary song exclusively written for the inmates to keep their spirits high and energetic. The song was a hit among the inmates as they would sing it at every gathering. In the tradition of a revolutionary song its tone is noticeably high and the idea of protest is enfolded in fortitude and buoyancy. The song envisages the ultimate victory of truth. The first stanza of the song goes like this:

*Darbar-e-watan mein jab ik din sab chaahney waley jayeingey*
*Kuchh apni saza ko pahucheingey, kuchh apni jaza lejayeingey*
*Aye khak nasheenon uth baitho wo waqt qareeb aa pahuncha hai*
*Jab takht giray jayeingey, jab taj uchhaley jayeingey*

The day all the devotees would reach the court of the motherland
Some would be sentenced, some would be rewarded
O, the humble souls, get to your feet, the time is close by
When the thrones would be toppled and the crowns would be tossed up

According to Ishaq, the third hue of Faiz's prison poetry was fully reflected in his famed poem *Mulaqat* that the poet started composing when he was admitted to a Karachi hospital and completed it in the Montgomery jail. The poem is exceptionally symbolic replete with arresting similes and alluring metaphors. It signifies a synthesis of pain[17] and respite. It extols the genius, resolve and spirit of the contemporary man who is on the verge of becoming the master of the universe. It remains one of Faiz's most significant poems. The fourth phase of Faiz's prison poetry, in Ishaq's view, commenced when he was shifted to Montgomery jail. Though all the comforts and facilities he had in Hyderabad jail continued to be available in the new prison as well, he missed many of his colleagues who were shifted to different jails of Pakistan. He was also flabbergasted because of the verdict that prolonged his internment. Prior to the judgement of the case he was certain of his release. That did not happen. The feeling of deprivation and loneliness that he had experienced in the initial period of incarceration returned that made him hyper sensitive about the environment he was forced to live in. Now he would keenly perceive all the animate and inanimate objects that surrounded his prison world. He internalised the revolutionary fervour of all those who were engaged in challenging the reigns of oppression and exploitation in different parts of the world and were similarly condemned to be in captivity or in some cases put to death. When the freedom fighters in Kenya were mercilessly tortured and murdered by the foreign rulers, Faiz composed a war-cry for the African revolutionaries, which is replete with passion and martial zeal. He named it after the slogan of the African freedom fighter—*Africa Come Back*:

*Aa jao main ne sun li tere dhol ki tarang*
*Aa jao mast ho gai merey lahu ki taal*
*Aa jao Africa*

Come across! I've heard the thump of your drum
Come across! The tempo of my blood got speedier
Africa! Come back

Likewise, when Ethel and Julius Rosenberg were executed in the USA as spies of the USSR, Faiz immortalised their martyrdom in a remarkably sensitive poem—*Hum Jo Tareek Rahon Mein Mare Gaye*:

*Terey honton ke phoolon ki chahat mein hum*
*Daar ki khushk tahni pe warey gaye*
*Terey haton ki shamon ki hasrat mein hum*
*Neem tareek rahon mein marey gaye*

We, in the love of the flowers of your lips,
Got hanged on the dry bough of the stake
We, in the unrequited affection for the glow of your hands,
Got killed in the dim-lighted streets

Then there are poems that may be categorized as patriotic. His Marxist leanings did not tone down his love for his land and its people. In this respect he was closer to Gramsci's insight rather than the blueprint provided by the classical Marxists. When he was briefly imprisoned in Lahore jail, he experienced a heightened emotional upheaval for the city, where he practically grew up, matured, went to college and university, made friends, fell in love, got disheartened, got employed and permanently settled was extremely close to his heart. He knew that his captivity in the city with which he had a strong emotional bond would bring back all the memories and made him miserable. For that reason he did not wish to be in a Lahore jail. However, for the dental treatment he was shifted to the jail of his beloved city and as a result an enchanting poem full of melancholy and remorse got created–*Ae Roshniyo*n *ke Shahr:*

> *Sabza sabza sookh rahi hai pheeki zard do-pahr*
> *Deewaro*n *ko chaat raha hai tanhai ka zahr*

> The pale noon is getting parched turf after turf
> The venom of loneliness is licking the walls

Another poem–*Nisar Main Teri Galiyo*n *Ke*–occupies a prominent place in the poetry that Faiz wrote in praise of his motherland. It condoles the misfortune of the land as well as the oppression and exploitation of the people.

> *Nisar mai*n *teri galiyo*n *ke ae watan ke jaha*n
> *Chali hai rasm ke koi na sar utha ke chale*
> *Jo koi chahne wala tawaf ko nikle*
> *Nazar chura ke chale, jism-o-jaan bacha ke chale*

> O my land! I offer myself as sacrifice to your streets
> Where none can dare to roam with his head held high
> If a lover of yours ventures out to go around
> (He should do so) with furtive eyes and watchful gait

# Chapter 5

# Faiz: A Free Man Again

> Freedom does not consist in any dream of independence from natural laws, but in the knowledge of these laws, and in the possibility this gives of systematically making them work towards definite ends.
>
> **—Friedrich Engels**

> Everything that is really great and inspiring is created by the individual who can labour in freedom.
>
> **—Albert Einstein**

The Pakistan Constituent Assembly could not frame a universally acceptable constitution for the newly created country even after more than seven years of deliberations and squabbling. Dismayed over the snail's pace with which the Assembly was working, the Governor General Ghulam Muhammad dissolved it on October 24, 1954. Muhammad Ali Bogra, a Bengali politician from the Eastern wing of the country, who was selected as the Prime Minister a year earlier in 1953 continued to hold his position. The significant development was that the Commander-in-Chief, Ayub Khan was inducted in the cabinet to serve as the Defence Minister. Taking advantage of the change in the political scenario, the defendants in the Rawalpindi Conspiracy Case challenged the very institution of the Special Tribunal in the High Court. The Court upheld their plea by declaring the Tribunal null and void and ordered the release of all those who were arrested in the case. Thus, Faiz became a free man again in April 1955.

Alys and the two daughters were obviously over the moon when he suddenly stepped into his home on a balmy afternoon in April. The elder daughter, Salima, was now in the final year of school. A few months later she passed the matriculation examination with distinction and got a gold watch from her beloved father as a reward. Moneeza, the younger one got very thrilled to embrace her 'Abbu'. Now, she wanted him to pledge that he would never go to jail again. Faiz tried to reason with her that he did not go to jail on his own. The authorities sent him there. However, she persisted with the demand of word of honour. So Faiz promised not to go to jail again—a promise that was to fall foul a few years later!

The same day he had an important visitor. It was Raja Ghazanfar Ali Khan who was at the time Pakistan's High Commissioner to India. He had come to invite Faiz for a *mushaira* that he was going to organise in New Delhi to celebrate 'Iqbal Day'. Faiz was sceptical about his participation for he was just out of prison and he had this apprehension that the authorities would not allow him to go abroad. Raja Sahab assured him that he would take care of everything. Faiz agreed. Within days he got clearance from the government and thus he went to New Delhi. Faiz was not aware that his five-year incarceration had made him a legend even in India. He had acquired an aura of a crusader for people's rights and liberty. The *mushaira* was planned on the lawns of the official residence of the High Commissioner of Pakistan that could not accommodate thousands of people who had turned up to see and listen to Faiz. There was no Doordarshan in those days. The organisers ultimately decided to install loudspeakers outside the bungalow. The President of India, S. Radhakrishnan presided over the *mushaira* that, on intense public demand, continued till the break of dawn. In the afternoon Raja Sahab informed Faiz that he could not invite Pandit Jawaharlal Nehru, the Prime Minister, because of protocol regulations. However, Nehru called the High Commissioner and asked him to arrange a special session that evening where he could listen to the poetry of Faiz and other poets from Pakistan. In deference of Nehru's wish the session was arranged wherein he met Faiz and exceptionally acclaimed his poetry.

He rejoined *The Pakistan Times* as its editor, the position that was held in his absence by Mazhar Ali Khan. He once again threw himself into the vortex of journalism. The same year he was asked to lead a delegation of journalists to the People's Republic of China. The other notable member of the delegation was Ahmed Nadeem Qasmi. By the time the delegation reached Hong Kong, the political set-up changed in Pakistan. Iskandar Mirza became the new Governor General and a bureaucrat sponsored by the Muslim League, Choudhary Muhammad Ali, was appointed the Prime Minister. Nonetheless, the new political establishment gave the green signal to the delegation to proceed to China, which was warmly welcomed by the Premier, Chou En-lai (new spelling Zhou Enlai)

There are two short poems in Faiz's fourth anthology, *Dast Tahe Sang* (Hand Under the Rock), which commemorates his visit to Communist China. The first one 'Peking' comprises barely seven lines. (When Faiz reached the Chinese capital its official name was Beijing. Faiz, however, dedicated his poem to the city by its earlier name.) Faiz sings the praises of the country and its capital that made rapid progress in the fields of technology, agriculture, economy, public welfare and so on as a consequence of the Communist Revolution. In the last four lines of the poem Peking proudly declares:

*Merey keesay mein hai raton ka siyah faam jalal*
*Merey haton mein hai subhon ki anan-e-gulgon*
*Meri aagosh mein palti hai khudai sari*
*Merey maqdoor mein hai mojaza-e-kun fikoon*

My pocket contains the magnificence of black nights
My hands hold the crimson reins of morn
In my being resides the entire godhood
I can carry out the miracle of 'Be and it was'

The other poem is dedicated to a province of China. Sinkiang (currently Xinjiang) is an 'autonomous' province in the north-west of the People's Republic of China. Urumqi is its capital. Eighty per cent of Sinking's people profess Islam and there is a deep impact of Turkey on its culture. The province is 'autonomous' only in name because as per Chinese regulations any region comprising a majority of a particular ethnic people different from the mainstream population of the Republic is called 'autonomous.' It does not give any political or economic autonomy to its people. Sinkiang became the part of greater China in 1884. Immediately, the local Muslim majority launched a '*jihad*' against the Chinese authorities and for long there remained a civil war kind of situation in the province. It still simmers albeit inertly. The Communist Revolution succeeded in subduing the subversive designs of the local people. Apparently peace prevailed when Faiz had visited the province that satisfied him ideologically. Underlining the fact that conflict and bloodshed were things of the past in the first seven lines of the poem, Faiz, in the last four lines, appeared confident of everlasting peace and for that reason, called for celebration. The four lines are:

*Ab koi jung na hogi, mai-o-saghar lao*
*Khoon lutana na kabhi ashk bahana hoga*
*Saqiya! Raqs koi raqs-e-saba ki soorat*
*Mutraba! Koi ghazal rang-e-hina ki soorat*

Henceforth, there will be no war, bring the cup and the wine
Neither will there be bloodshed nor wailing
O Saqi! Fix up a dance like the bop of zephyr
O Singer! Croon a ghazal doused in the hue of henna

Considering the current agitation for independence of the Muslims in Sinkiang it seems that Faiz's optimism has proved to be premature.

In October 1958, Faiz went to Tashkent to participate in the Afro-Asian Writers Conference. After the conference he went to Moscow. When he landed at Domodedovo, the old international airport of the city, he got the news that Ayub Khan had ousted

Iskandar Mirza and after packing him off to London, himself assumed the Presidency to enforce the first military dictatorship in Pakistan. Ayub Khan had also appointed himself as field marshal. The development saddened Faiz because it was a major setback to the nascent democratic forces that were trying to gain a foothold in a country that did not even have a constitution of its own. Alexi Surkov, a Russian poet, writer and translator, has written about his first meeting with Faiz first in Tashkent and then in Moscow.[1] Surkov had discussed the then prevailing political situation of Pakistan with Faiz and warned him about his imminent arrest in case he returned to Pakistan. The relevant part of the article goes like this:

In Moscow we were ensconced in a room that was assigned to the Writers Association of the city. Both of us were reciting poems and were also planning to bring out an anthology of Faiz's poems in Russian translation. Then, we found ourselves discussing the then political situation of Pakistan. I asked:

> 'What plans do you have for the immediate future?'
>
> Faiz looked at me with his black eyes whose depth had a shade of gloom and replied with a slight smile, 'First, I will go to London. There I will meet some of my friends who have just arrived from Pakistan. Thereafter, obviously I will go back to Karachi and then to Lahore.'
>
> 'However, you know that now there...'
>
> The slight smile was still on his lips. 'It is obvious that in such a situation I must go back to my motherland.'
>
> 'Then jail is the certainty...'
>
> 'Perhaps—and if a man has to go to jail for a greater cause then he must...'
>
> 'But if—there is something worse than jail in store then...?'
>
> The poet looked from the window at the garden in whose centre the statue of Tolstoy was installed. Then had a cursory glance at the cold and autumn-afflicted sky. All the while the smile was intact. After a few moments he spoke in his typical low voice, 'If there awaits something worse than jail then it will certainly be

very bad but, you know, struggle is after all struggle.' This was his calm and confident answer.[2]

The account is a testimony to two obvious facts: First, Faiz was expressly committed to democracy and freedom and the news of imposition of military dictatorship in his beloved country distressed him immensely. Second, he was a brave man who would willingly withstand state oppression for the sake of his principles. He was aware, as it is evident in the aforementioned description, that on reaching Pakistan he would certainly be jailed or might face something worse but he did not hesitate even for a moment to return to his motherland at a time when all the hopes and aspirations of establishing a people's rule were being trampled under the heavy and horrid military boots.

When Faiz reached London, he was mobbed by the students of Pakistani origin who were furious because of the military despotism that had been inflicted upon their country. They wanted to know from Faiz what they were expected to do and how democratic forces could regain the lost freedom. Faiz could only prescribe a hard and long struggle for people's liberty. On reaching Lahore, he was, as expected arrested and imprisoned in Lahore fort. The event is described by Alys: "Faiz came home from London on 12th December...He expected to be arrested at the Karachi airport, but was not. Karachi friends tried to prevail upon him to stay in Karachi, knowing that the orders for his arrest had been issued by the provincial government and that they were awaiting him. But 14th December was Salima's birthday and he wanted to be home for it. In Lahore, still no reaction apart from a call on the evening of the 14th, obviously from the CID verifying his presence. Time was catching up on him.

"Next day I was in my office when he called me. 'Can you come?' 'No, I'm busy.' 'Well you'd better...' I had taken a tonga (to home), 'My wife', Faiz had warned Habeeb Shahzada, the officer who had come to arrest him, 'will be very angry.' A typical Faiz understatement. With my mouth full of the choicest Punjabi lashings, I lightened my heart."[3] His earlier internment was on the basis of a trumped up charge but his imprisonment in 1958, was for no apparent reason. The military authorities did not even bother to invoke some fictitious accusation to justify his arrest. This perplexed him. Reacting to his second incarceration, Faiz had said: "Whether I have killed someone or am I a dacoit? Have I written against my country? Whenever something of consequence happens in the country I am sent to jail without a reason. What a put-up job is this!"

It was undoubtedly a period of mental torture to him being in jail with no rhyme or reason but the greater inconveniences were faced by Alys and the children. In the earlier stint, Faiz was in jail for almost five years but during the entire period his popularity as a poet went through the roof. The publishers and editors would lap up his ghazals or poems to increase the circulations of their magazines. The second time, however, the military rulers saw to it that no magazine published Faiz's poetry. It was an unwritten military edict whose violation would attract harsh consequences. During the five months' captivity, Faiz wrote a few poems, ghazals and a qata; this poetry was smuggled out of Lahore fort as well but there was hardly any publisher to buy it. Alys faced the adversity and privation with such steely resolution and dignity that spoke volumes about her extraordinary moral fibre. Faiz wrote his extremely popular poem *Aaj Bazaar Mien Pa-ba Jaulan Chalo* (Today Get Going in the Bazaar With Shackled Feet) in Lahore jail that is definitely one of the finest revolutionary poems in Urdu. Here is a stanza:

*Haakim-e-shahr bhi, majma-e-aam bhi*
*Teer-e-ilzam bhi, sang-e-dushnam bhi*
*Subh-e-nashad bhi, roz-e-nakam bhi*
*In ka damsaaz apne siwa kaun hai*
*Shahr-e-janan mein ab basafa kaun hai*
*Dast-e-qatil ke shayan raha kaun hai*
*Rakht-e-dil bandh lo, dik figaro chalo*
*Phir hamein qatl ho aaen yaro chalo*

The ruler of the realm, the throng of the people
The arrow of accusation, the stone of profanity

The forlorn dawn, the failed day
Who is their soul-mate save us?
Who is the pure one in the city of love save us?
Who is now fit for the smack of the killer save us?

O wounded hearts! Fasten the effects of heart (and) get going
O comrades! Let us get killed again, get going

After five months of custody, Faiz was released. Then, he got to know that his job at *The Pakistan Times* was gone because under the military despotism the daily was taken over by the government. In a week's time, Inspector General of CID, Nazir Rizvi visited Faiz. He promptly allayed the fears of the poet and Alys that his visit was not official and that he came as a friend with a request to make. He told Faiz that though the government had taken control of *The Pakistan Times*, the position of Chief Editor was still open for him. Faiz did not waste a moment telling Rizvi to "get lost." It was the absolute commitment to his ideals that despite being without a job and with no hope of getting one in the near future, Faiz turned down the lucrative offer. When asked about what plans he had in mind when he refused the government offer, Faiz had replied: "What plans I have or not is secondary. The real issue is that of principle. Sometimes, for the sake of the principles and for the protection of noble and sublime values of life one has to put together within himself a refined and sacrosanct fortification. In the absence of such a fortification a man is likely to be the victim of compromises. I think hunger can be won over. Similarly, man can also live through physical torture. Pain is within the prowess of man that can control it. Pain, in reality, is a scream to release some limb of one's body from frailty or disorder. When the man within you is in confrontation with death then physical agony becomes inconsequential."

Faiz had an abiding faith in the dialectical view of human existence and for that reason he would always be prepared to struggle against anti-people forces. In a struggle like this initially the oppressive and exploitative forces would always appear to be too strong against the exploited, weaker and unarmed masses.

Nonetheless, the masses ultimately win. History is testimony to the fact. Faiz believed that the October Revolution in Russia under the leadership of Lenin was in reality the height of the dialectical struggle of the classes. The revolution had shaken the foundations of the Church and monarchical order of the government and established in its place a new social order, created a new man with new ideals. He was hoping to see a similar revolution in Pakistan. That was not to be either in his lifetime or till now. Nonetheless, he tried to live for the success of the socialist ideals. His father, as it has been noted, led an aristocratic life and left behind huge property.

Though almost the entire urban property in Sialkot, Lahore and other towns was disposed to repay the money he owed to various creditors, substantial agricultural properties in the ancestral village were still under the family's legal control. Most tillers were Faiz's poor relatives from both sides of his parents. Faiz's elder brother, Tufail Ahmed Khan, who managed the properties, had died in July 1952 while Faiz was in jail. In 1959, when he came out of his second stint in jail he had made up his mind to hand over the ancestral agricultural land to the tillers. Though Faiz was released from jail, he was still under surveillance and the CID men were permanently stationed outside his home. One day he somehow managed to delude his watchdogs and without informing Alys left for Sialkot. There he convinced his mother, younger brother and other relatives and left for Kala Qadir along with the tehsildar and village patwari. He invited all the villagers who tilled his ancestral lands and announced that except for his ancestral home he was transferring the ownership rights of the agricultural lands to the tillers. Later, when Faiz's mother visited Kala Qadir, the villagers gave her the kind of reception that could be worthy of a queen!

His absence in Lahore had created an upheaval in the intelligence department. They panicked thinking that he had gone underground. Alys and his daughters were, sure enough, terribly worried. Three days later when Faiz reached home, his wife and daughters were on the verge of despair. He explained his absence to them. Then a high ranking intelligence officer dropped in to inform him that the Governor had invited him. The then Governor of Punjab, Mushtaq Ahmed Gormani, was a friend of Faiz for long. He would periodically consult Faiz to prepare orations. He was also concerned about Faiz's disappearance. Faiz narrated the entire episode. Gormani did not approve of Faiz's altruistic feat. He, however, added that there were many evacuees' properties that he could allot to anyone. He advised Faiz to identify the property of his choice and that would be allotted to him. Faiz replied, "I have just got rid of a curse and you want me to get embroiled into another one." The governor tried his best to persuade Faiz to accept his offer but the poet committed steadfastly to his socialist ideals politely refused the largesse.

An incident that happened in the second year of Ayub's marshal law, i.e. 1959 indicates how many people belonging to varied sections of society loved Faiz. The military authorities had decided to officially celebrate the birth anniversary of the Qaid-e-Azam. As part of the celebration a musical programme was organised in the central hall of Punjab University. Arrangements were also made to broadcast the programme live on Radio Pakistan. Almost all the renowned musicians and singers were invited. When the most popular singer of the country, Noorjahan, was invited on the stage, she started singing Faiz's poem, *mujh se pahli si mohabbat merey mehboob na mang*, the broadcast was immediately disconnected because Faiz's poetry was banned on the radio. The military officers present in the programme requested Noorjahan to sing some other song. She point-blankly refused. They tried to persuade her for quite some time but she stood her ground. Then somebody gave her a veiled threat that public performance involving banned poetry could put her in trouble. She shot back, "In that case you also send me to the jail where Faiz is." They ultimately conceded defeat and allowed her to sing Faiz's poem. Obviously, her performance was not broadcast on Radio Pakistan.

Faiz had been a chain smoker from his college days. Once when he was in the examination hall, he was just sitting idle. The invigilator was the famous poet Sufi Ghulam Mustafa Tabassum. He inquired why Faiz was looking forlorn instead of answering the paper. Faiz pleadingly asked for permission to smoke. At that moment the Principal, Patras Bukhari, the famous humorist and satirist, appeared in the corridor. Tabassum conveyed Faiz's unexpected request. Patras surprisingly asked Tabassum to allow Faiz to smoke. Thus, Faiz was perhaps the first student in Lahore who smoked while sitting in the examination hall.

In later years, nonetheless, his excessive smoking affected his health. Soon after coming out of jail he had a heart attack. It was Alys's alacrity that she immediately arranged for the medical care that saved Faiz's life. Alys put a restriction on his smoking. He could bear with it temporarily but could never give up smoking completely. He wrote a poem, *Heart Attack* to give expression to his feelings when he had it.

*Dard itna thha ke us raat dil-e-wahshi ne*
*Har rag-e-jaan se ulajhna chaha*
*Har ban-e-mu se tapakna chaha*
*Aur kahein door terey sahan mein goya*
*Patta patta merey afsurda lahu mein dhul kar*
*Husn-e-mehtaab se aazurda nazar aaney laga*
*Merey weerana-e-tan mein goya*
*Saarey dukhtay huye reshon ki tanaabein khul kar*
*Silsila war pata denein lagein*
*Rukhsat qafila-e-shauq ki tayyari ka*
*Aur jab yaad ki bujhti hui sham'on mein nazar aaya kahein*
*Ek pal aakhri lamha teri dildaari ka*
*Dard itna thha ke us se bhi guzarna chaha*
*Hum ne chaha bhi , magar dil na thaharna chaha*

That night the pain was so intense that the brutal heart
Coveted to wrangle with the network of veins
Yearned to drip from each root of the hair
And far away, as though in your courtyard
Every leaf bathed in my dejected heart
Seemed distressed by the beauty of the moon

As though in the ruins of my body
The fastening ropes of the throbbing hair got disentangled
Set off revealing in a sequence
The readiness of the caravan of longing to depart
And when there flashed in the dowsing candles of memory
A trice, the last moment of your love
(Yet) the pain was so intense that it too went by
Even though I wished but the heart declined to stay

## (II)

A high point of Faiz's life appeared in 1962 when he was chosen for the Lenin Peace Prize, which was considered the equivalent of the Nobel Prize in the socialist world. Pakistan was under military despotism and its foreign policy was out-and-out pro-American. The country was a member of the US-sponsored military alliances such as SEATO and CENTO. The military authorities of Pakistan forewarned him, obviously on cue from the US, not to accept the honour conferred by a 'godless' Communist regime and named after a leader who was not only 'anti-freedom but was also anti-Islam.' As Alys says, "there was an uproar led by the right-wing press, mainly the *Nawa-i-Waqt*. No term of abuse was left unsaid, no threat held back. He should not be allowed to leave Pakistan to receive the prize in Moscow!"[4] Faiz did not take note of the warnings and went to Moscow to receive the award. The problem was that on medical advice he could not fly so early after the heart attack. "Dr. Seltzer, our doctor, who had been solicitude itself throughout, said, 'by train and by sea only.' So long and ugly story cut a little shorter, Salima (on her way to England to study art) along with Faiz, prepared to board an Italian liner for Naples and then make the long overland journey to Moscow"[5] It is interesting to have a look at Salima's account of the long journey:

> When we reached Rome, a friend of Abba's had booked us into the Grand Hotel, this very fancy place. I pointed out the tariff to Abba. It was outrageously high and he said we can't afford

> this. So the next day we shifted to a more modest hotel. We boarded the train two days later and Abba being Abba, had no idea that the train journey was going to last three days. He had just looked at the arrival time, which was 9 am and he assumed it was the next day after we boarded. And, of course, it was my first time out of Pakistan so I was clueless. The train set off and we discovered that there was no restaurant car so there was no food to eat and the train didn't stop anywhere. At night we were hungry and tired but the train kept going. Finally, the next morning the train stopped somewhere, may be Vienna and we rushed off, ravenously hungry and finally found some sandwiches. When we finally got to Moscow, there was a reception committee to receive us. It was the first time that Abba and I had travelled alone together. It was also the first time I learned to wash his socks when I realised he didn't know how to do it.[6]

It must be stressed that he was the first Asian poet who was selected for the honour. Prior to him the other prominent persons who were conferred with the Lenin Peace Prize were Fidel Castro, Pablo Picasso, Berthold Brecht, Pablo Neruda, Mehmood Darvesh, Salvador Allende, Angela Davis et al. In his acceptance speech, which he delivered in Urdu, he hoped that mankind that had never surrendered to its enemies would once again be victorious and ultimately scourges such as hatred, oppression and war would give way to peace and universal brotherhood. Below the English rendition of his speech is reproduced:

> Honourable members of the Presidential Council, Ladies and Gentlemen!
>
> Creation and composition of words is the business of poets and writers. However, there come in life a few such occasions when this mastery gives in. Today, I am facing a similar predicament of lack of ability of expression. My mind fails to find a few proper words in which I must appropriately thank the Lenin Prize Committee, various institutions of the Soviet Union, friends and all the ladies and gentlemen for honouring me. The prominence of the Lenin Peace Prize is conspicuous in the very fact that the respectable name and revered word of Lenin is

associated with it. Lenin who, in the contemporary world, is the most revered standard-bearer of freedom and peace that are the first condition of human life and its beauty and goodness. In my writings and actions I do not see any such thing that meets the requirements of this illustrious honour. Nevertheless, one reason that comes to mind for the conferment of this honour on me is that, with the kind of longing and idealism my comrades and I are associated with the yearning for peace and freedom that in itself is so exalted that those who work for its attainment, however insignificant they might be, deserve to be honoured.

In this case, save the mentally retarded and criminals, all people believe that peace and freedom are very beautiful and magnificent things and all can imagine that peace is the fields of wheat and eucalyptus trees, the stole of the bride and the chuckling faces of children, the pen of the poet and the brush of the artist and freedom is the guarantor of all these virtues and slavery is the murderer of all these merits that distinguishes man from animal, i.e. awareness and wisdom, justice and truth, respect and courage, good deeds and broad-mindedness. For this reason, seemingly there should not be a difference of opinion on the issues of peace and freedom among the sensible people. Nonetheless, unfortunately it is not so because since the beginning of mankind till now, in every age, opposite factors and powers have remained confronted. These forces have been the forces of destruction and construction, progress and regression, light and darkness, justice and injustice. This is the situation even now and similar strife continues even today. Yet, there are differences of varied kinds between today's human problems and the tribulations of the human life of yore. In the contemporary age, war does not mean the reciprocal bloodshed of two tribes, nor does peace denote the end of bloodshed. Today, the meanings of war and peace are the survival of humankind and its annihilation. The perpetuation of human history and its end depends on the two words, i.e. survival and annihilation. On these words too depends the inhabitation of the people on the face of the earth or its destruction. This is the first variance. The second variance is that earlier human beings did not have much control over the natural resources nor did they have the kind of mastery over production that could take care of the needs and could ensure satisfaction of every group and community. There was, therefor, a justification for forcible snatching of things, pillaging and murder. Presently, however, this is not the case. Now, the human intelligence with the help of science and industry has reached the point where everyone can flourish and the needs of all can be taken care of. The rider, however, is that these valuable sources of nature, the unlimited harvests of produce should not be for the satisfaction of the voracity of a few monopolists and exclusive classes but should be made available for the benefit of all human beings. Moreover, all the inventions and capabilities of intellect, science and industry should be in use for constructive projects instead of destruction. This may also be possible that human society develops compatibility with these objectives and the foundations of the structure of human society be laid down on justice, egalitarianism, freedom and collective well-being instead of greed, exploitation and monopoly. Now, this is not an abstract or imaginative thing; it is a practical work. In this work the boundaries of struggle for peace and freedom run into each other. It is so because the friends and foes of peace and the friends and foes of freedom belong to the same tribe, form the same kind of forces. On the one side are the imperialistic powers whose interests and monopolies cannot stay alive without coercion and envy and for the protection of these monopolies they even go to the extent of sacrificing entire humanity. On the other side, there are forces which prefer human lives more than banks and industrial houses. They get more pleasure in mutually supporting each other and working in cooperation rather than lording over others. The conflict between construction and subversion, between humanism and anti-humanism keeps going in politics, morality, literature and art, in everyday life on many fronts and in varied forms. The people who love freedom and peace must pay attention to these fronts and each form of the conflict. For instance, apart from the struggle between imperialist and anti-imperialist forces, unfortunately there exist intense differences among those countries which got freedom recently. Such differences exist between our country, Pakistan and our nearest neighbouring country India; they exist amongst the Arab countries and also amongst the African governments. It is obvious that only those forces can benefit because of these differences that exist among the recently decolonised countries, which have an aversion to world peace and friendship and unity of humankind. Consequently, it is obligatory on the part of the reconciliation-friendly and peace lovers to contemplate the judicious resolution of these differences and help implement the resolution.

A little while ago when the reverberation of the latest stupendous achievement of the Soviet space project was strewn all across the world, I would often think over that today when we, settled in the world of stars, could look at our world then how absurd were the things such as the petty malice, self-centredness, the attempts to divide a few tracts of land, the craving for lording over a few clusters of people. Now, when all the ways of the universe have opened for us, the treasures of the world could be controlled by humanity, then don't we have a sizable number of conscientious, judicious and honest people among humankind that can prevail upon all others to wrap up the military establishments and sink the bombs, rockets, cannons and guns in the sea? And, instead of conquering each other let us get engaged in subjugating the universe. It may lead us there where there is no paucity of land, where there is no need for anyone to wrangle with others, where there are endless outer spaces and countless worlds. I am certain that despite all the impediments and difficulties, we will make our human brotherhood to agree to this.

I am certain that humanity that has never got beaten by its enemies till now will be triumphant again and ultimately in place of war and hatred, oppression and malice, the foundation of our common life will be the one about which the Persian poet, Hafiz, had instructed a long time ago:

*Khalal pazeer bawad her bina ki mi beeni*
*Magar binay muhabbat ki khali az khalal ast*

Don't you know that the base of all things is not without chink
Save the base of love that is without a chink[7]

The reaction of the junta in Pakistan was obviously antagonistic. Most newspapers and electronic media were loyally toeing the line of the military authorities. There was no dearth of self-serving journalists and 'literary critics' who had launched an anti-Faiz campaign. The thrust of their argument was that since Faiz had accepted the Lenin Peace Award conferred upon him by a godless and anti-Pakistan state (the USSR was labelled anti-Pakistan because it was anti-America and in the Cold War logic any state that had the slightest difference with the USA, was declared anti-Pakistan by the Pakistani junta), he was not only anti-Islam but also anti-national. The religious fanatics who were the paid lackeys of the junta were leading the campaign against Faiz. In the literary magazines which were controlled by the anti-progressive litterateurs, the so-called literary critics made malignant attempts to make their readers believe that the Lenin Peace Prize was essentially political and Faiz's poetry was not of the calibre that it could be honoured with an international award. They deliberately concealed the fact from the readers that the basic objective of the award was to honour those who should have a prominent position internationally in their respective fields and through their works, be it painting, music, poetry, performing arts or statesmanship, contributed immensely to the cause of international peace and freedom. The overwhelming majority of Pakistanis were, however, extremely delighted because of the honour conferred on their beloved poet. They were proud of him but because of the fear of persecution at the hands of the military authorities could not openly celebrate or give expression to their feelings of elation.

## (III)

From Moscow Faiz went to London with the apparent intention of making it home for as long as possible. It could be a joint decision or Alys might have insisted and Faiz had to give in but it could not possibly be Faiz's decision individually to settle in London. The reason could be traced in the account of Ayub Mirza who was in Nottingham at the time. On a cold afternoon he called Faiz who appeared to be extremely eager to meet him right away. Mirza along with a friend Eric went to Faiz's house that was located in a middle-class locality of London. Then, as Mirza reported: "Faiz hugged me. The room was an apology for a drawing room. Fire was on in a small singlenook... Faiz looked too disconsolate. He did not even open the topic of the Lenin Prize...Tea was served and we finished it quietly...I asked Faiz to have a stroll outside. Faiz said yes but Alys protested, 'Faiz has been coughing for the last two days and if he goes out he might catch cold.' However, Faiz did not listen to her. He picked up his overcoat and went out.

"We went to a pub. I invited Faiz to Nottingham so that he could meet his countrymen settled in other parts of England. He hastily asked, 'when?' I said soon enough...I felt that he was eager to meet his compatriots. I inquired why there was no cheerfulness on his face...'Is there any financial problem?' He said 'Nothing of the sort. Though the Prize money has not reached, I don't need it either'...I asked, 'you know London back to front. How have you found it this time?' He said; 'Brother! What sort of a country is it! It is too cold most of the time. I bear it for there is heat most of the time in my country and I bear that too. However, in this land of money, in this throng of slaves, wages, industries and offices, a quiet person cannot even walk with ease. People always keep scurrying. Take the bus, tube, rail, they keep rushing. There is no quietness anywhere. And there are rains that too I bear for I have borne the chill of winter and the incessant rains of my country. However, this overcast weather all through, you cannot see the sky at all. Not even the moon, stars or sun. Brother! What sort of a country is it, which does not have a moon, does not have stars, and does not have a sun of its own? In the absence of the sun, moon or stars, I cannot imagine life whatsoever.'

On returning to Pakistan in 1963, Faiz was appointed the Principal of Abdullah Haroon College, Karachi. During the India-Pakistan war of 1965, the anti-Faiz lobby in Pakistan started a malicious campaign against him that he was pro-India. Responding to the vilification, Faiz said: "This is claptrap. What is this pro-Indianness? India is a country which is bigger than our country.

In our country, there is suppression and oppression, violence and plunder right from the beginning. A sort of system has emerged here whose foundation is the ignominy, mortification of people and loot. There is a similar story in India too. It is a bigger country that is why such transgressions are done on a larger scale there. There, Tata, Birla, Dalmia like our Adamjis, Sahgals, Dawoods et al. are active against the interests of the people. There are two classes there too as they are here. One class comprises those who rule and plunder and armed with the political power seizes control of all means of production and wealth. And the other class is composed of the people whose fate is stowed with deprivation, poverty and disease. It does not control wealth but it produces wealth by tilling the fields and working in the factories. It grows foodgrains but its women and children do not get two meals a day. Dispossession is destiny. The two classes exist on the two sides of Wagha and Khokrapar. My sympathies have always been with the class that produces wealth but remains deprived of it. The class that pines for wealth and is ignorant of the marvels of its usage; the class whose children like cattle are oblivious of the finer aspects of life and like their ancestors they too get engaged in the production of wealth and get lost in the interminable labyrinth of starvation. It is a huge scam. The wars such as this one cannot end this scam. So far as the accusation (of being pro-India) is concerned, this trait is not mine; it is the peculiarity of 'great' people. I, therefore, am not qualified to get associated with this term nor do I like it...I do not treat this vile propaganda as a trifle. I do not consider these vulgar charges worthy enough to respond to. It is the kind of reality that overshadows humanity for thousands of years and it has reduced human civilisation to a moth-eaten state. If a paralytic mind or a wily and shrewd person shows the audacity to present it in a different hue then he publicises his bankruptcy of the mind's iniquity. This type of people are rascals."* Faiz was, in fact above the trivial cataloguing of patriots and traitors. Though he loved his motherland, he did not stretch his nationalist passion to the point of worship He seemed to believe in Rabindranath Tagore's saying: "Neither the colourless vagueness of cosmopolitanism, nor the fierce self-idolatry of nation-worship, is the goal of human history." [8]

Faiz's vision was too expansive to be contained within the confines of a particular nation. Like his works, he too belonged to the entire mankind. What Walt Whitman believed about himself was true about Faiz as well:

"Do I contradict myself? Very well, I contradict myself.
I am large. I contain multitudes."[9]

Despite being a believer in the ultimate revolution of the masses, Faiz was essentially a pacifist. He hated war. He strongly advocated that peace was not only necessary for all kinds of human development, it was also essential for establishing a brotherhood comprising all human beings. He upheld the view that a common man was by nature peace-loving; he would never fight despite being the victim of centuries of exploitation. Faiz particularly loathed the idea of a poor country waging war against an equally poor country to settle their mutual disputes. He believed that most Third World countries including India and Pakistan could not afford to play at an expensive exploit like war. The majority of their people had to suffer extreme poverty that consequently forced them to the level of subhuman existence. The teeming masses in such countries endure a life of deprivation, joblessness, illiteracy and malady. Most people in countries like India and Pakistan did not have access to clean potable water and hygienic toilets. An overwhelming number of people in the Third World did not have a roof over its head. The respective governments of these countries should launch welfare schemes to take the pressure off the agonised existence of their people. Instead the class that had an absolute control over power–political as well as economic–in these countries had the a penchant to frequently toy with a high-priced and extremely dangerous pursuit like war to divert people's attention from the real, pressing issues. Hundreds of soldiers who essentially belonged to the poverty-inflicted section of the masses got killed in the expensive escapade of the ruling clique. In the aftermath of the Indo-Pak war, Faiz wrote an elegy dedicated to the common soldier who with extreme sincerity and passion went all out to defend his motherland and in doing so laid down his life. Faiz's requiem, *Sipahi ka Marsiya* is a tribute to all the ordinary soldiers of the world who had been tricked to get killed for the satisfaction of the bestial egotism of their rulers. The diction of Faiz in this poem is closer to Hindi, a departure from his usual chaste Urdu.

*Utho ab maati se utho*
*Jago merey lal*
*Ab jago merey lal*

*Tumri sej sajawan karan*
*Dekho aai rain andhyaran*
*Neeley shaal, do shaaley le kar*
*Jin mein in dukhiyan akhiyan ne*
*Dher kiye hain itney moti*
*Itney moti jin ki jyoti*
*Daan se tumra jag jag laaga*
*Naam chamakney*

*Utho ab maati se utho*
*Jago merey lal*
*Ab jago merey lal*

*Ghar ghar bikhra bhor ka kundan*
*Ghor andhera apna aangan*
*Jane kab se raah takey hain*
*Baali dulhaniya, baankey veeran*
*Soona tumra raaj pada hai*
*Dekgo kitna kaaj pada hai*
*Bairi berajey raj singhasan*
*Tum mati mein lal*

*Utho ab maati se utho, jago merey lal*
*Hut na karo, maati se utho, jago merey lal*
*Ab jago merey lal*

Arise now from the dust
Wake up my son
Now wake up my son

To embellish your bed
Look! The dark night has arrived
Carrying blue shawls and wraps
In which, these aching eyes
Heaped up so many pearls
So many pearls whose lustre
offering has made your name shine
all across the world

Arise now from the dust
Wake up my son
Now wake up my son

The gold of the dawn is dispersed from house to house
Our courtyard is shrouded in thick darkness
Don't know since when the
young bride and the smart brothers
are looking out for (you)
Your realm is desolate
See! How much work is to be accomplished
The foe is seated on the throne
You lurch in the dust

Arise now from the dust, wake up my son
Don't be obdurate, arise from the dust, wake up my son
Now, wake up my son

## (IV)

The Fourth Congress of the Writers was held in Moscow in May 1967. Faiz from Pakistan and Krishan Chander from India were the special invitees. Pablo Neruda and Mikhail Sholokhov also attended the Congress. In the inaugural session, the President, Prime Minister and the Members of the Cabinet of the Soviet Union were also present but they were seated behind the row of the writers. This showed the kind of respect and dignity the writers enjoyed in the Soviet society. When Sholokhov reached the podium to deliver his talk, the entire audience including the political bigwigs rose and heartily cheered to give him a warm welcome.

In the evening of the first day, elaborate arrangements were made for the dinner. Many tables were laid in a huge dining hall. For each delegate a separate table was assigned on which a small flag of her/his nation was placed. Krishan Chander and his wife Salma Siddiqui arrived much earlier than Faiz. They noticed a small Pakistani flag on a table but Faiz was missing.When he finally arrived and spotted Chander sitting a short distance away, he picked the flag of his country and moved towards him. Chander too got up with the Indian flag and started towards Faiz. Both reached a centrally located table that was unoccupied. They kept the flags of their respective nations on the table and hugged each other so passionately as if the long separated brothers were meeting each other. All the delegates representing various countries were watching them with bated breath. They cheered and hailed excitedly when the two litterateurs from India and Pakistan embraced each other.

"What is the big issue after all," Faiz spoke animatedly, "are we the enemies of each other like the biased politicians? This enmity does not exist between us and how I wish it should not exist anywhere else." Then he added solemnly, "Nonetheless, unfortunately we cannot meet either in India or Pakistan. We meet only in Moscow." Then he lightly commented, "The organisers should hold the Congress of the Soviet Writers annually so that we can meet at least once in a year." In a short while many other delegates joined them at the table with the flags of their respective nations. At the valedictory function Faiz and Chander were accorded special honour by making them sit together in the centrally located table. When parting with each other both Faiz and Chander showed exemplary restraint in controlling their tears. Their eyes were dry but the eyes of about a hundred writers surrounding them were moist.

## (V)

The breakup of Pakistan and creation of Bangladesh was an event that tested Faiz's love for the exploited workers and peasants, the class that produces wealth but does not own it. He was deeply disturbed by the military brutality with which the heavily armed soldiers from the West wing of Pakistan slaughtered hundreds of unarmed people of the then East Pakistan. His poem, *Hazar Karo Merey Tan Se* reflects his mental agony. The poem is a frantic cry of a much abused, tortured, browbeaten, subjugated, oppressed and broken man who is about to become one of the victims of the genocide.

*Hazar Karo Merey Tan Se*

*Sajey to kaisey saje qatl-e-aam ka mela*
*Kisey lubhaye ga merey lahu ka wavala*
*Merey nazar badan mein lahu hi kitna hai*
*Charagh ho koi roshan na koi jam bharey*
*Na is se aag hi bhadkey na is se pyas bujhey*
*Merey figar badan mein lahu hi kitna hai*
*Magar wo zahr e halahal bhara hai nas nas mein*
*Jisey bhi chhedo har ik boond qahr e uf'ee hai*
*Har ik kasheed hai sadiyon ke dard o hasrat ki*
*Har ik mein muhr ba lub ghaiz o ghum ki garmi hai*
*Hazar karo merey tan se ye ghum ka dariya hai*
*Hazar karo ke mera tan wo chob e sahra hai*
*Jisey jalao to sahn e chaman mein dahkein ge*
*Bajaye sarva o saman meri haddiyon ke babool*
*Isey bikhera to dasht o daman mein bikhrey gi*
*Bajaye mushk e saba meri jaan e zaar ki dhool*
*Hazar karo ke mera dil lahu ka pyasa hai*

Be Vigilant Coming Up to My Body

In what way the fair of the fete of mass killing be adorned
To whom the howling of my blood would entice
How much blood after all is left in my frail body
(It can) neither light a lamp nor top up a goblet
It can neither fan the fire nor can quench the thirst
How much blood after all is left in my wounded body
But each vein is filled with a kind of deadly venom
Pierce anyone, its each drop is like the fury of a viper
(Each drop) is the brew of centuries of agony and deprivation
Each one holds, with sealed lips, the heat of indignation and anguish
Be vigilant coming up to my body as it is the river of poison
Be vigilant for my body is the wood of the desert
If you burn it then in the yard of the garden will flash
Acacia trees of my bones in place of cypress and jasmine
If you strew it in the forest and hills, there will spread
The dust of my drained self in place of musk air
Be vigilant for my heart is thirsty for blood

The unbridled genocide in the then East Pakistan had disturbed Faiz immensely. For weeks he would not talk to anyone. On the probing and coaxing of his doctor and a very dear friend, Ayub Mirza, he unburdened his heart by saying: "The heart piercing events of East Pakistan are such that have massively distressed me. I have not experienced a blow more severe because of any other tragic incident than the one that has happened in the Eastern wing of the country. There have been countless friends and admirers there. During the last few weeks I could not sleep. I feel that my faith in the sublime human values has been gravely shaken." When Bangladesh became a reality he was naturally upset but he was aware that the anti-people policies of Pakistan were mainly responsible for the catastrophe. He maintained that the real security of a nation depended on the internal system of the nation and that a country could only be protected by combined power of the masses.

In the new political scenario dominated by Zulfikar Ali Bhutto, Faiz was appointed the founding Chairman of Pakistan National Council of the Arts (PNCA). Culture, its history and its impact on human development were the themes that were closer to his heart. In his view the term culture before the eighteenth century was not used in the sense as it came to be used in the twentieth century. Culture, courteous behaviour, etiquette, decorum etc. were considered to be the qualities of lords and nawabs. The common man was bereft of them. Faiz thought that objectively speaking culture had two aspects. The first is the one that influenced our customs, traditions, lifestyles, conventions, beliefs, dresses, languages, cusines, behaviors and the ways people interact with each other. The second aspect comprised the fine arts. In this sphere the feelings and intellect of human beings played the major part. For instance poetry, fiction, pottery, painting, architecture and sculpting are the areas in which human talent and geographical conditions play a pivotal role. He also pointed out socio-political and economic conditions too had a bearing on this particular aspect of culture. He admitted that religion was one of the factors in the orientation of culture but the other factors were of prime importance. For instance, he exemplified that the culture of Egyptians was different from that of Pakistanis despite the fact that both the peoples profess the same religion. In this context he emphasised the role of language which, according to him, was the backbone of any culture.

Being the founding Chairman of PNCA, Faiz along with the proactive support of his wife, Alys did the seminal work particularly in rediscovering the folk culture of different regions of Pakistan. It was through PNCA that Faiz could popularise folk theatre, folk music, art and artifacts and paintings. In the capacity of the Chairman of PNCA, Faiz also undertook a project to establish an Academy of Letters in Pakistan. He faced various hurdles in translating his dream into reality. Nonetheless, it was his perseverance that ultimately helped him establish the Academy of Letters of Pakistan.

Faiz was also a part of the first official delegation led by Bhutto to Bangladesh. He was very happy to be part of the delegation for he thought he could meet his many Bengali friends and admirers. On arrival, the delegation was given a warm welcome. Mujeebur Rehman hugged Faiz and implored, "Faiz *Bhai!* Write something." Faiz informed him that he had written a lot, whereupon Mujeeb said, "Faiz *Bhai!* Write something about us too." The warm reception accorded to the Pakistani delegation on arrival died out very soon. The differences in the positions of the two nations on a number of issues were too knotted to be resolved. Consequently no joint communique resulted and the diplomatic relations between the two countries could not be immediately established. Faiz took the plane back to Pakistan with a heavy heart. It was during the flight that he composed his famous poem *On Return from Dhaka.* Here are the first two couplets:

*Hum ke thairey ajnabi itni mulaqaton ke baad*
*Phir baneingey aashna kitni mulaqaton ke baad*

*Kab nazar mein aayegi be daagh sabzey ki bahar*
*Khoon ke dhabey dhuleingey kitni barsaton ke baad*

We have been classed as strangers after so many meetings
We will be friends again after how many meetings

When will the spring of unblemished verdure be visible again
The blood stains will be washed away after how many rainfalls

Faiz, his wife and many of his friends and admirers contributed tremendously to make PNCA a cultural hub of international standing. Nonetheless, this institution was running on an ad hoc basis. It was still to be made an official institution of the government, which could only be possible if the Bill pertaining to its establishment was passed by the Parliament. Faiz was on a visit to the Soviet Union in 1973 when the Bill of the Pakistan National Council of the Arts was passed. When he came back he got to know that he was no more the Chairman of the PNCA because as per a provision of the Act the Minister of Culture and Education could only be the ex-officio Chairman of the Council. Accordingly, the PNCA was made a government department, whereas Faiz was expecting it to be an autonomous institution on the lines of the universities. Thus, the then Minister of Education, Abdul Hafiz Peerzada was appointed the Chairman. In the new set-up, Faiz was offered the post of Director General. Faiz politely declined to accept the offer with the excuse that he did not want to be a government servant. On Bhutto's request he agreed to be the Honorary Advisor to the Council.

## (VI)

Faiz had also made infrequent forays into film making. He strongly believed that film was essentially an art medium and, therefore, he was very critical of the proclivity of the film journalists to designate the film world as an industry. He argued that film was the only art form that was degraded to the level of an industry though other fine arts such as painting, sculpting, music and even poetry also have commercial strings attached to them. He was particularly critical of the kinds of films that were being made in Pakistan. Whenever he was asked how and when a good film would be made in Pakistan, he would reply half in jest, of course, "when instead of shooting films, the film-makers would be shot."[10] He strongly upheld the view that a film could reflect ecstasies and agonies of the real life and at the same time it could be entertaining; it entirely depended on the creative brilliance of the writer and director to make realism appealing to the audiences.

When he was released after serving his term in the Rawalpindi Conspiracy Case, he thought for the first time to make a film on a story by Manik Bandopadhyay which had appealed to him greatly. Ayub Mirza in his book erroneously mentioned that the first feature film that Faiz produced was *Jago Hua Savera* based on Manik Banerjee's novel *Boatman of the River Padma.* First of all, the correct name of the novelist is Manik Bandopadhyay and secondly, Faiz's film *Jago Hua Savera* (The Day Shall Dawn, the English version) was not based on Bandopadhyay's famous Bengali novel *Padma Nadir Majhi* (Boatman of the River Padma) It was based on a story by Bandopadhyay depicting the arduous lives of Bengali fishermen in the village of Saitnol, not very far from Dhaka, and how they had to survive against the manipulations of the unethical and avaricious moneylenders. In the credits, Faiz's name appeared as screenplay and dialogue writer and not as the producer as Mirza has reported. He had also written the lyrics of the film. A.J. Kardar (son of the famous filmmaker and director, A.R. Kardar) and Nauman Taseer were respectively the director and producer while the film's music director was the prominent Indian composer, Timir Baran. The cinematographer of the film was Walter Lassally who later won an Oscar for Best Cinematography in 1965 for *Zorba the Greek.*

When the film got completed, the new military dictatorship of Pakistan under Ayub Khan stopped its release because of its leftist content and also because the writer of the film was a marked man. Soon after the film's completion, Faiz was imprisoned without being informed about the reasons for his arrest. However, the film's director, Kardar, somehow managed to arrange its premier in London and defying the instructions of the martial law dictator, Pakistan's High Commissioner to Britain attended it. The film was very well received by the film critics who wrote approving reviews in international newspapers and magazines. In view of this, the military dictator of Pakistan changed his stance on the film and *Jago Hua Savera* was allowed to be released in Pakistan. Nonetheless, it was not very successful at the box-office for the Pakistani film goers, like their Indian counterparts; love their inane melodramatic, over-the top films replete with songs and perplexing dances. *Jago Hua Savera* was an art film. However, it was critically acclaimed and the reputed Indian film critic Saibal Chatterjee wrote, "it is the only known neo-realist film produced in Pakistan at that time."

The film's English version was made with the title *The Day Shall Dawn* and was selected as the official Pakistani entry for the Best Foreign Language Film category at the 32$^{nd}$ Academy Awards but could not be selected for the final list of the nominated films. Nevertheless, it won a Golden Medal at the First Moscow International Film Festival in 1959.

Subsequently Faiz made quite a few documentaries. The first one was a tribute to the leading painters entitled *Symphonies of Expression* that paid rich homage to the art of Abdur Rehman Chughtai, Sadiqain, Zainul Abideen, Musawwara Zubaida Agha and Laila Shahzad. It was ultimately bought by the Library of Congress, Washington DC. The second was a joint venture, *Operational Readiness: Sialkot, 1965,* with the financial support extended by the government of Pakistan. He also made a documentary in collaboration with the Pakistan Atomic Energy Commission entitled *Karachi Nuclear Plant.* Then in 1971 he made two documentaries, *The Great Conspiracy* and *Dark is Light Enough.* Both of them were about the unfortunate developments in the then East Pakistan. The only English poem of Faiz, 'The Unicorn and the Dancing Girl' (See Appendix) served as the screenplay of his documentary, *Mohenjodaro,* that was sponsored by UNESCO in 1963. It was screened at the Locarno International Film Festival and fetched a prize. A similar type of documentary that Faiz made was *Taxila,* which was also honoured with the Golden Dolphin Award. Another documentary, *Northern Areas* was about the socio-cultural life of the people living in the northen parts of Pakistan.

Faiz had to give up filmmaking because of the rancorous circumstances he was forced into by the wiliness of his film colleagues whom he had blindly trusted. Faiz was very impressed by a novel by Muhammad Khalid Akhtar, *Chakiwada Mein Visal* and decided to make a feature film based on it. He wrote its screenplay, dialogue and lyrics, chose a title of the film, *Door Hai Sukh Ka Gaon,* and selected his trusted director, A.J. Kardar to direct it. The newly established National Film Development Corporation (NAFDEC) agreed to finance the project only on the condition if Faiz was its producer. The filmmaking was delayed because of a combination of many factors over which Faiz did not have any control. Kardar argued that he wanted to screen the film at international film festivals and for that he had to develop its prints and soundtrack in London. In the meantime, Bhutto's government was overthrown by a fanatic military dictator, Zia-ul-Haq. In the changed circumstances, the NAFDEC served a legal notice to Faiz because the financial assistance was given to him as the producer of the film. The negatives of the film were in London and Kardar was nowhere on the scene. NAFDEC went to the court against Faiz to recover its money. Faiz was in real trouble because in the fanatic military dictatorship he had no sympathisers. The prolonged litigation had disturbed him terribly and there were rumours in the media that he might commit suicide. Then, Agha Nasir, a devoted admirer of Faiz became the Chairman of NAFDEC and helped him wriggle out of the arduous situation. Nonetheless, the fate of *Door Hai Sukh Ka Gaon* is not known.

## (VII)

Faiz has always been a very popular poet in India where he is, as per estimation, read more in Hindi transliteration than in Urdu. There have been many celebrations in his honour during his lifetime and since his death in cities like Delhi, Mumbai, Hyderabad, Lucknow, Kolkata, Allahabad, etc. Among all the fiestas held in honour of Faiz in India the most impressive was Jashn-e-Faiz (Faiz Festival) at Bhopal organised by the Faiz International Committee (FIC) headed by I.K. Gujral who was at the time Indian Ambassador to the USSR. The FIC whose Secretary was the famous critic Qamar Raees, was approved and sponsored by the government agencies and the celebration at Bhopal was its first event in a series of other programmes in honour of Faiz that were held at different cities in India. Gujral was an influential political figure who later (1996) became India's Prime Minister. He was a student of Faiz and an ardent lover of Urdu. An important scholar and literary critic, Gopi Chand Narang was also a member of the FIC and it was he who went to Pakistan to invite Faiz along with his wife and Ayub Mirza.

The celebration was held on September 15, 1978, in Tagore Bhavan and was presided over by the Chief Minister of Madhya Pradesh, Virendra Kumar Sakhlecha. Many scholars including Qamar Rais made learned assessments of Faiz's poetry in their orations. Faiz, in his address said that though being a poet his main concern was to arrange and rearrange words, he could not find suitable words to thank the organisers of the event for the grand manner in which they had honoured him. He observed that he was visiting the historical and beautiful city of Bhopal for the second time though the first visit was too short. He had always wanted to visit the city a second time to see it more closely, to spend more time with its wonderful residents and to enjoy their hospitality. He recalled that Bhopal was the city that had extended its hospitality also to the great poet Iqbal during the last years of his life. He called Bhopal a place of pilgrimage, in particular, for writers, poets and intellectuals. He wished to see an atmosphere of amity and friendship between India and Pakistan so that the people from India could freely travel to Pakistan and vice versa. He acknowledged that India had taken the lead in that direction by organising the event and expressed his optimism that this would continue. Speaking about himself, he modestly quoted Ghalib's line—*hum kahan ke dana thhey, kis hunar mein yakta thhey*—(What type of intellectual have I been, in what craft have I been unparalleled), and that he neither had political power nor the riches; he knew only to cause his heart burning and transform it into poems. He thanked all those who had conferred so much love and respect on him, which would always be part of his best memories.

Then he also narrated an incident that once when he was flying out of Moscow and waiting at the airport for the plane of his daughter who was to arrive from London, many friends and admirers had gathered there to say adieu to him. When he finally boarded the plane, an old man asked him whether he was a minister of some country. Faiz replied in the negative whereupon the old man asked whether he was a businessman. When Faiz again said no, the old man exclaimed in wonder then why so many people had come to say goodbye to him. Faiz had replied that they were his friends who loved him and in return he too loved them a lot.

He mentioned that many writers and poets often complained that they did not receive the kind of love and recognition that they truly deserved. He said that such writers speciously thought of recognition in terms of possessions of material things. He had only loved people and in return got their love. There could not be a much greater recognition of an artist than that. Then he concluded the address with his lines:

> *Gham e jahan ho, rukh e yar ho ke dast e adu*
> *Sulook jis se kiya hum ne aashiqana kiya*

> Be it the worries of life, the face of the beloved or the hand of the nemesis
> I treated with love whosoever I had to

## (VIII)

Faiz was offered to edit the Afro-Asian literary magazine *Lotus* that was published under the patronage of the Palestinian leader Yasser Arafat from Beirut. In order to accept the assignment he first went to England from India and then to the Soviet Union for a medical checkup. On getting a satisfactory medical report he went to Beirut. In those days, Beirut was the headquarters of the Palestinian Liberation Organisation (PLO), which was labelled as a terrorist outfit by Israel as well as the USA. It was obviously a dangerous assignment because the members of the PLO would make frequent raids against the outposts of Israel from Lebanon and Beirut was the centre of their freedom struggle. As a result of it, Israel, a much superior military power would invariably bombard Lebanese villages and the main city, Beirut. Faiz was, however, very keen to be in Beirut because he wanted to be part of the Palestinians' struggle in some way. The Palestinians' struggle was based on truth as they were striving for having their homeland in their own territory which was usurped by Israel. Faiz's sympathy for their cause was not because of his Islamic connection but because of his belief in Marxism and enlightened humanism that taught him to be the supporter of all freedom-loving people whose rights were badly emasculated by the neo-imperialist power, the USA and its lackeys.

Faiz was the Chief Editor of *Lotus* and his office was within the precincts of the PLO headquarters. The place was obviously on the radar of Israel. Faiz was aware of the imminent threat to his life but he did not show much concern about it. He said that the attack on the PLO headquarters was a foregone eventuality. The only uncertainty was about its timing and the magnitude of the attack. Faiz thought that the Israeli forces would limit their raids to the southern parts of Lebanon and would not expand their aggression beyond that. Faiz had reasons to think this way. First, he thought Israel would not dare to ignore international pressure that was building up against its aggression. Second, the Lebanese government had its relations with Palestinians as well as pro-US Western powers. Third, Faiz could not imagine the extent of the reckless military adventurism of Israeli forces. He thought that Israel would at least pretend to be a civilised nation and for that reason would restrain itself to disregard world opinion.

Israeli forces eventually attacked the PLO headquarters on June 6, 1978. It was the third day after Faiz's arrival in Beirut and as a result of the bombing his office of Lotus was completely destroyed. Faiz pointed out that in the very first air bombardment by the Israeli air force more than a thousand people were killed. Israel justified the barbaric bombardment by claiming that an Israeli soldier was killed because of the land-mines that were laid down by the PLO and secondly because an Israeli painter was shot at in London. In the cruel logic of Israel to avenge the death of a single Israeli soldier it was necessary to kill more than a thousand Palestinians and without ascertaining the identity of the person who shot at the Jewish painter, it should also be treated as a crime of the PLO! Thereafter, on 8$^{th}$ June, the Israeli armed forces entered Lebanon and the PLO headquarters came under constant raids and aerial bombardment. It was not the PLO headquarters that was completely destroyed by the Israeli armed forces but the entire city of Beirut had been damaged. Consequently thousands of Palestinians, Lebanese and other people were killed and many villages, towns and most parts of Beirut were turned into rubbles. Palestinian freedom fighters despite heavy odds continued to fight against the Israeli armed forces for two weeks. Syria, which initially came to the rescue of the Palestinians, had declared a cease-fire on the third day itself. Faiz was very impressed by the courage and conviction of the Palestinian people and the excellent leadership of Yasser Arafat who would constantly move from place to place during the course of the battle.

Two weeks after the beginning of the armed conflict, efforts were started for the armistice by Philip Habib[11] and his colleagues. The ticklish issue was the American envoy's insistence that all the PLO fighters should first lay down their weapons and then negotiations might commence. Yasser Arafat resisted this condition which prolonged the peace efforts for more than a week. During these trying times, Faiz continued to attend his office which was shifted to a new location. The significant point was that no Muslim State or the Organisation of Islamic Countries (OIC) did not extend any support to the PLO nor did they pass a resolution condemning the merciless bombardment of civilian areas of Lebenon by Israel. It was the sheer valour of the PLO fighters and resilient leadership of Yasser Arafat that Israel failed to completely rout the Palestinian combatants. Though Israel had three armed conflicts prior to this one against the armed forces of Egypt, Jordan and Syria with the proactive backing of most of the Muslim states, the Jewish state could defeat them with comparative ease with minimum loss of its soldiers. In 1978, however, Israel had to face tremendous difficulty in subduing an opponent which was just an organisation of freedom loving volunteers. Israel had also to suffer heavy losses in terms of its soldiers. Faiz was witness to the courage and conviction with which the Palestinians including young boys and girls fought against Israel. People of Palestinian origin from abroad had also landed in Lebanon to join the battle against a state which came into existence by displacing the original people of the land. The famous poet Mehmood Darvesh had also reached Beirut to be a part of the freedom struggle of his people. Faiz, besides editing *Lotus*, could also interact with other prominent poets such as Darvesh and Moeen Bseiso who had dedicated their lives and works for the creation of an independent state for the Palestinians. The three poets would write poems to boost the morale of the freedom fighters. One such poem of Faiz is given below:

*Main jahan bhi gaya aye arz e watan*
*Teri tazleel ke daghon ki jalan dil mein liye*

*Teri hurmat ke charagon ke lagan dil mein liye*
*Teri ulfat, teri yadon ki kasak sath gayi*
*Tere naranj shigoofon ki mahak sath gayi*
*Sarey un-dekhey rafeequon ka jilu sath raha*
*Kitney hathon se hum-aaghosh mera hath raha*
*Door pardes ki be-mehr guzar gaahon mein*
*Ajnabi shahr ki be naam-o-nishan raahon mein*
*Jis zamein par bhi khula merey luhu ka parcham*
*Lahlata hai wahan arz-e-Falastein ka alam*
*Terey a'da ne kiya ek falastein barbad*
*Merey zakhmon ne kiye kitney falastein aabaad*

O motherland! Wherever I went
With the vexation of your disgrace in the heart
With the love of the esteem of your lights in the heart
Your love and the pain of your memories went along
The fragrance of your orange buds went along
The company of all the unseen colleagues was together
My hand embraced countless hands of others
Far away in the streets of foreign land
(In) the unidentified streets of an alien city
In whatever land the flag of my blood got unfurled
The flag of the land of Palestine is waving there
Your enemies have destroyed one Palestine
My wounds have populated several Palestines

Faiz edited *Lotus* for three years during which time the magazine had acquired international recognition. He had plans to launch an Urdu edition of it from Islamabad and had discussed the issue with prominent Pakistani writers when he was on a visit to Lahore. Ayub Mirza was to be the editor of the Urdu edition. Regrettably, the idea remained unrealised because of his failing health. His departure from Beirut was under hazardous and equally dramatic circumstances. The Israelis bombarded the building wherein the office of *Lotus* was shifted. Faiz was in the office but miraculously survived. This was not known to anyone though they had the knowledge that the office of *Lotus* was bombarded. The international press was asking, "where is Faiz?" Alys noted that when she heard about the bombardment of the apartment block she had almost given up hope of his survival. Then she added:

> He was left alone in the apartment after the bombing–no lights, no water, no lift–until at last Mousa came to him and took him away to Moeen's house with just one suitcase hurriedly packed because the city by then was almost under siege. And there he stayed until the PLO told him he must leave, that he was too precious to them to be at risk.But how? With whom? All roads were closed and he was a 'name on a list'. Then a Pakistani UNO official came to his rescue having heard that he was stranded, and he left at an hour's notice with a family, to whom one must be eternally grateful...he passed the Green Line, several Israeli posts and Maronite guards–how, he never quite understood. It was assumed that he was a diplomat...After a long and tedious journey, unshaven, unbathed for days...he arrived in Damascus. His first thought was to put our minds at rest. He telephoned London and London phoned us–Iftikhar Arif was on the line. I happened to pick up the telephone. One wept, part joy for Faiz's safety, part sorrow for his friends left behind.[12]

Finally he arrived in Pakistan but his three years' stint in Beirut living under extremely uncertain and perilous conditions damaged his health. Faiz was admitted to Mayo Hospital in Lahore for loss of breath and other complications in March, 1983. He remained alive with an oxygen mask and IV drips for a week. Then surprisingly he recovered almost completely. He also wrote a poem in the hospital itself:

*Is waqt to yon hai ke kahein kuchh bhi nahein hai*
*Mehtab na suraj na andhera na savera*
*Aankhon ke dareechon pe kisi husn ki chilman*
*Aur dil ki panahon mein kisi dard ka dera*
*Mumkin hai koi wahm tha, mumkin hai suna ho*
*Galiyon mein kisi chaap ka ik aakhri phera*

*Shakhon mein khayalon ke ghaney ped ki shayad*
*Ab aa key karega na koi khwab basera*
*Ik bair, na ik mehr, na ik rabt, na rishta*
*Apna koi tera, na paraya koi mera*

*Mana ke ye sunsaan ghadi sakht kadi hai*
*Lekin merey dil pe to faqat ek ghadi hai*
*Himmat karo jeeney ko to ik umr padi hai*

At the moment it is like there is nothing anywhere
Neither the moon nor the sun, neither the darkness nor the dawn
(Neither) is there a screen of some beauty hanging on the windows of the eyes
Nor is there the dwelling of any pain in the refuge of the heart
Maybe it was an illusion, perhaps I might have heard
The sound of footsteps of someone's last round
On the branches of the dense tree of thoughts
Perhaps no dream would make its abode now
Neither is there malice nor is there warmth, neither is there a link nor is there a bond
Neither is someone of mine yours, nor is someone unknown mine

Agreed that this bleak hour is too harsh
Yet for my heart it is merely a moment
Muster courage for being alive there is a lifetime

Despite the apparent recovery, the medical advice was that Faiz would have to take utmost care about food and drink. Smoking was completely prohibited. He was required to follow a strict regimen about getting up, eating timings and the time to retire. Alys was very strict to make him follow the regimen. Nevertheless, he had always been a heavy smoker which had severely damaged his lungs. With such a state of health it was neither possible for Faiz to go back to his editing table in Beirut nor could he do something concrete to launch the Urdu edition of *Lotus* from Pakistan. In mid-November he was admitted again to Mayo Hospital but the doctors could hardly do anything to save his life. Ultimately the final hour arrived and he breathed his last on November, 20, 1984. A couple of days later his funeral procession attracted thousands of mourners despite the fact that the reigning military dictatorship was on the look out to detain anyone having even a remote connection or sympathy with a communist poet even if he was no more alive.

# CHAPTER 6

# Faiz: The Critic

> Literary criticism can be no more than a reasoned account of the feeling produced upon the critic by the book he is criticising.
>
> **—D.H. Lawrence**

> The most common mistake students of literature make is to go straight for what the poem or novel says, setting aside the way that it says it. To read like this is to set aside the 'literariness' of the work–the fact that it is a poem or play or novel, rather than an account of the incidence of soil erosion in Nebraska.
>
> **—Terry Eagleton**

Literary criticism in Urdu, like the novel and short sory, is imported from the West and for that reason is comparatively a young genre. Maulana Altaf Husain Hali (1837-1914) is the first critic in the true sense for his preface, *Muqaddama-e-Sher-o-shayeri*, to his collection of poems, is the first essay written with a composed, scientific objectivity in the true traditions of literary criticism that were prevalent then in Europe. Since then, quite a few significant poets had tried their hands writing critical appreciation about varied literary issues including their own oeuvre or of other poets. It must also be pointed out that the poets who had seriously studied Western or at least English literature usually attempted to write literary criticism, which can be called worthy of note. Among Faiz's contemporaries, Raghupati Sahay Firaq Gorakhpuri (1896-

1982) is another example whose book *Andazey* (Estimations) is also a significant volume of literary criticism.

Faiz's collection of critical essays on various topics of Urdu literature, *Meezan*, (Criterion) came out in 1962 that contained 31 articles divided thematically into 4 sections. All these articles are not of equal literary value. Quite a few are really insightful helping the reader to comprehend the core aspects of the topic under consideration while a few of them are commonplace written in a pedantic style of a teacher of literature. The probable reason for the uneven standards of these essays is the considerable extent (the gap between the earliest one and the latest is more than two decades) of time during which they have been written. Secondly, as Faiz has explained in the Deebacha (Preface): "To have an analytical discussion on literary issues (I) neither had the time nor the predisposition. However, there were occasions to reflect on these issues in radio talks and various literary gatherings. These essays are the collections of those reflections. In these (essays), therefore, the address is not to the scholars but the common readers who wish to know a little about literature."[1] It explains why a few essays sound like class-room lectures. Nevertheless, Faiz, in his characteristic modest style has made it plain that these essays have not been written in the overbearing mode replete with abstruse terms which is usually the hallmark of professional literary critics.

The first section is named *Nazariya* (Theory) comprises 7 articles, which are, as the designation of the section suggests, about literary issues of fundamental nature principally in Urdu literature. The first article, *Adab ka Tarraqi Pasand Nazariya* (The Progressive Theory of Literature) written in 1938, when Faiz was teaching English at the Anglo-Indian (MAO) College, Amritsar, and had recently attended the inaugural conference of the Progressive Writers Association (PWA) at Lucknow. Since the first conference of the PWA held in 1936, almost every notable progressive writer has written about what exactly is the theory of progressive literature. A few books also appeared dealing with the topic. Aziz Ahmed (1914-1978) was the first to publish a book on progressive literature followed by Ali Sardar Jafri (1913-2000). Sajjad Zaheer, a prominent figure of the PWA, has also explained the theoretical framework of progressive literary writings. Nonetheless, it is in Faiz's essay that the true essence of progressive literature was revealed in a coherent and logical manner. The other writers needlessly derided the literary output of their predecessors as well as ridiculed the writings of their contemporaries. Faiz's essay is absolutely focused. He does not revile the point of view of the non-progressives, he presents his own. The sincerity and grace with which Faiz has developed the arguments in illuminating the theory of progressive literature are reflected throughout in all the essays of *Meezan*.

Faiz, first of all, makes it clear what he means by progressive literature. For him it must satisfy two criteria: First, by progressive literary writings, he means, those literary works that help progress society and second, such writings must also satisfy artistic standards of literature. Additionally, he asserts: "Progressive literature represents such writings that should generate the kind of motivations in the political and economic conditions of society that help promote culture and the revisionist literature is the one that counters these inclinations and because of which impediments are created that retard culture."[2] By a progressive culture, Faiz means, the culture of a social order that gives preference to the fundamental values of life. Now, fundamental values are those that sustain and bequeath meanings to other values. For instance, all values of life carry any meaning so long as human beings survive. Thus, the values that help human beings not only survive but also improve upon the existing living conditions are fundamental. They must have preference over other values. Such an arrangement is possible only if a kind of eco-political order is created that endorses and preserves fundamental values for the interest of society at large.

I think all well-balanced readers of Urdu literature support this point of view. An enviable culture generates and grows in a healthy social order. If large sections of people suffer from abject poverty, disease and deprivation, talking of culture in such miserable socio-economic conditions is nothing but playing a cruel joke on the starving masses. The critics of progressive literature erroneously accuse the writers of PWA for two reasons. First, the accusation is that the progressives only propagate about the issues of workers, peasants, exploited women, sex workers and in short the subaltern section of society and in doing so they get dictated by the bosses of the Communist Party. Second, the progressive literature is bereft of artistic and aesthetic values. If we analyse Faiz's definition of progressive literature and its two dimensions then the accusations of the critics fall flat. Reflecting on the acute problems and miserable conditions of the half-naked, half-starved masses does not make someone a communist. Most litterateurs of PWA were not communists. Faiz himself was not a member of the Communist Party. This accusation that the PWA has been a literary front of the Communist Party is, therefore, a canard and it deserves to be contemptuously dismissed. The second accusation is equally flawed. The second dimension of the definition that Faiz has stipulated about progressive literature stresses that it must satisfy artistic and aesthetic values. It must also be underscored that aesthetic values are social values. They do not grow in a vacuum. Insisting on that a creative writer need not bother about social realities is, therefore, claptrap and nothing else.

An objective study of progressive literature is suffice to reveal the fact that all notable progressive poets, short story writers and novelists have enriched Urdu literature by their creative writings. This enrichment would not have been possible if their writings were devoid of artistic and aesthetic merit. The fact is that in the post-Iqbal period, the poetic and fiction output produced by the progressive writers is recognised as truly valuable. So far as Faiz is concerned, despite having Leftist leanings, he remains the only Urdu litterateur who has ever been nominated for the Nobel Prize.

An incidental charge is also levelled against the progressives by some detractors of the PWA. They contend that the progressive litterateurs who write about workers, peasants or prostitutes are not themselves workers, peasants or sex workers! The silliness of the charge is obvious. They are actually insisting that if you are not a king yourself then you have no right to write a poem, story, novel or drama about kings. Similarly, if you are not a woman you must not write about women! Faiz quips that as per this yardstick,

Shakespeare should have been born a thousand years earlier to write historical plays about the fifth and sixth centuries. Workers and peasants, in most cases do not have the time and the necessary skills to create their own literature. This is also true about sex workers. In the social order of the Indian subcontinent the workers and peasants had always been forcibly kept deprived of education and civility. More often than not they were treated like animals. Their problems, angsts, agonies, joys and aspirations have always been written about by the litterateurs who belonged to the middle or lower middle classes. This is true not only about Urdu but the literary traditions of almost all languages.

The second essay in the collection, *Sha'er ki Qadrein* (Values of Poet), seems to be an extension of the first one. In this Faiz returns to the controversy whether a literary piece should only have aesthetic value or must also accentuate the values of the social order to which it belongs. The disparagers of the progressive literature insist that other merits–social, political and economic– that emanate from the theme or content of the piece should be avoided or outrightly ignored. Faiz obviously rejects this viewpoint. He avers that a poem should reflect the feelings and sentiments of the people so that they can share the perception of the poet. This could only be possible if the poet's observation is sharp and his comprehension about the society he is living in has depth. For Faiz, both aesthetic merit and utilitarian value are equally important. In his concluding words, "An absolutely good couplet is the one that should not only satisfy the artistic standards but also that of life."[3]

As the title of the third essay, *Adab aur Jamhur* (Literature and the Masses) suggests that thematically it too belongs to the first two articles. In this, Faiz only adds historical dimension that how with monarchy and feudalism becoming the things of the past and with the rise of democracy the literary writings started reflecting the life of the masses. It is not a profound analysis of the relationship between literature and the masses. Faiz has surprisingly ignored the fundamental issue that the literature created by the masses or about the masses can be better described by the term 'folk literature'. This is usually created by the creative genius of the masses over a long period of time in dialects rather than proper, polished language. So far as Urdu is concerned, its affiliated dialects, Dakhani Khari Boli, Biraj, Avadhi, Bhojpuri, Maithili, Haryanvi, Rajasthani, etc. are common to both Urdu and Hindi. So, the folk literature which may be called closer to Urdu or Hindi belongs to these dialects. Faiz has obvipously missed this point.

The next essay, *Hamari Tanqidi Istelahat* (Literary Terminology of Our Literary Criticism) sounds more like a classroom lecture than a worthwhile critical assessment. While listing literary terminologies such as similes, metaphors, effusion, symmetry, spontaneity, coquetry, humour, pathos, etc., Faiz has also included *tassawuf* (mysticism) as one of the literary terminologies. This is clearly incorrect. Though *tassawuf* has been a popular theme in the classical poetry and prose of Urdu but it cannot be technically called a terminology. It belongs to the thematic aspect of literature and cannot be included as a terminology specific to literature. The next three essays in the collection are written in an imparting and pedantic style which lack insight.

The first essay of the second section [*Masaael* (Issues)], though not accurately about Urdu literature but is about culture that too the culture of Pakistan. Yet it can be argued that language and literature have linkages with the overarching scope of culture. This particular essay, *Pakistani Tahzeeb ka Masa'la* (The Issue of Pakistani Culture) is significant in many ways. To begin with, it raises the question of a fundamental nature, i.e. is the culture of Pakistan different from the culture of India? If yes, then could religion, the basis on which a separate homeland was created for a section of the Muslims of the subcontinent, be treated as the sole defining factor of culture? If yes again, then how could one explain the creation of Bangladesh? Moreover, is the culture of Pakistan similar to Iran, Saudi Arabia, Turkey, Indonesia, Malaysia and so many other Muslim dominated countries because of a common religious bond? Obviously the answers to all these posers are in the negative. Faiz, as is apparent from the essay under discussion, is very much aware of this anomaly. He is also aware that though religion may be one of the factors but it is not the only essential factor in the structure of a particular culture. He rightly mentions music, painting, literature, film, theatre and so one as the crucial constituents of culture.

Faiz's problem that has muddled his line of argument in this particular essay is that he could not obviously declare that the creation of Pakistan had divided the territory of the subcontinent into two but failed to divide the culture because it is indivisible. At times he seems to admit that the sources that count in shaping the culture of the subcontinent including the area that got designated as Pakistan, are common. Nonetheless, he restrains himself in admitting that Pakistani culture is similar to that of India. We can understand his dilemma. At the beginning of the essay he finds fault with many measures that were officially implemented immediately with the emergence of Pakistan. For instance, the broadcast of Hindustani classical musical modes such as Dadra and Thumri were banned. Next, emerged the bizarre attempt of singing the ghazals of Mir and Ghalib in Egyptian and Irani tunes. Faiz calls it "massacre of the ghazals"[4]. Thereafter, the Muslim zealots stated that the national language of Pakistan should be Arabic because languages such as Urdu, Bangla, Punjabi, Sindhi, and Pashtu were all iniquitous! Subsequently, *dholak ke geet* (lyrics sung usually by women on the beats of a small drum), dances and public performances by film stars were branded as the activities of the debauchers, vagabonds and libertines who were likely to pollute the salubrious environment of an Islamic state.[5]

Faiz himself raises the question–is there something like Pakistani culture? He is right to figure out that for the existence of a national culture, the presence of a nation is necessary and it must have its history, its territory and also its distinctive social order. This is one area where Faiz's attempts to make clear the contours of Pakistani culture are painfully unconvincing. It seems that he is anxious to come across an acceptable answer to the query that according to him is a political poser, whether Pakistanis constitute a nation? He maintains that the political experts have failed to provide a reasonable answer that is widely agreeable. In the context he quotes the position of the pan-Islamists who completely reject the idea of a nation or a national territory because it is, in their opinion, contrary to the teachings of Islam.[6] It must be noted that Faiz wrote this article before the creation of Bangladesh. He, therefore, argued that despite the fact that there was hardly anything common between the people of the Eastern wing of Pakistan and the West Pakistanis save the bond of religion. However, the people of West Pakistan did share this bond with many other countries such as Iran, Central Asia, Somalia, Indonesia, etc. Why then did the West Pakistanis not join the people of any of these countries to make a nation? Why was it thought necessary, in spite of a vast distance between the two wings, to join with the people of East Bengal to create a nation of Pakistan? He believed that there had to be some other bond rather than religious between the two peoples and he seemed convinced that it had to be a political bond that provided the basis for the creation of a nation.[7] The fallacy of his argument is palpable because he rightly ruled out the adequacy of a religious bond for the constitution of a nation, he missed the apparent point that undivided India in every respect–historical, social, cultural, economic, political–had always been a nation. He, for obvious reasons, could not admit the fact. Admitting it would have invited the wrath of the fanatics who created Pakistan by propagating that Hindus and Muslims constituted two separate nations. Faiz's dilemma was that he did not believe in the canard yet he could not admit it!

Nevertheless, his identification of the components that go into making a national culture is flawless. He argued that the cultural history of the region that ultimately came to be known as Pakistan was more than five thousand years considering the artifacts of Mohenjo-daro and Harappa. He further argued that if the cultural history of Pakistan began with Mohenjo-daro and Harappa then it should also include the cultural heritage produced by Vedic, Brahmanic, Buddhist and Greek societies. He, however, was aware that the fanatics would not agree with it because for them the history and culture of Pakistan began only with the arrival of the Muslims in the subcontinent. He accurately pointed out that the Muslim traders or invaders arriving in the Indian subcontinent were not a socio-cultural monolith. They included Arabs, Turks, Iranians, Afghans and Mongols and each one of these groups had its own distinct history and culture. The intermixing of these cultures with the local cultural traditions, which themselves were cosmopolitan over a long period of time produced the culture which could be truly called the culture of the region that got labelled as Pakistan.[8] No one could possibly reject this historical scenario and process of cultural amalgamation. The fundamental point, however, is that the process of cultural intermingling was not confined to the regions of West Pakistan and East Bengal. This was all pervading across the entire Indian subcontinent that consequently produced a culture, which despite the presence of linguistic diversity, had major commonalities and is widely known as Indian culture. When Faiz chose to write on the issue of Pakistani culture, he should have objectively acknowledged that despite creating a separate political entity, the Pakistanis shared the same culture with their Indian counterparts. He did not do it for doing so would have questioned the very rationale for Pakistan!

The next article in the collection, *Jahan-e-Nav Ho Raha Hai Paida* (The New World is Emerging) is an extension of the previous article on Pakistani culture. The only difference is that in this piece Faiz has fixated his reflections on the development of the Urdu language and the vicissitude of its literature. Faiz was conscious of the limited presence of Urdu in his country, the language that was declared to be the national language of Pakistan and the one in which he was writing poetry and criticism. It was not the spoken language of any region of Pakistan. He movingly observed that the Urdu litterateurs of Pakistan had neither heard a child taking offence in Urdu nor any mother singing a lullaby in the language. They did not even know when two men fight what swear words they would express or when a boy and girl met each other what words of love they would exchange. Obviously, an overwhelming majority of Pakistanis did not use, and they still don't, Urdu as a medium of expression in their day-to-day interactions. Faiz justifiably concluded that a new language would only emerge when Urdu that was confined only to books would become the spoken language of the majority of Pakistanis. We sadly notice that wish has not been translated into reality till now.

A presidential address that Faiz had delivered at a function of the Oriental College, Lahore, from where he had completed his Masters in Arabic is also included in the collection. Besides Faiz, the other prominent alumnus of the College was Muhammad Iqbal. The most interesting aspect about the College is that it was founded by Pandit Navin Chandra Rai, a preacher of Adi Brahmo Samaj in 1876. The address does not strictly fall into the category of literary criticism, so it does not need further consideration.

Who is a poet? How does he write poems that stir human beings emotionally and, at times, intellectually? Why does a poetic creation motivate or awaken a man more often than a piece of prose? What factors influence a poet to give expression to ideas in his poetry that keep varying from time to time? These are fundamental issues that are frequently reflected upon in literature. Faiz too writes about them in the article, *Urdu Shaa'eri ki Purani Riwayatein aur Naye Tajrubat*, (The Old Traditions of Urdu Poetry and New Experiments) that along with the next two articles, viz. *Jadeed Fikr-o-Khayal ke Taqazey aur Ghazal* (The New Demands of Thought and Imagination and Ghazal) and *Jadeed Urdu Shaa'eri Mein Ishariyat* (Symbolism in Modern Urdu Poetry), constitutes a thematic trilogy.

In the first article, Faiz speaks of the ancient times when a poet was thought to be a sort of mysterious if not super-natural being who would receive ideas from celestial sources which were beyond the constraints of time and space. Gradually, this irrational view about poets and poetry vanished. In the contemporary world the prevalent idea is that a poet, like any other person, is a member of society and his poetry is also a social product. Since society keeps changing so does a poet and his poetry. There is nothing fundamentally erroneous about this dominant viewpoint that is widely regarded empirical too except the difficulty we often face in bracketing the poetic genius and inspirational thought of a few poets with their respective times and contemporaries. The most prominent example from Urdu poetry is that of Ghalib whose art and ideas cannot be explained within the straitjacket of his times or the characteristics of the society he lived in. The usual penchant of most analysts in such cases, be it Amir Khusro or Ghalib, is to declare, "he was ahead of his times." It hardly explains anything about the masterminds and their poetic brilliance except reiterating the ancient drivel in a different mode that "a poet is a mysterious being who receives ideas from celestial sources".

Faiz, in the first piece, maintains throughout that how constantly changing socio-political forces produced the poets whose poetry reflected the social, economic and political realities of their respective times. He speaks of feudalism when poetry was confined to the courts of kings and nawabs, the situation that was altered because of the loss of political power by Indians. British colonialism forced Indians to learn to live like a subject people and the more enlightened among them had also launched the social-educational reform movements. Persian that had remained the official language and medium of instructions for eight hundred years was replaced by English. An emerging middle class that also had the benefit of modern education cautiously started speaking for a better treatment for their countrymen by their foreign masters. Gradually this led to national awakening and the national struggle for independence. Faiz has, by and large, rightly analysed different trends of Urdu poetry in the background of socio-political changes that were taking place in India. Nevertheless, it does not explain the poetic genius of Ghalib who, as pointed out above, cannot fit into the straitjacket of his time and space. Ghalib's society is described by most analysts as decadent, innately debauched in which the Indians had no control over political power and the feeling of loss was particularly intense among Urdu speakers that included Ghalib. A cursory look at the Urdu poetry produced by the contemporaries of Ghalib may suffice to conclude what Faiz describes as "the circumstance of the court was fake. The precinct of the Red Fort was considered to be the Asian continent. The whimsical and debauched nawabs were known as Kay-Khusrow and Nausherwan. Like the personality of a poet his poetry too would be muffled under the etiquette and rituals of the court."[9] Then what was it that made Ghalib different from his contemporary poets?

Though Faiz was a Marxist, he overlooked the observation of Marx, "The materialist doctrine that people are products of circumstances and upbringing, and therefore, changed people are products of other circumstances and changed upbringing forgets that it is people that change circumstances...the coincidence of the changing of circumstances and of human activity can be conceived and rationally understood only as revolutionising practice."[10] Invoking this *thesis* we can explain Ghalib's political genius who did not belong to the category of "products of other circumstances and changed ubbringing" but was among those whom Marx calls the "people that change circumstances." In the history of Urdu poetry, Ghalib was the first poet who endowed the traditional genre of the ghazal (which till then was being treated as a love poem and occasionally used as a vehicle to give expression to mystical thought, *tassawuf*) with his philosophical gems and insightful intellectual ideas. His scepticism about traditional wisdom and irreverence towards things and ideas that were commonly held sacrosanct by the conformists brought in the billows of fresh air and intellectual freedom in a society that had been suffocatingly conservative for long. Ghalib proved to be the precursor of people like Altaf Husain Hali and Syed Ahmed Khan who had systematically begun a renaissance among the Urdu speakers of North India. Faiz was definitely aware of Ghalib's modernity and secularism as he wrote and spoke about it elsewhere but in this piece (written in 1937) he did not underscore this particular point.

Faiz has justifiably written an entire paragraph about the contribution of Nazeer Akbarabadi to Urdu poetry. Nazeer was contemptuously ignored by his contemporaries and even later many professional critics of Urdu poetry expressed reservations about his unique impact on the language of Urdu poetry. Faiz pointed out that Nazeer's "poetry is a powerful protest against the traditional language and contrived themes of court poetry. Nazeer's entire poetry is in the language of the people and his themes too represent the viewpoint of the people." It was during the height of the Progressive Writers Movement that Nazeer's poetry was re-experienced and his position as a poet was firmly established in the history of Urdu poetry.

The next article in the trilogy is a brief piece in defence of the ghazal, the most popular genre of Urdu poetry. During the reform movement chiefly led by Hali and Syed Ahmed Khan that was largely devoted to the spreading of modern and scientific education mainly through the medium of English, the genre of the ghazal was unfairly censured for engendering a debased and corrupt culture wherein the poets would only write about a make-believe world of love and licentiousness that hardly had any connection with the social realities. This, according to the critics of the ghazal, produced a people of Urdu speakers who despite being the most deprived and lowliest segment of society imagined to be still living in the feudal culture of nawabs. The reformers had their reasons to stir the people of North India, in particular, the Muslims, out of the stupor and superstitions they had been living in, and motivate them to bring about social and educational reforms. The diagnosis of the reformers about the disease with which the people, they wanted to be reformed, were suffering was right but they miserably failed to identify the main cause of the disease. The ghazal is just a poetic genre, which by no stretch of the imagination, can be blamed for the degeneration of successive generations of the people. Faiz has correctly dispelled the misgivings about the ghazal. He has asserted that though the ghazal's form places a few restrictions on a poet, it provides complete freedom to him so far as content or theme is concerned. What is required is the competence of a poet. He must be aware of the depth and space the ghazal provides to reflect on any theme in a symbolic matrix. Nonetheless, this piece is too brief to do justice to the most popular genre of Urdu poetry. A more comprehensive article with much deeper analysis of the form and themes of the ghazal was expected from Faiz, who is counted among one of the notable poets of the ghazal.

The last article in the thematic trilogy is on symbolism in Urdu poetry. In fact, true poetry is only possible in oblique and symbolic expression. In a direct and expounding style it will end up as versified journalism. Therefore, a symbolic expression is an intrinsic trait of poetry. Faiz has distinguished between the constantly changing symbols that are used in poetry because, like the nature of poetry itself, symbols too are products of constantly shifting socio-political scenarios. In classical Urdu poetry, Faiz has pointed out, symbols such as *raqeeb* (rival in love), *darban* (doorkeeper), *sahab* (lord), *qatil* (assassin), *jallad* (executioner), *gul* (flower), *bulbul* (nightagle), *saaqi* (cup-bearer), *paimana* (goblet), *shama* (lamp), *parwana* (moth), Qais, Laila, Shirin, Farhad, etc. were extensively used.[12] During the reformative phase many of these symbols were retained but poets like Hali and somewhat later, Akbar Allahabadi assigned them different connotations. The former was mainly concerned about the honour of the community while the latter was about its lifestyle. Iqbal too retained most of the old symbols but used them in different meanings. His core idiom was *ishq* (love) but he did not use it in the sense of love of a man for a woman or vice versa. By love he meant the kind of a draw, a power that keeps a man restless for social and ethical progress. Iqbal has also used symbols such as Parvez and Farhad which keep changing their meanings according to the context. In a political poem Parvez becomes the symbol of a capitalist and Farhad is used in the sense of a worker. In the context of an ethical poem Parvez assumes the symbol of materialism and Farhad represents idealism.[13]

With the rise of anti-colonialism and national awakening, quite a few poets started writing poems that were alive with patriotic fervour and revolutionary zeal. Josh Malihabadi was the most significant of this group who, having ascribed new connotations to the old idioms, had also created new symbols for his poetry of protest. Thus, symbols such as *badal* (cloud), *barq* (lightning), *ra'ad* (thunder), *aandhi* (hurricane), *zalzala* (earthquake), *khoon* (blood), etc. were widely used by the school of nationalist poets and a little later also by some of those who belonged to the Progressive Writers Movement. A mention must also be made of Akhtar Shirani whose major contribution to modern Urdu poetry was abstaining from the usage of masculine gender for the beloved which was, with the exception of early Deccani poetry, widely in use in Urdu love poetry because of the influence of Persian. Shirani called a girl a girl and also christened her by the name Salma that became a popular symbol for a gorgeous beloved. The progressive poets, according to Faiz, more often than not, refrain from making their poems obscure by excessive use of symbols. They use simple language as their fundamental goal is to impact on the common people. The symbols, if at all they are used by a progressive poet, are never far-fetched or personal. With a slight focus they convey the meaning to an average reader of poetry. In a comparatively brief article, Faiz has done a commendable job in sketching the changing phases of symbolism in Urdu poetry. This is the best piece of the thematic trilogy.

The last two articles in the section, *Adab aur Saqafat* (Literature and Culture) and *Film aur Saqafat* (Film and Culture) are thematically interlinked. In the first, Faiz identified the constituents of culture such as literature, music, painting, architecture, handicrafts, etc. Having done so, he insists that among these, literature occupies a position of prominence because, first, it requires the minimum paraphernalia for its creation, second, its dissemination is easier and simple and third, it can be appreciated by larger addressees. In the second piece, Faiz reflects on filmmaking as a serious and responsible art form because its impact on any society is far greater than any other art. He detests the practice of calling filmmaking an industry because it is one art form that bands together almost all other art forms be it poetry, fiction, music or painting. Faiz seems to be totally disenchanted by the kind of films produced in the subcontinent. His disillusionment is justified but there are no simple or workable remedial solutions to alter the trend. The situation in Hollywood is more or less similar because the massive cost of making a film and the anxiety of recovering it hardly leaves any room for creating an artistic movie. Faiz knew the art of filmmaking perfectly because he himself had produced quite a few documentaries and at least one feature film. Despite his familiarity with filmmaking, he does not suggest a method through which one can make a truly artistic film that can also ensure a reasonably acceptable profit for its maker to remain in the field.

The third section of *Meezan* is named *Mutaqaddamin* (Predecessors) that includes critical assessments of six litterateurs and an article on the Urdu novel. The first essay is on Nazeer Akbarabadi and Altaf Husain Hali who were apparently different kinds of poets and Faiz was aware that making a joint appraisal of the two would not be regarded as a proper exercise. Yet, he could find common ground between the two by calling both of them 'rebel poets' as they showed contempt for 'court poetry', both aimed at inventing a new poetic expression, both attempted to purge fake and ritualistic content from poetry by reinfusing in it genuine feelings and realism, both, in their distinct ways, tried to reduce the gap between life and poetry and both made efforts to release poetry from the control of a privileged class and let the masses enjoy its elegance.[14] Having said this, Faiz also pointed out the differences between the two that conspicuously concern their respective diction, themes and different poetic style. He writes, "Hali has the solemnity of old age. Nazeer's poetry has the passion and coquettishness of youth, Hali usually looks at the heartrending and instructive aspects of events. Nazir mostly expounds their funny and mirthful facets. Satire and humour, to some extent, is also found in Hali's disposition. He jeers at the sermoniser and does not refrain from shaming a deceitful scholar. Nevertheless, his satire does not go beyond disdain or a trifle smile. He does neither laugh uproariously nor does he applaud like children. Hali is fond of abstract ethical topics. Nazeer, however, is a materialist; he believes that the ethical values of things depend on their material value and he examines ethical issues as per their material benefits."[15]

Dealing first with the poetry of Nazeer, Faiz fittingly comments that his poetry is a protest, a kind of reaction against formulaic and contrived poetry that was very popular among the nawabs of Delhi and Lucknow. Nazeer was essentially a poet of the masses. He selected his themes from the life of the common people and presented them in the diction and poetic style that could easily be grasped by the masses. He did not conceal the distasteful or harsh realities while portraying the life of common people. He tried to underscore the fact that a romantic viewpoint about life could be an escapist outlet for the privileged classes but the masses had to face the bitterness and evil aspects of life. Nazeer presented the events, experiences and manifestations of life in their original mode and colours without camouflaging the ugly and unpalatable aspects in syrupy or saccharine diction and romantic style. Nazeer is ruthless in exposing the pains and agonies with which the masses confront almost daily. It makes him a sincere poet too. Though the ghazal was the popular genre of Urdu poetry during the times of Nazeer but, as Faiz indicated, his temperament was not suited to the genre of the ghazal. Despite this Nazeer wrote quite a few ghazals and some of them were worthwhile too. In a brief appraisal, Faiz has put the significance and contribution of Nazeer Akbarabadi in the proper perspective.

Faiz begins the evaluation of Hali by saying that he is usually regarded as the father of modern Urdu poetry He, however, adds that Nazeer was the first to make the beginning in this regard and sincere and truly captivating feelings found expression in Ghalib's poetry. Nonetheless, Hali was the first writer who wrote about the essentials, need and worth of modern Urdu poetry. In this respect, Hali was the first scientific critic of Urdu poetry. Faiz's estimation of Hali is worth mentioning: "In my opinion Maulana's literary and historical significance is more because of his *qaul* (what he said about poetry) rather than his *fa'el* (the poetry he produced). The reason for this is that with the exception of *Musaddas* (a long poem that he wrote about the rise and fall of the Muslims that has six-lines in each stanza) all other poems that he has written, as per his principles, do not contain poetry more than ten to twenty per cent...These poems are not true reflection of his personality; they are the result of his rational and cerebral beliefs and poetry is not a product of principles and rules but of experiences and feelings."[16] Faiz remarks that there are merely two concens that have inspired Hali to write genuine poetry. The first one is the anguish about his community and the second is the love for his country. It was his anguish about the degradation, ignominy and humiliation of his community that made him compose *Musaddas.* Faiz appropriately concluded that Hali was not a sermoniser but essentially a poet but the pathetic condition of his countrymen, in particular, of the Muslims would compel him, against his poetic disposition, to write reformist and didactic poetry. Besides *Musaddas,* there are quite a few ghazals that are notable for their simple diction and exquisite charm that makes Hali a significant poet. Faiz has not adequately assessed the worth of Hali's ghazals.

The next piece in the section is entitled *Ghaib aur Zindagi ka Falsafa* (Ghalib and the Philosophy of Life) that has been written in a form that seems closer to drama but is not exactly so. It is more akin to 'dialogues' popularised by Plato. As has been suggested above, Faiz held Ghalib in high esteem for his thoughtful content, unique style, spacious vision and the insightful mindset towards life. In this piece, Faiz, through posers and counter-posers proposed and discarded by four persons with appropriate couplets of Ghalib, has brought into focus three salient aspects of Ghalib's poetry, viz. first, nostalgia about the ornateness and wholesomeness of the bygone age and melancholy about its termination, second, listlessness and crankiness and third, hopefulness about a better future. In closing the course of dialogues through the submission of a participant, Mirzaji, Faiz infers, "The specific excellence of Ghalib is that he is not an individual but an entire generation. He is not the spokesperson of a few fascinating moments but a representative of an entire age."[17]

The next four essays pertain to the Urdu novel and novelists so they can be considered together because of thematic unity. The first article, *Urdu Novel,* as per the endnote was written in 1942 and for that reason it could not examine a few important novels that were written afterwards. For instance, *Khuda ki Basti* (Shaukat Siddiqui) was first published in 1957, *Aag Ka Darya* (Qurratulain Hyder) first appeared in 1959, and *Udas Naslen* (Abdullah Husain) was first printed in 1964. These are the three most prominent novels that appeared subsequently and, therefore, could not be evaluated by Faiz. The novel (in Urdu there is no separate term to denote this particular genre of fiction) has its roots in Western literature and it is not an off the mark observation that Urdu fiction writers were mainly influenced by English works of fiction. Though we had a long tradition of *Dastan* (fable) and the custom of oral storytelling (*Qissa Goi*), these belonged essentially to folk literatures and had very little bearing on the genres like the short story (*Afsana*) and novel.

Faiz rightly pointed out that apart from the total number of novelists, the total number of good novels in Urdu could not exceed twenty. He pointed out that next to Nazir Ahmed's reformist novels, entertaining novels of various sorts were written which could be classified into three broad categories viz historical, social/romantic and the detective. His comment about the detective novels: "Among the three, the detective novel is the last and most inferior product and so far no adept detective novelist has appeared,"[18] is true only because Faiz wrote these lines before Ibne Safi and his series of detective novels became extremely popular among the Urdu readers. His observation about the historical novel that this genre ended with the demise of Abdul Halim Sharar is also incorrect because (as he himself acquiesces in an essay written on Sharar and included in this collection), Sharar is not a novelist in the true sense of the term. His writings can be placed in the category of claptrap journalism with religious fanaticism and historical warp as its prominent features. He fantasises about a glorious past of Islamic sovereignty over almost half the world and seems to have extremely regressive views about socio-political issues. Counting him as a novelist is not appropriate. The fact is that there is no worthwhile historical novel in Urdu.

Faiz's assessment of Premchand that his technique of writing a novel is worn-out and he lacks the expertise to interconnect the plot despite having the skill of story-telling is though, by and large, true; yet equating him with Nazir Ahmed is inappropriate. Premchand's novels despite having the Gandhian brand of social reformism are better than the novels of his precursors in terms of technique, themes and style. In the post-Premchand scenario, Faiz has also mentioned that Sajjad Zaheer's novel *London ki Ek Raat* (A Night of London) is noteworthy because of its new technique and "the exclusive political candour of the new generation." This estimation could have been true in 1942, when this essay was written. In retrospect, however, Zaheer is not even counted among the leading Urdu novelists. Krishan Chander, Rajinder Singh Bedi and Upendra Nath Ashk have also been named by Faiz and their novels have been marked as "not more than the early experiments." Krishan Chander's *Shikast* (Defeat) is now counted as an above average novel but it is perplexing whether Ashk has written a novel by the name *Qafas* (Cage of Birds/Jail) as has been pointed out by Faiz. There is an anthology of short stories by Ashk entitled *Qafas* and in all probablity, Faiz has incorrectly called it a novel. If it is so, then the question arises whether Faiz has really read the book at the time of writing the essay?

Ratan Nath Sarshar is definitely a prominent name among the earliest Urdu novelists. Faiz's piece on Sarshar written with empathy and competence is extremely valuable because it encompasses Sarshar's oeuvre which is not usually acknowledged. Faiz, at the beginning of the essay has made an interesting observation. He observes that despite the popular perception, Urdu novels began depicting social realism and afterwards they espoused romanticism and escapism from realism. In the context, Faiz mentions that in the novels of Nazir Ahmed social realism is too conspicuous while Sarshar whose novels appeared a little later has intermixed social realism with dollops of imaginery locales. The romanticism and escapism from reality, Faiz insists, has started dominating the novels in the post-Sarshar period. The trend has changed only with the Progressive Movement, when social realism has once again got a fillip.

In the last section, *Mua'asirin* (Contemporaries), of the book, there are two articles on Iqbal. Both the articles evaluate Iqbal as a poet while deftly skirting his ideology and politics for which he is not only admired but revered among a large number of people both in India and Pakistan. For a Pakistani writer it is very difficult to critically assess Iqbal's view on religion, philosophy and politics because it was Iqbal who first thought of a separate homeland for Muslims of India that was later concretised as Pakistan. It is for this reason Iqbal enjoys the status of a national poet in Pakistan and many simpletons both in India and Pakistan, on account of his Islam-centric poetry, have put him on a sacrosanct pedestal by calling him Rahmat ul-Allah Alaih (Mercy of God be upon him). It is thus, comprehensible why Faiz has avoided commenting on Iqbal's philosophy, religious outlook and politics.

In the first piece, *Iqbal Apni Nazar Mein* (Iqbal in His Own Eyes), Faiz, with the help of appropriate couplets and stanzas of *nazms* from Iqbal's poetry, makes an attempt to prove that despite his status as a philosopher-poet and Islamic thinker, Iqbal considers himself to be an ordinary man and not an "absolute, autonomous or omnipotent" entity. Faiz, therefore, argues that Iqbal's primary concerns have been similar to the affairs of a common man. Initially his poetry is full of nature and its beauty. Later the poet expresses his anxieties, composes poetry on perpetual struggle and like most people he too yearns for better rewards. The second essay, *Jazbat-e-Iqbal ki Bunyadi Kaifiyat* (The Fundamental Condition of Iqbal's Emotions) is, on the whole, based on a line of a poem by Iqbal, *Jibreel-o-Iblees* (Gabriel and Satan) wherein when Gabriel asks Satan, *Hamdam-e-dereena kaisa hai jahan-e-rang-o-bu* (O old companion! How is the world of colour and fragrance?), then Satan replies, *Soz-o-Saz-o-Dard-o-Dagh-o-Justajoo-o-Aarzoo* (Misery and Music, Pain and Scar, Struggle and Yearning). This latter line, according to Faiz is the summation of Iqbal's emotions that have been expressed in many of his poems and ghazals. There cannot be a dispute on the issue of Iqbal's poetic competency. He is rightly considered to be one of the top three prominent Urdu poets. Nevertheless, Iqbal, in the later phase confined himself within the narrow sphere of Islam with the absolute faith in the exactitude of his religion. Moreover, his separatist political agenda led to the greatest tragedy of the Indian subcontinent, i.e. its partition. It is hardly unfair to expect from a progressive poet like Faiz to critically assess Iqbal's religious and political ideas too. Regrettably it is missing.

The essay on Josh Malihabadi, *Josh Sha'ar-e-Inquilab ki Haisiyat Se* (Josh as a Poet of Revolution), is perhaps the best critical assessment of Josh's poetry. Though it was written in 1945 and Josh lived 37 years more after its publication during which time he had written a vast amount of poetry, the basic thrust of Faiz's essay remained sound and convincing. The reason is that there were no changes in the style, diction, form, perspective or even themes of Josh's poetry from beginning to the end. He grandiosely declared himself to be an anti-ghazal poet as the genre was a relic of the past and he and his oeuvre, as per his own assertions, belonged to the modern age. With the establishment of the Progressive Writers Association, he would frequently made it known that he was a part of the PWA. The self-conferred title of *Sha'ar-e-Inquilab* got permanently associated with him thanks to his dim-witted admirers who would often pitch him against Iqbal. In fact, Josh's mindset, values, poetic style and the overall milieu in which he was brought up was decadent and feudalistic. He would never lose any opportunity to pompously declare that the "Urdu language is a female-serf of his household" to proclaim his command over the language. For him excessive use of extravagant Persian and Arabic words was the highpoint of 'great' poetry.

As a matter of fact, Josh started emulating the poetic style made popular by the elegists of Lucknow, in particular, Mir Anis and Mirza Dabir. His early poem, *Husain aur Inquilab* (Husain and Revolution) is a poor replication of Anis's style of elegy writing. Thereafter, he conferred on himself the title of *Sha'ar-e-Inquilab,* which has been rightly looked into by Faiz. On account of repeated claims by Josh that he belongs to the progressive school of poetry, Faiz goes along the claim and by irrefutable arguments developed with the help of Josh's poetry, proves that his poetry "may perhaps be the reflection of the mindset of eulogists of the courts of nawabs but it is not the representative of communistic consciousness."[19] Though Josh was intensely anti-British, his opposition to the colonial rule was primarily because it had worn away the feudal economy and its values which were very dear to him. Faiz has accurately pointed out that in a few poems that are usually counted as the revolutionary poems of Josh, the poet exults that despite centuries of oppression and repression certain comforts and pleasures of life have survived. In some of the pretended revolutionary poems, Josh attacks the traditional beliefs and sham ethical norms. This poetic output hardly meets the requirements that make a poet truly revolutionary.

There is also a sketch of Patras Bukhari, *Ke Goher-e-Maqsood Guftagoo Ast* (That the Reward of the Objective is Conversation), who was Faiz's teacher, mentor and later a friend. Though Pir Syed Ahmed Shah Bukhari Patras has written a handful of humourist essays, he is one of the two finest humourist writers in Urdu. The other one is Mushtaq Yusufi. His pen-name Patras is the Persianised version of 'Peter'. The story goes that one of his school teachers would call him Pierre instead of Pir. Pierre is French for Peter. When Bukhari started writing, he adopted the Persianised version of Peter, i.e. Patras as his pen-name. Incidentally, Peter is called Patras in Greek too. In Faiz's sketch, Patras emerges as an amazing man with multilayered merits. He was a polyglot hving an astonishing command over six languages, viz. Urdu, Punjabi, English, Persian, Kashmiri and Pashtu. Before the partition of India he was the Director General of All India Radio. In Pakistan he first became the Principal of Government College, Lahore and later was appointed the permanent representative of Pakistan to the United Nations.

From 1954 till his death in 1958 he served as the Under Secretary of the United Nations. Though he never had a formal training in diplomacy, he proved to be a very successful diplomat and his major contribution to the UN was to fight for the continuation of UNICEF that was marked for closure by the Western nations because in their view it had accomplished its objectives. Patras forcefully argued that UNICEF could play a much more productive and valuable role in the decolonised under-developed and developing countries than what it did in the European nations after the end of the Second World War. His advocacy for affording a permanent status for UNICEF convinced even Eleanor Roosevelt to change the US stance in favour of UNICEF. Acknowledging his enormous contribution to the international organisation, Ralph J. Bunche, the UN Secretary General and Nobel Peace Laureate paid a tribute to him in these words: "Ahmed Bokhari was, in fact, a leader and a philosopher, a savant, indeed, even though not old in years, a sort of elder statesman. His true field of influence was the entire complex of the United Nations family.... He was acutely conscious of the aspirations of people throughout the world for peace, for better standards of life, for freedom and dignity, but no one was more soundly aware than he of the difficulties and obstacles to be overcome in bringing about a broad advance of humankind along these avenues."[20] And his student-friend, Faiz Ahmed Faiz, has to say this about this astounding personality: "He was a scholar, a writer, a teacher, a companion, a witty person, an elegant calligrapher, an exacting administrator, a carefree smart man and to end, a sagacious statesman too. Nevertheless, enlisting all these attributes does not help describe him truly. The basic facet of his life has been that no moment of him has passed useless or purposeless, as each moment of his time has been spent in extricating and enjoying the worth, beauty and elegance from every manifestation of existing objects."[21] This piece is not a critical assessment of Patras's writings but Faiz, through his sketch, has at least provided a glimpse of a genius of a man.

Israrul Haq Majaz was a talented poet with a promise of becoming one of the prominent names in the history of Urdu poetry. Regrettably he died young. A slim volume, *Aahang* (Voice), is the sole anthology of his poems, which has been reviewed in *Meezan*. The key to the evaluation of Majaz's poetry for Faiz is the opening couplet in the anthology: *Dekh shamseer hai ye, saaz hai ye, jam hai ye/ Tu jo shamsheer utha le to bada kaam hai ye* (Look! This is a sword, this is a musical instrumrnt, this is a goblet/ If you lift up the sword it will be a great job) In Faiz's opinion the three things, sword, musical instrument and goblet are the basic constituents of Majaz's poetry. In fact, they indicate only two positions of the poet. The sword is a metaphor for revolution while the musical instrument and goblet symbolise a life of pleasure and gratification.

Majaz was a very popular poet when *Aahang* was published. He got associated with the PWA but continued to compose mostly romantic poems primarily because musicality was an innate quality of his oeuvre and the young crowd at the Aligarh Muslim University (where he emjoyed the status of a hero), in particular his female admirers, would induce him to write the poems of love and romance. In *Aahang* there are barely a few poems that could be associated with progressive ideology. Faiz has also mentioned that Majaz is basically a poet of musicality because of which his poetry is bereft of the high sounding oration and fiery incitement that are the hallmarks of some over zealous progressive poets. Faiz seems to be impressed by the musicality of Majaz's poetry which is its natural quality. In a few poems that can be called progressive or revolutionary, according to Faiz, "Majaz's revolutionist zeal is different from the common revolutionary poets. The common revolutionary-poets boom and rumble about revolution, they call out, thump their chests (but) cannot sing about revolution. In their minds the perception of the arrival of revolution is composed of with hurricane, lightning and thunder; not encompassed in a thousand songs and colours of spring. They grasp merely the terror of revolution; cannot recognise its beauty... Majaz is not the town crier of revolution; he is the singer of revolution."[22] Faiz himself is a far better singer of revolution and precisely because of this he appreciates the musicality and soft tenor of Majaz. Nevertheless, Majaz's outlook about revolution seems to be extremely sentimentalised and impulsive. He was also not a very well-read person. He could have become a significant progressive poet had he lived longer. In the poetry of *Aahang,* he appears only as a good enough romantic poet.

Latterly, there are five forewords by Faiz to five different books. These are most likely pieces that have been written on request. So, an attempt to explore Faiz's critical vision in them may be a futile exercise. It is, however, required to glance through these writings as well. First, is the foreword to *Misr ki Raqqasa* (The Dancer of Egypt), which is, in fact, the Urdu translation of Jules Massenet's opera based on Anatole France's famous novel *Thaïs.* Patras Bukhari who had an amazing command over both Urdu and English has translated this world famous opera. The second, *Kham-e-Kakul* (Curled Lock of Hair), is Saifuddin Saif's anthology of ghazals. Faiz's foreword serves as a piece of advice and encouragement to a junior poet who has shown the promise to adeptly interlace social realism with romanticism without losing the musicality of his ghazals. The third one, *Meeraji ka Fann* (The Art of Meeraji) is a brief prelude to Meeraji's articles that were published posthumously. Meeraji's poetry has been starkly different from the poetry of Faiz and other progressive poets. In fact, Meeraji is regarded as the forerunner of the Modern School of poetry, which vociferously denounces progressivism. Obviously Faiz was not a great admirer of Meeraji's poetry. In this foreword, however, he commends Meeraji's style of prose as well as the topics of the essays. Meeraji had written a series of essays on the prominent (mostly foreign) writers and poets when he was associated with a literary magazine, *Adabi Duniya*, in Lahore. Faiz comments: "If, in the light of the critical stance and convictions of these essays, Meeraji's poetry is revisited, then perhaps some of its facets appear dissimilar to the ones which are in vogue."[23] The fourth foreword is to a collection of plays *Wo Log* (Those Folks) by Hajira Masroor. Urdu drama is not very advanced even compared to other languages of the Indian subcontinent. Most plays that get published or staged are either the adaptation or translations of mostly foreign plays. It is, therefore, necessary to applaud the appearance of an anthology of Urdu plays. Faiz has exactly done that. Hajira Masroor is basically famous as a short story writer. *Wo Log* was her first collection of plays which, according to Faiz, "in addition to their literary merits also possess the attributes and requisites to make the grade of stage plays. This collection is a valuable addition to dramatic literature in Urdu."(p. 249) The last foreword is to a collection of short stories, *Chand Roz Aur* (A Few Days More), the third one by Khadija Mastoor. Faiz speaks of three noticeable characteristics of Masroor's stories. The first one is that most of the stories are about the poorest people who have to cope with abject destitution, hunger, feebleness and are perpetually struggling for survival. The second one is that Masroor refuses to be judgmental about the people and their vulnerable existence of her stories. The last one, according to Faiz, is that she loves portraying the details of the locales within which her characters inhabit. Moreover, Faiz also acclaims her choice of the issues that she has drawn attention to in the stories. They are war, peace, riots, tragedies, etc. which crop up from the class struggle, though in Faiz's, opinion, Masroor has yet to accomplish the expertise in manifesting all the facets of these issues. In a nutshell he approves of the stories included in *Chand Roz Aur* as well as the competence of the storyteller.

# CHAPTER 7

# Faiz: The Poet

> They (the poets) are to us in a manner the fathers and authors of the wisdom.
>
> **—Plato**

> The poet's eye, in a fine frenzy rolling, doth glance from heaven to earth, from earth to heaven; and as imagination bodies forth the forms of things unknown, the poet's pen turns them to shape, and gives to airy nothing a local habitation and a name; such tricks hath strong imagination.
>
> **—William Shakespeare**

Faiz is among the most popular poets in the subcontinent. If one refers to the books of Urdu literary criticism, he may come across a very short list of the most significant poets that usually contains the name of Faiz Ahmed Faiz. According to a latest estimate, 'the most loved and quoted poet after Ghalib' among speakers and writers of Hindi and Urdu is Faiz. The writer of the piece also observes that "in the past five decades, Faiz has perhaps been read more in Hindi than Urdu."[1] The statement seems to be true because Urdu, during the last five decades, has been hijacked by the Muslim fanatics who are passionately working on a project to Islamise the language and as a part of the mission promote, publish and project only religious books and articles. Literature and that too 'literature with a leftist slant' is completely taboo. Consequently, most of those who still continue to write poetry and fiction in Urdu, have also started churning out 'literature' that is in tune with Islamic values. This is a calamitous development and apparently there seems to be no end to it because according to the dominant view of the publishers of Urdu books and magazines, it is only religion (Islam) that sells.

Coming back to Faiz's popularity, the situation in Pakistan might be more or less the same. The only difference would be that Faiz's name might appear after Iqbal pushing Ghalib to the third place. It is essential, however, to clarify that popularity is not the valid criterion for assessing the literary significance of a writer. Conversely, unpopularity is also not an indication of literary prominence. We must, nonetheless, think over what makes Faiz a very popular poet not only among the Urdu/Hindi speakers but also the speakers of other Indian as well as some foreign languages including English. This is a complex issue and for that reason it cannot have a straight and linear explanation. So far as popularity goes, it must be borne in mind that Ghalib was not a popular poet during his lifetime. His popularity evolved with the spread of education and unprejudiced literary values. In contrast, Dagh Dehlavi and later, to some extent, Jigar Moradabadi were extremely popular poets when they were alive. Today, they are barely known outside the circle of Urdu speakers and for most Urdu critics, though they are good enough but not counted among the major poets. It only confirms that popularity or lack of it is a variable that can hardly help in assessing the true worth of a litterateur. One fact, should however, be underscored with some caution that the popularity that a writer attains posthumously may be genuine as it is because of his works and not because of the self-promoting machinations which many writers resort to during their lifetime. Faiz is somehat exceptional in the sense that he was a much admired poet during his lifetime and his popularity increased manifold after his death.

A very significant factor in making Faiz's poetry popular is its musicality. The lines of his poems are marked because of their soft tone and low pitch. As a progressive poet he interlaces socio-political and revolutionary topics in his poems but he never raises his pitch or loses touch with the musicality that is his hallmark. He waits for revolution in the manner as a true lover waits for his beloved. His diction is almost bereft of words that have rough and rasping sounds. It is the reflection of his personality that we see in his poetry. Contrary to T.S. Eliot's dictum that a writer has to negate himself in his works, Faiz's poetry is in fact a mirror image of his gentle and even-tempered disposition. It is the soft, almost whispering and melodious expression that has gradually acquired acceptance and admiration among the Urdu/Hindi readers.

Then there is the content of his poetry that appeals to most people breaking across the linguistic barrier. Dealing with socio-political topics, protesting against all types of persecution, oppression and exploitation of the masses, protesting against imperialism and injustice and hoping to bring about a revolution that may usher in an era of equality, liberty, peace and justice for all are not the themes typical of Faiz's poetry. All progressive poets have written poems on these subjects. Then why could they not attain the kind of fame and recognition that has been accorded to Faiz? The mystery could be bared in the poetic treatment of a particular theme. Faiz never allows any theme to overshadow the aesthetic excellence of his poetry. At the height of the Progressive Writers Movement he had to face sarcastic comments and rebuffs of his fellow progressives for his melodic expressions.

In a *mushaira* held as part of Jamia Millia Islamia's silver jubilee celebrations in 1946, in which Faiz had recited his poem *Siyasi Leader ke Naam* (To a Political Leader) and the audience, most of which comprised the writers associated with the PWA and their aficionados, did not appreciate the poem at all. "In fact, Faiz till then was not a significant poet for Sajjad Zaheer and Sardar Jafri. This is not all, in a book (*Tarraqi Pasand Adab* by Sardar Jafri), published in 1952, he (Faiz) is sparsely mentioned and in it he is not even praised as much as Kaifi Azmi had been. Refer to the books written by the progressive critics, one after the other, the name of Faiz is hardly mentioned."[2] Major Ishaq was an admirer of Faiz and spent years with him in jails. His *Rudad Qafas* (Account of the Days in Jail) has been incorporated in *Zindan Nama*—the third anthology of Faiz in which he, despite being an unfaltering enthusiast of Faiz's personality and poetry, does not lose the opportunity to remark: "In the poetry of Faiz there is passion and fervour of a chivalrous man. The heart of the entire nation throbs in it but strangely the hitch is that in its essence the warmth of the propitious blood and sweat of Pakistan's working classes has not yet been fully mixed. The kind of adoration with which (he) has recollected jasmines and roses, the wretched and ill-fated people have not been reminisced with similar affection and detail... His poetry has yet to come out of drawing rooms, schools and colleges and extend to roads, bazaars and fields."[3]

The extremist faction of the progressives imperiously led by Sardar Jafri and some of his cohorts who dominated the fifth All India Progressive Writers Conference held in May 1949, at Bhimdi (now Bhiwandi) continued to not only ignore Faiz but also disparage his poetry. In the aftermath of the fifth conference that had fundamentally overhauled the aims and objectives of the PWA determined in the first conference held at Lucknow, the first attack on Faiz was made by Sardar Jafri who found fault with Faiz's poem *Subh-e-Azadi* thus: "Faiz, in his poem on 15$^{th}$ August, has laid such veils of idioms that it becomes difficult to fathom who is seated behind them. Its first couplet is: *These blotches of light, this night-nibbled dawn/ This is not the dawn that was being anticipated*, and the last line is: *Keep moving for the destination has not arrived yet.* However, the Muslim League leaders can also say this."[4] Taking no notice of Jafri's inability to appreciate nuanced literary works, one can point out that here he is speaking like a Congress Party man who is in raptures because of the transfer of power from the *gora sahibs* to the Indian elite. Faiz's poem is written from the Leftist point of view; and for the Leftists of the Indian subcontinent the purported independence in 1947 was moth-eaten. Quite a few poets have composed poems on the theme of independence. Faiz's poem is unquestionably the best of them all. One must also mention Makhdoom Mohiuddin's poem *Chand Taron Ka Bun* that is also an excellent one appraising the struggle for freedom and its aftershock.

Despite unkind remarks and hurtful criticism, Faiz did not go against his poetic virtuosity as Majrooh Sultanpuri did albeit briefly. Majrooh's entire oeuvre comprised ghazals, a poetic genre frowned upon by the extremist faction of the progressives. Additionally, Majrooh's vocabulary was also censured because of its feudal origin, sophistication and Persianised roots. So, in order to be a 'true' progressive in the light of the new charter of 1949, Majrooh made conscious efforts to overtly contend with political themes in his ghazals and make use of a language that sounded closer to sloganeering. He could write only a couple of ghazals with such lines: *Lenin ke paigham ki jai ho, Stalin ke naam ki jai ho* (Long live the message of Lenin, Long live the name of Stalin)/ *Lal phurera is duniya mein sab ka sahara ho ke rahe ga* (The red flag will be the succour of all the world over)/ *Ye bhi koi Hirler ka hai chela maar le saathi janey na paye* (He too seems to be a follower of Hitler, strike him comrade don't let him get away). Thank goodness, Majrooh realised his folly soon enough and went back to his original style. Faiz's disposition was such that he did not write poetry according to the whims of the critics. He remained true to himself that ensured musicality and aesthetic attributes of his poetry.

The title of Faiz's first anthology, *Naqsh-e-Faryadi*, is borrowed from the first couplet of *Diwan-e-Ghalib* (Collection of Ghalib's Urdu Ghazals). In Ghalib's couplet the word *naqsh* is without appendage, whereas Faiz, by affixing an appendage to it, makes it govern *faryadi*. The consequent compound word *naqsh-e-faryadi* cannot be accurately translated into English. There are variants such as 'Imprints', 'Supplicating Images', 'Remonstrance' and so on. Evidently, none of them conveys the spot-on meaning for it remains elusive. If we refer to Ghalib's complete couplet, i.e. *Naqsh faryadi hai kis ki shukhi-e-tahreer ka/ Kaghzi hai pairahan har paikar-e-tasveer ka,* then we get the word *tasveer*, which explains the word *naqsh* in the preceding line. Therefore, *naqsh* (image, portrait) is protesting or griping. In view of this, I prefer to interpret the compound word *Naqsh-e-Faryadi* as 'Portrait Remonstrates'.

*Naqsh-e-Faryadi* (Portrait Remonstrates) was first published in 1941 with an introduction by Nazar Muhammad Rashid (Noon

Meem Rashid) who had rightly pointed out: "*Naqsh-e-Faryadi* is the collection of poems and ghazals of one such poet who stands at the confluence of romance and reality." This assessment applies to all the subsequent anthologies of Faiz because he never abandoned his proclivity of coalescing romance with reality. Nevertheless, the first part of *Naqsh-e-Faryadi* [in the beginning Faiz has quoted a couplet of the famous Persian poet Urfi: *Barau aye aql-o-minah mantiq-o-hikmat darpesh/ Ke mera nuskha-e-ghambaay falan darpesh ast* (O intellect! Go away. Don't submit your logic and wisdom before me. Don't make attempts to teach me. / Presently, I'm confronted with quite a few griefs and I've to find out their alleviation which you don't possess) comprising couplets, segments, ghazals and poems is essentially romantic. Some of these poems date back to his college days when as a teenager Faiz had, for the first time, experienced the ecstacy and agony of love and failure. Faiz had confided that for the first time he intensely fell in love with an Afghan girl who was one of his relations. However, because of his bashful personality and reticent nature he could never muster the courage to express his love to her. She was married to someone and a heartbroken adolescent poet transferred his agony to the poems. There are 29 poetic pieces comprising the first part of *Naqsh-e-Faryadi* which do not exemplify the synthesis of romance and reality; they are solely romantic.

A critical appraisal of these earliest poems and ghazals makes one realise that Faiz had an amazing grasp of writing ghazals and nazms (poem) with equal felicity. This has always been a rare quality, in particular, among the progressive poets. As Baqar Mehdi pointed out: "Among the progressives, Faiz is the only poet who can be called equally successful in writing both genres (nazms and ghazals) because Firaq while writing poems goes astray. Faiz, even if he loses his poise in a few political poems, while composing ghazals, upholds the customary values with absolute firmness."[5] In actual fact, in the poetry of Faiz the differentiation between nazm and ghazal is blurred thanks to the basic merit of his poetry, i.e. musicality. It must be underscored here that the genre of nazm (poem), which became popular among the Urdu poets after the

*Jadid Sha'ri* (modern poetry) movement launched by Hali and Azad, could properly be dealt with by a handful of poets. Faiz is one of them. Since he was a keen student of English literature, he was well aware of the technique of writing a poem. From beginning to end, in every stanza he develops the theme of the poem. He shuns the tendency, which is very common among Urdu poets, to repeat with new poetic styles the aspects/ facets/ issues that have already been dealt with in the preceding stanzas. He is a strict disciplinarian in this respect. Despite musicality and silky tone, which are the innate qualities of his poetry, his nazms do not appear like ghazals only because he knows the technique of writing poems. Kalimuddin Ahmed, a very blunt critic and extremely frugal in praising any litterateur, says this about Faiz's expertise in writing poems: "Faiz is aware of the the exigencies of the craft of poem-writing and he intends to satisfy the requirements of the craft. Other progressive poets are not aware of the demands of the craft of poem-writing and this inadequacy is the reason of their failure."[6]

Faiz writes in the Preface to *Naqsh-e-Faryadi*: "The publication of this anthology is a kind of confession of defeat. In it there are a few poems that are bearable." This is the characteristic modesty for which he was famous. In the first section itself, there are about half a dozen poems [*Khuda wo Waqt na Laaye...*(May God Never Send Out the Time...), *Surood-e-Shabana* (Nocturnal Melody), *Aakhri Khat* (The Last Letter), *Intezar* (Expectation), *Yaas* (Despair) *Ek Rahguzar Par* (At a Pathway) and a couple of ghazals that can be counted as fine pieces of Urdu romantic poetry. Additionally, there are a few qatas (poetic segments) that are also exceptional. Though the poems are written in the conventional style of romantic poetry, the themes are also the usual ones and the diction is also not innovative, there is a kind of freshness that makes them charming. If we go deeper to explore the mystery of their appeal we end up recognising the musicality and smooth, silky tone of the poet. In this sense Faiz is basically a poet of an alluring soft and silky tone that gives his poetry an enchanting pitch and mesmerising resonance.

The second section of *Naqsh-e-Faryadi* begins with a line of the Persian poet Nizami: *Dil-e-ba'farokhtam, jaan-e khareedam* (I've traded my heart and in return I've procured life. (Life here means the everyday affairs of living.) signifying the ideological shift in Faiz's poetry. Henceforth, in most poems there is a distinct fusion of romance and socio-political realities. As already pointed out Faiz got committed to scientific socialism after his encounter with Sahabzada Mahmood-uz-Zafar and his wife Rashid Jehan in Amritsar. Though he worked among workers who were affiliated to the All India Trade Union Congress (AITUC), workers' wing of the Communist Party of India, he never became a card holder of the Communist Party. He believed in the core values of Marxism and was convinced that a society can only be transformed to an egalitarian, truly democratic and peaceful social order only through a people's revolution (not necessarily a proletariat one). He had an abiding faith in the humanistic contents of Marxist ideology. As a poet, however, he was an incorrigible romantic with a matching soft, velvety and musical tone, which he could alter only at the cost of ravaging his poetry. Gratefully, he did not do that. He started romancing with the idea of revolution. Attempting a blend of his Marxist ideology and the romantic crux of his poetry, he set off on a salubrious poetic excursion. He seems to expect the arrival of the dawn of the revolution as a lover waits for his beloved.

*Mujh se Pahli si Mohabbat Meri Mehboob na Maang* (O My Beloved! Do Not Ask Me for the Previous Kind of Love) is the first poem of the second section of *Naqsh-e-Faryadi*. Having confessed the reduction of intensity of love to the beloved in the opening line, in the next five lines Faiz endorses his love like a romantic. The seventh line is the expression of a realistic perception that love may not ensure the state of bliss one expects from it. In subsequent lines the poet speaks of the other worries that a man has to confront apart from love such as the dark conjuring that comes wrapped in satin and brocade, the bodies spattered with dust and bathed in blood, on sale all around. He says that though his beloved is still extremely beautiful, he cannot evade these miserable spectacles. This poem became a rage soon after its publication which proved that Faiz's experiment of fusing romance and reality was appreciated by his readers.

Besides *Mujh se Pahli...* there are six more valuable poems in the second section of *Naqsh-e-Faryadi* of which two, viz. *Raqeeb Se* (To the Rival) and *Tanhaai* (Loneliness) are counted among the best poems of Urdu literature, which can even be compared with the best poems of world literature. *Tanhaai* is a very short poem comprising only nine lines but subsequent to its publication Faiz reached the height of popularity and came to be counted among the leading poets of undivided India. Though it belongs to the second section wherein most compositions exemplify the synthesis of romance and political reality, *Tanhaai* is not overtly socio-political. Most critics including the commended ones, who are violently opposed to PWA and Faiz's association with Wazir Agha, acclaim the poem as a priceless addition to Urdu poetry. Kalimuddin Ahmed says:

> *Tanhaai* has depth as well as individualistic grandeur. Where *Intezar* (Expectation, a poem in the first section of *Naqsh-e-Faryadi*) culminates, this poem initiates at that point. The eyes get tired because of perpetual awaiting...in the meantime a footfall could be heard but no one comes. The night has slipped, the cloud of stars is about to be scattered, the drowsy lamps are faltering in the houses, every pathway has gone to sleep after expecting for long and the hope withers away. 'Now no one, no one will come here'. These are not the moments of waiting that perhaps every young man has to endure. Here, the veins of the heart get splintered, there is extreme intensity of despair, a deep sense of deprivation...Here (in the poem) the distress of thought, and grief of eyes is depicted with the help of external objects." Though Ahmed has largely rephrased the poem in prose, the ultimate opinion he gives about the poem is significant. He concludes: "In *Tanhaai* the Urdu poem has got rid of the ghazal. *Tanhaai* is Faiz's best poem and has a significant place in Urdu poetry.[7]

Likewise, other critics, Mumtaz Husain, Baqar Mehdi, Gopi Chand Narang, Nazeer Siddiqui, Muhammad Ali Siddiqui, Ateequllah et al. have unanimously commended the poem. It is true that Faiz has been successful in linking the nine lines of the poems with such enchantment that it transfixes the reader and he is overwhelmed with a kind of delight that is absolutely ethereal. When he recovers from the allure of the poem, he feels gloomy because pathos is the real strand of *Tanhaai.* The significant point, which quite a few critics have pointed out, is that as a socialist Faiz has not burdened the poem with any ideological content and in its tone and tenor it is not even soaked in progressivism.

Nonetheless, Ludmila Vasilieva, the Russian biographer and critic interprets the poem in entirely progressive terms. She writes:

> On the surface, the poem describes the apex of loneliness with no reward for waiting, but on closer inspection, the entire atmosphere of the poem is suffused with life. Take the language. How many of the verses contain verbs which signify movement, itself a symbol of life and action. Someone is coming or not coming, a traveller's going somewhere else, the night is declining, the stars' cloud scattering, the lamp flickering, the highways sleeping...and when the night is ending, obviously day break is near with its promise of new hope and yet another wait.[8]

*Tanhaai* is subjected to the varied interpretations because it defies an ideological trap. Consequently, the critics can interpret the lines of the poem as per their socio-political preference. In most other poems though Faiz gives expression to the socialist themes like the miseries of the working class, the greed and ruthlessness of the big land owners and the capitalists, the grit and tenacity of the browbeaten people, the cunning ways of exploiters to grab political and economic power, the need for the unity of the disadvantaged sections of society, the ultimate defeat of the manipulating forces and the eventual victory of the common people through the means of a revolution, his diction and tone never sound like propaganda. There are two reasons for this. First, Faiz never composes a poem in a loud pitch. His natural poetic expression is akin to whispering, a half-sleepy sound like resonance. Secondly, as pointed out already, musicality is the innate quality of his poetry. He can never write a line that may sound jarring or earsplitting. Quite a few poets associated with the PWA had a skewed notion about revolutionary poetry. They believed that it ought to be composed in a louder pitch and invariably in journalistic jargon. Faiz scores because he is a genuine poet and even in dealing with the revolutionary themes he does not sacrifice his original poetic expression.

The other outstanding poems of *Naqsh-e-Faryadi* are *Raqeeb Se* (To the Rival), *Chand Roz Aur Meri Jan!* (A Few Days More, My Love!), *Bol* (Speak), *Mauzu-e-Sukhan* (Themes of Poetry) and *Hum Log* (Our Kind of People). Some critics also include *Kuttey* (Dogs) among the finest poems of the first anthology of Faiz. *Kuttey* is not a bad poem, however, it, one way or another, does not gel with the other beautiful poems of the anthology. It is overtly political. That is fine. However, its tone and tenor is different from the soft pitch and musicality that are the hallmarks of Faiz's oeuvre. In *Kuttey* the tone is frantic and at places heated. The method of dealing with the theme is direct that hardly spares any room for poetic niceties.

A poem that has been very well received by the notable connoisseurs of Urdu poetry besides *Tanhaai* is *Raqeeb Se* (To the Rival). Firaq Gorakhpuri has declared that it is not only one of the best Urdu poems but also of world literature. One cannot dispense with Firaq's opinion by calling it an exaggeration as some poets and critics of the Jadeediyat (the so-called 'Modernist' school) have done. Firaq, besides being a very significant poet and critic, was a conscientious student of European literature. So when he says that it is very difficult to find such a beautiful poem in world literature, he must have valid reasons to make such a claim. A major component of Faiz's Leftist ideology has been his conviction in humanism. It is the humanistic factor of Marxism that gets exposure in his works and it is from a humanistic point of view he addresses his rival in love in this poem. For most critics, it is a new, almost original viewpoint to think about the rival. Baqar Mehdi, however, points out that such a perspective about the rival in love can be traced to Ghalib.[9] The couplet of Ghalib that Mehdi has hinted at is:

*Zikr us pari vash ka aur phir bayan apna*
*Bun gaya raqeeb aakhir thha jo razdan apna*

Her exquisite beauty's portrayal and that too in my consummate expression

Has created such an effect) on my confidant that he has ended up as my rival

Here, Ghalib does not revile or swear at his confidant-turned-rival but gives an acceptable reason for the conversion of a close friend into an adversary in a credible way. The confidant, in any case, is also a human being. The impressive narrative of a gorgeous beloved by the poet influences his intimate friend so much that he too falls in love with the beauty. This is absolutely a human failing that should not be reproached. Ghalib, in fact, extols the marvellous depiction of an equally elegant beauty. Ghalib was among the most favoured poets of Faiz and, therefore, he might have drawn inspiration for his poem from him as Mehdi pointed out.

In *Raqeeb Se,* Faiz too has an absolutely humanistic approach when he addresses his rival in love. He does not hate or despise the rival. In fact, through him the poet recalls the beauty that has made his heart a fairy-home and in her love he has stopped thinking about the world. The humanistic approach of the poet gets expressed in second and subsequent stanzas. The poet reminds the rival that his feet too have been accustomed to the paths that have been honoured by her youth; the darling winds infused with the faint scent of her attire have also teased him; he too has been soaked in the brightness of the moon that has showered from her rooftop; and, he has also seen her forehead, cheeks, lips and eyes that have livened up the entire life of both of them. Then pointedly the poet addresses the rival that the grief of love has presented countless favours to both of them. Hereafter, the poem adopts an overtly humanistic-socialistic hue. The common favours have taught them the meaning of powerlessness besides the protection of the poor; they have also learned the sense of grief and anguish, the denotation of the moanings of the pale faces; they have grasped the problems of the defenceless people. In the last two stanzas, Faiz says how he feels restless and agitated whenever he witnesses the extreme exploitation of the oppressed workers and persecuted, weak and poor people. This poem is a fine example of how Faiz can effectively fuse romance ith reality.

Another poem *Bol* (Speak) is entirely political wherein Faiz exhorts all those who are conscientious and alive to speak the truth so long as the truth is alive. It is a short and condensed poem that makes it very intense and penetrating. The romance and reality get fused once more in *Mauzu-e-Sukhan* (Themes of Poetry), another exquisite poem. The first twelve lines of the poem touch on the subjects that are frequently expressed in romantic poems. Faiz, therefore, speaks about a grief-stricken, blazing evening turning into a moon-lit night; fervent eyes expressing feelings; the yearning fingers caressing the equally craving hands; the hued stole, the bright cheeks and the dazzling attire making the curtain multicoloured; the earrings sparkling in the fuzzy, dense shadow of her tresses. He adds that today the stunning beauty will again adorn herself by lining her dreamy eyes with kohl, daubing her cheeks lightly with powder and smearing a faint trace of henna on her whitish hands. In the thirteenth and fourteenth lines, Faiz observes that the world of poetry and thought of a poet is replete with these matters. Hereafter, in the subsequent lines, the poem depicts the real sights that are usually neglected in the traditional poetry. A typical poet rarely thinks about what sufferings have come about to the progenies of Adam and Eve during the course of black and bloody centuries; he does not pay attention to our fate nor does he think about what might have transpired to our ancestors in the day-to-day scuffle between life and death. A conventional poet neither inconveniences his mind about why most residents of the glittering cities continue to survive only in the expectation of death. He avoids reflecting about why the blooming farmlands grow only after death; he refuses to grasp the import of the enigmatic enclosures wherein countless youths have perished and a conformist poet skips even the ubiquitous abattoirs of the dreams, which radiate the minds of innumerable people. In a line Faiz apprises that these are some and there may be many more similar topics which are usually dear to a poet. Then, satirically he concludes that a middling poet recalls the slow parting of his beloved's lips and loses himself in the magnetism of her shapely body.

*Mauzu-e-Sukhan* is a very significant poem not only because of a remarkable synthesis of romance and reality but also because of its technique. Faiz rarely experiments with the form of the poem. This poem too is composed in the conventional form. Nonetheless, the theme of the poem is gradually uncovered. There is a beginning, a climatic point, a summing up stanza and the ironic culmination. He has a complete command over the composing of a poem, which is not true about many of his contemporaries and quite a few later poets.

*Chand Roz Aur Meri Jan!* (A Few Days More, My Love!) is a significant poem wherein the poet addresses his beloved to endure the oppression for a few more days. The encouraging words are meant to soothe the lady-love who is forced to live on with fettered limbs and chained feelings. Nevertheless, it is an enigma whether the addressee is the poet's beloved or his beloved motherland. A few lines strongly indicate that Faiz has written this poem to mollify the flustered emotions of the lovers of the motherland whose 'bodies are fettered and feelings are chained'; 'whose thoughts are confined and the speech is stifled'. Moreover, two more lines, i.e. 'the unspecified dreadful oppression of the foreign hands' and 'we have to bear today not forever' strongly call to mind that the poem is focused on the freedom fighters. The usage of the word *ajnabi* (foreign) epitomises the British rule. Along with *Kuttey*, this poem too has been composed with nationalist commitment.

*Hum Log* (Our Kind of People) is beyond doubt one of the finest poems of Urdu poetry. The poem may be interpreted as a sorrowful divulgence of the weak, poor, browbeaten, persecuted and suppressed people who were condemned to live in the darkness of deprivation for so long that they are now apprehensive of facing the sunshine. At another level, the poem may be expounded as an acknowledgement of disillusionment of the revolutionaries who have started with changing the world by finishing the exploitation and the exploiters, the plunder and the plunderers, the tyranny and the tyrants. Their struggle, however, has lost its course either because of their own failure 'to convert terrible pain into a song' of revolution or because of the manoeuvring of their adversaries.

The point to be underscored is that *our kind of people* (including Faiz) are in a state of despondency and confusion. Though they are in a miserable condition they still 'long to be in a desert or prison with a torn collar', and they attach importance to find a solution (to transform their dreams into reality). The poem does not lose sight of the harsh political realities that have challenged the revolutionaries of the earlier period and of the present who too face up to the antagonists. *Hum Log* accentuates that it is the commitment that counts.

Faiz's second anthology, *Dast-e-Saba* (The Hand of Zephyr) appeared more than a decade after *Naqsh-e-Faryadi*. In the ensuing period, the most extraordinary event that had happened in Faiz's life was, of course, his incarceration. He was arrested on March 9, 1951 and he was in jail when *Dast-e-Saba* got published. As a result, some poems and ghazals of *Dast-e-Saba* and the entire poetry of the subsequent anthology, *Zindan Nama* (Prison Book) were composed in different jails of Pakistan. It was, therefore, natural that the poems of the second and third anthology differed from the compositions of the first one in terms of the pitch and treatment. The tone of the poems of *Dast-e-Saba* and *Zindan Nama* is somewhat louder than those which are included in *Naqsh-e-Faryadi* The second anthology opens with a finely composed confronting *qat'a* that has become an apothegm of protest poetry. It is:

*Mata e loh o qalam chhin gayi to kya gham hai*
*Ke khoon e dil mein dubo li hain ungliyan main ne*
*Zaban pe muhr lagi hai to kya ke rakh di hai*
*Har ek halqa e zanjeer mein zaban main ne*

If the assets like the tablet and pen are snatched away, what worry is it?
For I've dipped the fingers in the blood of the heart.
If the tongue is sealed, so what! As I have placed
The tongue in each ring of the chain

The outstanding poems of *Dast-e-Saba* include *Subh-e-Azadi* (Dawn of Independence), *Tumharey Husn ke Naam* (Saluting

Your Beauty), *Do Ishq* (Two Loves), *Irani Talba ke Naam* (To Irani Students), *Nisar Main Teri Galiyon Ke* (Could I Sacrifice Myself to Your Streets?), *Sheeshon ka Masseha Koi Nahi* (No Messiah of Glass), *Zindan ki ek Shaam* (An Evening of the Prison), *Zindan ki ek Subh* (A Daybreak of the Prison) and *Yaad* (Recollection). The dawn of independence has already been commented upon above. Here, it must be added that even after more than 70 years, the poem has not lost its appeal. Though the images and similes in *Tumharey Husn ke Naam* are mostly conventional, they sound different because of the manner Faiz has interlaced them in conjoining human beauty and the vistas of nature. The hues of her attire from the rooftop refine phases of the day–daybreak, noon and nightfall–the clothing on her tall frame help adorn cypress and juniper trees in the garden and the ghazal happens when the poet drops his heart in the goblet filled with the wine of her cheeks and lips. In view of this the poet salutes her beauty. In the second stanza the poet gets inspiration from the henna of her hands and believes that so long as her loveliness is young fate will be kind to him and her presence assures the congeniality all around. Then the poet suddenly realises his miserable condition yet upholds that her memory turns the bitterness of his situation into pleasantness. It is a complete romantic and very charming poem.

It must be underscored here that Faiz, despite being a profound student of world literature, restricts himself to compose poems only on those themes that are closer to his heart. Consequently, there seems to be a recurrence of certain themes if we peruse his collected works. Nonetheless, the thematic reiteration does not deter the reader from taking pleasure in the poems that may have identical themes. The reason is that the treatment, diction, similes, metaphors, symbols and the overall poetic milieu differ markedly between the poems with similar themes. Each of his poems exudes freshness that is seductive. The theme of *Do Ishq* is similar to that of *Mauzu-e-Sukhan*. Here too the dichotomy of romance and revolutionary passion is present but with a difference. The variance is not too glaring. The two stances seem to be coming closer. In the last stanza of section 1 of the poem alludes to his restlessness when the loneliness draws attention to the memory of his beloved. It goes like this:

*Tanhai mein kya kya na tujhey yaad kiya hai*
*Kya kya na dil-e-zar ne dhondein hain panahein*
*Aankhon se lagaya hai kabhi dast-e-saba ko*
*Dali hai kabhi garden e mahtab mein bahein*

What modes have I not taken to remember you in solitude!
What shelters have not been searched by my frail heart!
At some point I've caressed the eyes with the hand of the waft
At times I've placed the hand round the moon's neck

In the second section of the poem, Faiz mentions his devotion to his beloved motherland. The intensity of emotions and intimacy of love towards his revered country are similar to those that got expressed for his ladylove. The first stanza of the second section is:

*Chaha hai isi rung mein laila-e-watan ko*
*Tadpa hai isi taur se dil us ki lagan mein*
*Dhondi hai yunhi shauq ne aasaesh-e-manzil*
*Ruksar ke kham mein kabhi kaakul ki shikan mein*

In the same manner I've loved my beloved motherland
In the same fashion my heart fidgeted for her
In the same mode my fixation sought a place of comfort
In the curve of her cheek, at times in the curl of her ringlet

Now, romance and reality seem to be merging in each other. This poem, though divided in two sections, has mainly obliterated the distance and distinction between the poet's two loves. This assimilation even goes further in *Mulaqat* (Meeting), a remarkable poem included in Faiz's third anthology, *Zindan Nama.* In *Mulaqat* the wall of separation between romance and revolutionary vision has almost collapsed. Although there are two sections of the poem, there are no separate stanzas dealing with romance and revolutionary content. The entire poem is a thematic unit wherein romance and revolution are compressed blurrily. The poem is also noteworthy because it is a departure from the soft and musical tone that has been the typical attribute of most of his poems. In *Mulaqat,* Faiz has distinctively raised the pitch of his tone and does not seem to make any conscious effort to compose the melodic lines. We find the entire poem full of metaphors and symbols which click beautifully with the theme of the poem. The stance of certitude that is present throughout the poem is obviously the outcome of the poet's firmness in his ideology. He is now fully convinced of the truth of his conviction and absolutely confident about the success of his revolutionary mission. *Mulaqat* is one among his lengthiest poems comprising 43 lines, yet neither are the ideas repeated nor are the lines composed to clarify any aforesaid thought. In the progressive poetry night usually symbolises oppression and the period of inequality and injustice, whereas day as a rule epitomises the age of egalitarianism, justice and people's freedom. In view of this most progressive poets ridicule night and extol day. Faiz, nevertheless, in *Mulaqat,* does not deride night but positions it at a higher pedestal than the individual who might be a revolutionary but cannot circumnavigate night, a necessary stage that leads to daybreak. Faiz had a much deeper understanding of Marxism than many of his contemporary progressive poets and writers. Considering that capitalism is an inevitable stage of political economy to make the workers realise their exploitation after which they unite and bring about revolution, night is also an unavoidable time-period that will ultimately give way to daybreak. Another noteworthy point is that Faiz underscores the unity of the revolutionary class as opposed to individual striving. No individual can do away with the stages that lead to the socialist revolution or, in other words, no individual is greater than the cause of the revolution. The poem opens thus:

*Ye raat us dard ka shajar hai*
*Jo mujh se tujh se azeem tar hai*
*Azeem tar hai ke is ki shakhon*
*Mein lakh mish'al bakaf sitaron*
*Ke karvan ghir ke so gaye hain*

*Hazar mahtab is ke saaye*
*Mein apna sab noor ro gaye hain*

This night is the tree of the agony
That is greater than you and I
It's greater for in its branches
The caravans of lakhs of torch-wielding
Stars have got lost
Thousands of moons, under its shadow
Have moaned their glow

The pain—exploitation. oppression, persecution and injustice—that the underclass has to endure during the phase of capitalism (in case of undivided India, feudalism), symbolised creatively as night, is an inevitable period on the way to revolution and, therefore, it is greater than the two lovers who are also among those who are wronged. The torch-bearing stars and thousands of moons epitomise the earlier revolutionaries who got whitewashed in their encounter against the phase of night. The opening stanza of the second section is so wonderful that the feelings that the poet intends to convey cannot be conveyed any better in any other manner. It is the poetic composition at its best:

*Bahut siyah hai ye raat lekin*
*Isi siyahi mein ru-numa hai*
*Wo nahr-e-khoon jo meri sada hai*
*Isi ke saye mein noor-gar hai*
*Wo mauj-e-zar jo teri nazar hai*

This night is too dark, yet
There manifests in this darkness alone
The channel of blood that's my voice
In its shadow alone there illumines
The surge of gold that is your vision

It is evident here that the poet's ladylove is his comrade in the fight against oppression and injustice. There is no need for the poet to ask his ladylove, 'O my love! Do not ask me for that love again.' They are together now in the revolutionary mission. Faiz closes the poem with his characteristic optimism:

*Ye ghum jo is raat ne diya hai*
*Ye ghum saher ka yaqeen bana hai*
*Yaqeen jo ghum se kareem tar hai*
*Sahar jo shub se azeem tar hai*

The anguish that this night has handed over
This anguish has developed into the certainty of the dawn
The certainty that's more gracious than agony
The dawn that is greater than night!

There remains no scepticism about the success of the revolutionary struggle. The night will go by giving way to the inevitable dawn of a socialist order. *Mulaqat* is one of the finest revolutionary poems.

We must revert back to *Dast-e-Saba* as I intend to briefly comment on at least four poems that have enriched Urdu poetry by apportioning it a global sensibility. The poems are *Irani Talba ke Naam* (To Irani Students), *Nisar Main Teri Galiyon Ke* (Could I Sacrifice Myelf to Your Streets?), *Zindan ki ek Shaam* (An Evening of the Prison) and *Zindan ki ek Subh* (A Daybreak of the Prison). The subtitle of the poem *Irani Talba ke Naam* is 'For those who got martyred for peace and freedom. The background of this poem is the modern history of Iran. In the aftermath of the Second World War, the Western Powers got involved in the internal affairs of Iran. In protest against the imperialist designs of the Western Powers, the Irani students took to the streets, held demonstrations and ultimately faced bullets and got martyred for the peace and freedom of their motherland. Faiz's poem is a tribute to those students.

*Nisar Main Teri Galiyon Ke* is an expression of grief for his beloved motherland that has come under the rule of self-seeking dictators who have trampled not only on the rights of the people but even the façade of civilised governance under their loathsome boots. The tragedy of Pakistan has been that its institutions of governance have been under the absolute control of a crooked nexus between the military and the mullahas. Faiz's lamentation written in jail in the early 1950s has always been justifiable as true democracy was never allowed to succeed in Pakistan. The poem opens with the lines:

*Nisar main teri galiyon ke aye watan ki jahan*
*Chali hai rasm ki koi na sar utha ke chale*
*Jo koi chahney wala tawaf ko nikley*
*Nazar chura ke chaley, jism-o-jaan bacha ke chaley*

*Hai ahl-e-dil ke liye ab ye nazm-e-bast-o-kushad*
*Ki sang-o-khisht muqqaiyad hain aur sug aazad*

O motherland! Could I sacrifice myself to your streets, where
A custom is now in vogue that no one should walk with head held high
If any lover of yours ventures out to see around
Should walk with stealthy looks, and caution to protect body and life

For the people of hearts now the new ground plan is
That the stones and bricks are imprisoned and the dogs are free

The poem written in *mussadas* (each stanza of six lines) form is outright political but with the alluring diction and musicality that make Faiz's poems stand out. Though the poet is in jail, he is fully aware of the coercion and cruelty the people are exposed to outside. He keeps the sense of time by the arrival of dusk and dawn. In an extremely enchanting stanza he remembers his motherland at different hours of the day. It goes like this:

*Bujha jo rauzan-e-zindan to dil ye samjha hai*
*Ki teri maang sitaron se bhar gayi hogi*
*Chamak uthhey hain salasil to hum ne jaana hai*
*Ki ab sahar terey rukh par bikhar gayi hogi*

*Gharaz tasawwur-e-shaam-o-sahar mein jeetey hain*
*Girift-e-saaya-e-deewar-o-dar mein jeetey hain*

When the prison vent has gone dark, my heart grasps
That the stars must have filled in your hair-parting
When the shackles have sparkled, I got to know
That the dawn must have spread out on your face

In brief, I live on with the thoughts of dusk and dawn
I live on in the shade of the confines of wall and door

The translation merely conveys the approximate meanings of the lines; the real beauty of this stanza can only be appreciated in the original. The poem, like most of his poems, closes with the distinctive optimism with the expectation that the poet would be free again and though presently the adversary has an upper hand but this will certainly end soon.

Two more poems of *Dast-e-Saba* are also about the sense of time or we may call it the counting of days and nights that ought to be a forced pursuit of someone who is constrained to live within the four walls of a jail. The poems, *Zindan ki ek Shaam* (An Evening of the Prison) and *Zindan ki ek Subh* (A Daybreak of the Prison) captivatingly depict the arrival of dusk and daybreak from the point of view of an inmate who zealously loves his freedom. The poet's imagery in these poems is creatively breathtaking. Added to it the poet's perilous position as an inmate wrenches the reader's heart so much that he is likely to gasp for air. A few opening lines of *Zindan ki ek Shaam* are:

*Shaam ke pech-o-kham sitaron se*
*Zeena zeena utar rahi hai raat*
*Yun saba paas se guzarti hai*
*Jaisey kah di kisi ne pyar ki baat*

By the circuitous stars of the dusk
The night is descending step by step
The zephyr passes by in such manner
As if someone expresses love

This exquisite imagery illustrating the scenic ambience continues and only after a dozen lines the poet's mind revisits his hapless condition but with a firm belief:

*Zulm ka zahr gholney waley*
*Kaamran ho sakeingey aaj na kal*
*Jalwagah-e-visaal ki sham'ein*
*Wo bujha bhi chukey agar to kya*
*Chand ko gul karein to hum janein*

The blenders of venom of oppression will
Neither be victorious today nor tomorrow
The lights of the rendezvous of the union
Even if they've snuffed out, so what
If they could turn off the moon, then we would concede

*Zindan ki ek Subh* too has the equally fascinating imagery with a spectacle at the beginning:

*Raat baqi thi abhi jab sar-e-baalein aa kar*
*Chand ne mujh se kaha "jag sahar aai hai*
*Jag is shab jo mai-e-khwab tera hissa thi*
*Jam ke lab se tah-e-jaam utar aai hai"*

The night was yet to be over, when, coming to the head of my bed,
The moon spoke to me, "get up, the dawn has arrived
Get up, for this night the wine of dreams that was your share
Has gone down from the lip of the goblet to the bottom of the goblet."

Though the poem is incomplete, the sparkling imagery all the way through makes it a very captivating piece of poetry. In these poems, *Zindan ki ek Shaam* and *Zindan ki ek Subh* the political content is not overtly present but the very fact that the poet is in prison because of his political views makes it obvious that despite persecution and harassment his revolutionary intensity has not faded away. *Sheeshon ka Masseha Koi Nahi* (No Messiah of Glass), and *Yaad* (Recollection) are also very charming poems that have made *Dast-e-Saba* a truly enriching volume.

*Zindan Nama*, the third collection of Faiz's poetry appeared when he continued to be in jail. A much respected critic speaks about this collection that it is not the account of the life in jail of our sagacious and outstanding poet but is the distressed call of the wounded soul of the contemporary age whose impact makes elegant the beauty of life and helps revitalise the faith in humanism and progress.[10] The most outstanding poem of this collection, *Mulaqat,* has already been critiqued. The volume encompasses more ghazals than poems. Besides *Mulaqat,* the other significant poems in the volume are, *Ay Raushniyon ke Shahr* (Oh City of Lights), *Hum jo Tareek Rahon Mein Marey Gaye* (We, Who Got Killed in the Dark Alleys) and Africa, Come Back. *Ay Raushniyon ke Shahr* is addressed to Faiz's darling city, Lahore. Since the authorities would keep Faiz shifting from one jail to another, at the beginning of 1954, he found himself in Lahore, the city he adored and with which many of his poignant memories were associated. His despair was at its peak because though he was in the city he loved, the city where he spent the major part of his youth, the city where he worked as a teacher, an army officer, an editor and the city where he had his friends, lovers and his family, but he could not walk freely on its roads and streets, he could not meet his wife and daughters and he could not visit the homes of his friends. He was in prison and that too unjustifiably. This acute sense of helplessness made him write this poem. The first two stanzas depict his pain of being in solitude, incarcerated in an unkind prison located in his charming city, the city of lights. After the second stanza his anxiety is expressed:

*Aaj mera dil fikr mein hai*
*Ay raushniyon ke shahr*
*Shabkon se munh pher na jaye armanon ki rau*
*Khair ho teri lailaaon ki, un sab se kah do*
*Aaj ki shab jab diye jalayein oonchi rakein lau*

Today my heart is filled with anxiety
Oh city of lights

Let not the surge of desires turn its face away from the night attack
May your darlings be in good form, speak to them all
This night when they light the lamps, let the flames be high

Thus the despondency of the opening stanzas gives way to hope and fortitude.

*Hum jo Tareek Rahon Mein Marey Gaye* is a poem that happened because of the letters of Ethel and Julius Rosenberg. It will, however, be an inaccuracy if we restrict the backdrop of the poem only to the lives of the American-Jewish wife-husband duo that were convicted of espionage for the USSR and executed in June 1953. During the Cold War years, in the Soviet bloc, both Ethel and Julius had emerged as cult figures, as heroes who were inexcusably executed and for the Leftists of the world they were a source of inspiration. While in jail, they wrote a series of letters to each other and to their two sons, a few of them got published in the *New York Times* and some other American publications. In the letters both of them strongly declare that they were innocent and unjustly framed by the American authorities. Though they were aware of their imminent execution, they did not show any penitence or weakness. Instead they took pride in the values they believed in. The most surprising thing is that when a few of their letters first appeared in the *New York Times*, Faiz was in jail and when they first appeared in the form of a book (New York: Jero Publishing Company, Inc., 1953.) in 1953 he was still incarcerated. *Hum jo Tareek Rahon Mein Marey Gaye* was composed in May 1954 when Faiz was in Montgomery jail. It is amazing how quickly Faiz got hold of the volume in jail and finished it as he mentioned in the note that accompanies the poem: 'This has been written after having been inspired by the letters of Ethel and Julius Rosenberg.' During one of the functions held at Karachi, Faiz declared that *Hum jo Tareek Rahon Mein Marey Gaye* was his favourite poem. The entire poem is replete with similes and metaphors. The martyrs address to the revolution that they sacrificed their lives for the flowers of its lips, for its intoxicating hair, for its shiny hands and so on. In the last part of the poem Faiz says:

*Qatl-gahon se chun kar hamarey alam*
*Aur nikleingey ushshaq ke qafiley*
*Jin ki raah-e-talab se hamarey qadam*
*Mukhtasar kar chaley dard ke fasley*
*Kar chaley jin ki khatir jahan-gir hum*
*Jaan ganwa kar teri dilbari ka bharam*
*Hum jo tareek rahon mein marey gaye*

Having gathered our standards from the killing fields
The caravans of the devotees would move on further
For the sake of their expedition our footfalls
Have cut down the painful distances
For their sake we have made extensive,
Having given up our lives, the repute of your love
We, who got slain in the dark alleys

This poem belongs to the group of compositions like *Irani Talba ke Naam* comprised in *Dast-e-Saba*, a martial song, *Africa! Come Back* and many more in the future anthologies that are significant because they show Faiz's interest in all the Leftist resistance movements across the world. No other Urdu poet, till then, showed such alacrity and passion about the revolutionary drives beyond the confines of the Indian subcontinent. The awareness that all revolutionary movements that set sights on the setting up of people's power structures must be reinforced and hailed was Faiz's major gift to the poets and writers associated with the PWA. *Africa! Come Back* was the most popular slogan of African freedom fighters who were engaged in throwing out the imperialistic forces from the entire continent. Faiz has made it clear that *Africa! Come Back* has been the slogan of the African freedom fighters. On January 14, 1955, the day this poem got completed, the freedom fighters in Kenya were in confrontation with the British imperialists and Faiz was incarcerated in Montgomery jail. Despite his personal pains and problems, Faiz was disturbed about the enslavement and torments of all the colonized people of the world and dreamt of their freedom. This poem is the reflection of his concern about humanity.

*Dast-e-Tah-e Sang*, (Hand Under the Rock) was Faiz's fourth anthology. Most poems and ghazals in this collection belong to the period when he was released from prison but had to face varied mental dilemmas and the real problems such as looking after the needs of his family. During this period he was briefly incarcerated again though slightly before that he was allowed to visit the Soviet Union as part of the official delegation to the Afro-Asian Writers Conference. Writing about this period, Faiz says: "The period after *Zindan Nama* has been a period of mental turmoil during which I lost my journalistic career and was imprisoned again. The martial law phase arrived that helped generate again, in the mind and all around, a feeling of terminating a track and an exigency for the new paths.[11]

The pronounced ambience of most compositions in *Dast-e-Tah-e Sang* is of suppressed fury and protest because, though he was out of jail, he could hardly do anything to put into action his preferred political ideology. He could not revive his trade union work because there were no unions of workers. He was witness to the oppressive regime of a military dictator who was trampling on all rights of the people and democratic values under his heavy army boots but could not even protest because even an inoffensive word of dissent was construed to be un-Islamic and hence, anti-national. 'Hand Under the Rock' was an appropriate name for the collection of that period because the poet's mental condition was indeed like that of a person who was in terrible agony because his hand was crushed under a heavy piece of rock. The only fruitful thing that he could do was to give expression to his bottled-up rage in the form of poems and ghazals. These are compiled in this anthology. I would like to particularly mention only one poem that is representative of those days of suppression and oppression. The poem is *Aaj Bazar mein Pa-ba-jaulan Chalo* (Today Walk in the Marketplace with Fetters On). Its opening stanza is:

*Chashm-e-nam, jaan-e-shorida kafi nahin*
*Tuhmat-e-Ishq-e-poshida kafi nahin*
*Aaj bazar mein pa-ba-jaulan chalo*

The wet eyes, the fiery soul are not enough
The allegation of covert love is not enough
Today, walk in the marketplace with fetters on

It is not a very long poem. There are three more stanzas of three lines each goading the comrades to go to the marketplace with stretched hands and dancing, they should not worry about the dust in the hair and bloodied vests. Walk in the same state as the city of the sweethearts is in expectation. Besides common people, the tyrant ruler with his arrows of accusation and stones of abuse and also the ill-fated dawn and the failed day are anticipating arrival of the fellow travellers. In the third stanza the poet reveals that only he and his comrades are worthy of being executed. The poem closes with a gem of a couplet:

*Rakht-e-dil baandh lo dil figaro chalo*
*Phir hamein qatl ho aayein yaro chalo*

O comrades of wounded souls! Fasten the gear of heart and walk
O friends walk forward to be slayed once again

In *Sar-e-Wadi-e-Sina* (At the Mouth of the Valley of Sina) there are poems and ghazals in almost equal number. The title of Faiz's fifth anthology is symptomatic of the fact that in the late 1960s, in particular after the Arab-Israel war, Faiz started taking keen interest in this Middle Eastern flashpoint that still has the potential of getting converted into a major war involving many states of the Middle East as well as other nations. Though there are no poems or ghazals set in or about the Middle East, Faiz seems to be making a common cause with the Arab freedom fighters, in particular the members of Yasser Arafat's *Al-Fatah*, who have been struggling against the stooge of the imperialistic powers, Israel. In subsequent anthologies this phase of Faiz's life will be sharply in focus.

In my estimation the most noteworthy poems of *Sar-e-Wadi-e-Sina* are: *Intesab* (Dedication), *Yahan Se Shahr ko Dekho* (Look at the City from This Point) and *Dua* (Supplication). *Sochney Do* (Let Me Think) is also a significant poem. Of these *Intesab*, though an incomplete poem is of great value in many ways. First, its narrative is without decorative similes and metaphors. Secondly, the tone is simple and direct, which is surprising because it lacks Faiz's typical musical pitch. Thirdly, its canvas is vast because Faiz intends to dedicate it to all the oppressed, suppressed, exploited, wronged, persecuted, enslaved, victimised, ill-treated, aggrieved and wounded persons and sections of society. It is for this reason the poem is incomplete and such a poem is unlikely to be complete at any point of time as exploitation keeps changing its strategies and targets. A few opening lines of the poem are:

*Aaj ke naam*
*Aur*
*Aaj keg ham ke naam*
*Aaj ka gham ke hai zindagi ke bharey gulsitan se khafa*
*Zadr paton ka bun*
*Zard paton ka bun jo mera des hai*
*Dard ki anjuman jo mera des hai*

For today
And
For the name of today's grief
Today's grief that is annoyed with the entire garden of life
The forest of pale leaves
The forest of pale leaves that is my homeland
The congregation of pain that is my homeland

The anxiety and fretfulness dominate the entire ambience of the poem but the poet is not melancholic; instead he salutes the commitment, devotion, courage and nerve of those who have faced all kinds of injustice without compromising their convictions. A similar restless streak continues in *Yahan Se Shahr ko Dekho* wherein the entire city/country seems to have been converted into a prison and the verve and warmth that define a vivacious, lively city are conspicuous by their absence. See the first stanza:

*Yahan se shahr ko dekho to halqa dar halqa*
*Khinchi hai jail ki soorat har ek samt fasil*

*Har ek rahguzar gardish-e-aseeran hai*
*Na sang-e-meel, na manzil na mukhlisi ki sabeel*

Look at the city from this point there appears, ring after ring,
A rampart like in a jail spread out in all directions
Every path is like a spherical corridor for the inmates
Neither a milestone, nor a destination, nor an egress

It is strange for a Marxist and a revolutionary to supplicate to an unseen, omnipotent entity that is commonly known as God. This point needs an explanation. Languages are geographically bound as they originate in particular geographical regions and for that reason their genius is embedded in the regions of their origin. The popularity of a language, which depends mostly on political and historical factors, may expand the sphere of that language beyond the confines of its region of origin. But for the external users that language will always remain a received or acquired language. The status of English today is a case in point. There are more students of English in countries like China and India than the entire population of England; many of them are also good speakers and writers but the genius of English is entrenched in England. If we look closely at the vocabulary of English then we may find quite a few words and expressions that have their roots in English socio-cultural and religious traditions. The users of the English language use these words and expressions in the normal course without being conscious of their roots. It is quite likely that an atheist might use the expression 'O my God' or 'O Jesus!' because these come naturally in his expression as an English speaker. We must not read anything more in that. It does not mean that an atheist has become a believer because of the usage of these words and expressions. Similarly, Urdu which originated in undivided India has many words and expressions that are deeply ingrained in the socio-cultural and religious traditions of the Indian subcontinent. Since a sizeable section of Muslims of the subcontinent are Urdu speakers many words, idioms and expressions that have their origin in Islam or Islamic history are an incontrovertible part of the Urdu lexis. It is quite likely that an atheist or a non-Muslim speaker of

Urdu might use expressions such as 'Bismillah keejiye' (let us begin/ literal: in the name of Allah), Alazmatullah (to express wonder or gratefulness/ literal: greatness is for Allah) or Alhamdulillah (to express that he is fine/ literal: praise be to Allah). In the same way words such as 'dua', 'salam', 'khuda hafiz' (nowadays, because of ever-increasing religious fanaticism the religiously extremist Muslims have switched over to 'Allah hafiz' with the idiotic argument that 'khuda' is a Persian and not an Arabic word. By that line of argument they must expel almost 80 per cent words of Urdu because of their non-Arabic origin) are part of lexis and colloquial. In Faiz's poetry we also come across expressions like bismillah, dua, salam and even saugandh because these are Urdu lexis and nothing else.

His poem *Dua* is a supplication in the cultural tradition and not a religious one. There is no mention of Allah, Khuda or Ishwar in the poem. The poet supplicates to '*Nigar-e-hasti*' which may be translated as 'beautifier or sustainer of existence'. This is not in contradiction of his Marxist ideology. In the very first stanza Faiz underscores that he belongs to the group that believes in love:

*Aaiye haath uthaein hum bhi*
*Hum jinhein rasm-e-dua yaad nahin*
*Hum jinhein soz-e-muhabbat ke siwa*
*Koi but koi khuda yaad nahin*

Come, let us also lift our hands
We, who don't remember the ritual of supplication,
We, who save the passion of love,
Don't remember any idol, any god

The most wonderful stanza of the poem is the fourth one:

*Jin ka deen pairawi-e-kizb-o-riya hai un ko*
*Himmat-e-kufr miley, jurrat-e-tahqeeq miley*
*Jin ke sar muntazir-e-tegh-e-jafa hain un ko*
*Dast-e-qatil ko jhatak deney ki taufeeq miley*

Those whose faith comprises deceit and hypocrisy,
May they get the courage of rejection and mettle of enquiry,
To those whose heads are in anticipation of the sword of injustice,
May they get the power to shake off the hand of the killer

In this stanza too there are words such as 'deen' 'kizb', 'kufr' that are often used in Islamic religious texts but Faiz has used them to enflame his comrades to revolt against them to establish a social order with freedom and egalitarianism as its characteristics. In a section of *Sar-e-Wadi-e-Sina*, Faiz has published the poetic Urdu translations of a few poems of Rasul Hamza (in the original Avar language his name is spelt as Rasul Gamzatovich Gamzatov), probably the most important poet of Daghistan (Dagestan) writing in the Avar language. We are not in a position to compare the original poems with Faiz's Urdu versions but one thing can be said that the Urdu renditions have all the literary merits.

Faiz's sixth collection, *Sham-e-Shahr-e-Yaran*, (Evening of the City of Darlings) came out in 1978. Most poems and ghazals in this anthology are bereft of the enchanting melodious tone that has always been the hallmark of Faiz's poetry. In terms of subjects too one feels a very faint trace of acquiescence with the surroundings including social conditions. It is not the outcome of mental peace because his ideology over the years has been squarely discredited not only in Pakistan but also in some other parts of the world. The socialist revolution by this time looked like a utopia rather than a possibility. Faiz was not yet despairing but a muffled sense of resignation may be noticed in poems such as *Jis Roz Qaza Aayegi* (When the Death will Arrive), *Merey Dard ko jo Zaban Miley* (If My Pain Speaks), *Aye Shaam Mehrbaan Ho* (O Evening! Be Merciful), *Tum Apni Karni Kar Guzro* (Do Whatever is Expected of You) and so on.

A poem in ghazal format is, nonetheless, extremely poignant and full of aggrieved feelings. This is so because *Dhaka Se Wapsi Par* (On Reurn from Dhaka) is about a very painful episode in the life of Faiz. The dismemberment of Pakistan and the creation of Bangladesh left an emotional scar on the hearts of an overwhelming majority of Pakistanis. Faiz was no exception. However, when he first visited Dhaka as part of the Pakistani delegation led by Z.A. Bhutto, he had imagined to establish cordial domestic relations between the two nations. This did not happen and the dejection that engulfed him forced him to write this poem. The poem is very touching because the feelings expressed in it are genuine. The first few lines of the poem are:

*Hum ke thahrey ajnabi itni mulaqaton ke baad*
*Phir baneingey aashna kitni mulaqaton ke baad*

*Kab nazar mein aayegi be-daagh sabzey ki bahar*
*Khoon ke dhabbey dhuleingey kitni barsaton ke baad*

We have been classed as strangers after so many meetings
We will be friends again after how many meetings

When will the spring of unblemished verdure be visible again
The blood stains will be washed away after how many rainfalls

*Sham-e-Shahr-e-Yaran* also includes a few Punjabi poems and some translations of Turkish poet Nazim Hikmat's poems. For the progressive poets and writers, Hikmat was a source of inspiration because his poetry, plays, novels and films also reflected socialistic and revolutionary ideas. Like Faiz, he was also a 'romantic revolutionary' and he too had spent a long time in prison. Urdu readers may have a foretaste of Hikmat's poetry through these translations.

*Merey Dil Merey Musafir* (My Heart, My Travel-Companion) was published two years after *Sham-e-Shahr-e-Yaran*. This was a difficult period for Faiz and his family. Zia-ul-Haq, the forbidding dictator was tearing apart the remnants of civility and forbearance by making attempts to convert Pakistan into a fundamentalist theocracy wherein more than the fourteen hundred-years-old *Sharia* laws of a desert society were supposed to be introduced. Faiz spent most part of these years in exile living in Beirut, Moscow and London. The title of the collection is indicative of his physical state i.e. a person constantly on the move in search of a safe haven. He lived in Beirut for almost two years supporting the struggle of the Palestinians against the combined forces of the US and Israel. He had close interactions with the Palestinian leader Yasser Arafat and for that reason this anthology is dedicated to Arafat. In reality it was the last proper anthology of Faiz. In his Collected Works, *Nuskha hai Wafa* (Book of Commitment/Destinies in Love) *Ghubar-e-Ayyam* (Dust of Times) has been included as a separate anthology but it should be treated as the addendum of *Merey Dil Merey Musafir*

The poetry compiled in these two slim volumes does not contribute to enhance Faiz's stature as a poet. Yet these collections are significant from the point of view of his activism for revolutionary causes, his exertion to support Palestinian freedom fighters, his personal suffering for being an intimidated refugee at an advanced age and, of course, for his perplexed feelings about his life and unexecuted mission. We can easily detect these influences on the poems and ghazals of Faiz's last two anthologies.

Despite homelessness and disparaging conditions, Faiz did not renounce the revolutionary ideas, the belief in changing the oppressive and exploitative social conditions into a social order based on justice and equality. Though the revolutionary message is not pronounced in this poetry, a discerning reader may feel a faint yearning for a better world muffled in Faiz's poetry of the last phase too. While living in Beirut and other places in Lebanon, Faiz wrote a few poems dedicated to or about Palestine that are included in *Merey Dil Merey Musafir* as well as in *Ghubar-e-Ayyam.* These poems include *Do Nazmein Falastin ke Liye/ 1. Flastini Shuhda jo Pardes mein Kaam Aaye/ 2. Falestini Bachchey ke liye Lori* (Two poems for Palestine/ 1. To Palestinian Martyrs Who Laid Down Their Lives in a Foreign Land/ 2. A Lullaby for a Palestinian Infant), *Gaon ki Sadak* (Pathway of a Village), *Kya Karein* (What to Do) *Ek Naghma Karbala-e-Beirut ke Liye* (A Lyric for the Karbala of Beirut), *Ek Tarana Mujahideen-e-Falestin ke Liye* (An Anthem for the Warriors of Palestine), etc. He also gave expression to his sorrow about the circumstances that forced him to lead the life of a refugee in some poems like *Dil-e-Mann, Musafir-e-Mann* (My Heart, My Travel-Companion), *Phool Murjha Gaye Sarey* (All Flowers Have

Withered Away), *Ye Maatam-e-Waqt Ki Ghadi Hai* (This is the Hour to Mourn Time), *Paris,* and *Merey Milney Waley* (My Acquaintances). A hint of despondency about the unresolved ideological mission gets expressed in these poems: *Lao to Qatl Nama Mera* (Bring Here My Execution Order), *Hum to Majboor-e-Wafa Hain* (We're Helpless Owing to Fidelity), *Tum hi Kaho Kya Karna Hai* (You Tell What is to be Done), *Is Waqt to Yun Lagta Hai* (At this Hour it Senses Like) and *Ye Kis Dayar-e-Adam Mein* (In What Region of Void).

Lastly, a brief appreciation of his ghazals needs to be done. Among the progressive poets, Faiz is the most prominent ghazal writer after Firaq. Most critics have pointed out that Faiz has faithfully put up with the standards of the classical ghazal including the vocabulary. They, however, concede that he has assigned a new meaning (revolutionary and political) to the traditional phrases and symbols that have always been used by the leading classical poets. This observation is largely true but usage of traditional diction is a widespread phenomenon. Many progressive poets who were the contemporaries of Faiz also did that. According to Shamsur Rehman Faruqi, Makhdoom Mohiuddin was the first among progressive poets who had used the vehicle of the ghazal to spread his political/revolutionary ideas.[12] Majrooh Sultanpuri was another significant progressive poet who exclusively used the form of ghazal to disseminate his politically loaded ideas using the traditional vocabulary of classical ghazal writers. Then why could the other poets not be given the kind of admiration and appreciation that the ghazals of Faiz have drawn out. What is more, the form of the ghazal is such that a topic or theme must be expressed in two lines of a couplet. Each couplet of a ghazal is a complete unit in terms of an idea which may or may not have a thematic linkage with other couplets of the ghazal. So, whatever the subject or theme, a poet has to convey it transforming the limited words into symbols. The formulaic restrictions give Faiz as much scope to convey his ideas through the couplets as they give to other progressive ghazal writers. Yet, Faiz's ghazals score over the ghazals of his contemporary poets. According to Faruqi, "The way Faiz has enlivened the classical colour in ghazals is the brilliant chapter of our poetry. In his ghazals the precise refinement of the Urdu ghazal gets expressed that is marked by intermingling of ideas and delight."[13]

In *Naqsh-e-Faryadi* there are thirteen ghazals. Reading these ghazals along with the poems in his first anthology, the first quality the reader may discern is that Faiz has diminished the distinction between the ghazal and nazm (poem) to a certain extent. Most of his poems, as pointed out earlier, are also replete with musicality and enchantment, the qualities that are usually associated with ghazals. The major point of distinction between Faiz's poems and ghazals is formulaic. Additionally, the ghazals are richer in musicality than the poems. Though many of these ghazals were written when Faiz was a college student, there are a few couplets that can be counted among the memorable assets of the Urdu ghazal. See these couplets:

*Ik fursat-e-gunah mili wo bhi chaar din*
*Dekhey hain hum ney hausaley parwardigar key*

(We) got a very short leisure time for going wayward
(We) have tried out the mettle of the Providential God

*Na janey kis liye ummidwar baithha hoon*
*Ik aisi raah pe jo teri rahguzar bhi nahin*

Nobody knows why I'm seated with expectation
On the path that is not even your pathway

*Pa-posh ki kya fikr hai, dastar sanbhalo*
*Payaab hai jo mauj guzar jayegi sar sey*

Forget worrying about the shoes, care for the headgear
The wave that's under the feet might go over the head

In *Dast-e-Saba*, Faiz seems to be much more comfortable in dealing with the form of ghazals. Though the number of ghazals included in the second anthology is also thirteen if we discount the tribute paid to Mirza Muhammad Rafi Sauda and Mirza Ghalib which are written in ghazal format, the lines of ghazals appear more chiselled and ringing. There is a distinct expertise with which Faiz has coalesced political issues symbolically in the couplets without damaging the genre of ghazals. Below are given some of the famous ghazal couplets from his second anthology:

*Tum aaye ho na shab-e-intezar guzri hai*
*Talash mein hai saher baar baar guzri hai*

You haven't turned up, so the night of waiting hasn't moved out
The morn is in quest, has come and gone over and over again

*Wo baat sarey fasaney mein jis ka zikr na thha*
*Wo baat unko bahut na-gawar guzri hai*

The issue that got no mention in the entire story
That issue has caused offence to him massively

*Saba ney phir dar-e-zindan pe aakey di dastak*
*Saher qareeb hai, dil sey kaho na ghabraye*

Zephyr has knocked again on the prison-door
(Whispering) 'the morn is close by; ask the heart don't panic'

*Tum aarahey ho ke bajti hain meri zanjeerein*
*Na janey kya merey deewar-o-baam kahtey hain*

You're turning up or my chains are ringing out
None knows what my doors and roof chatter

*Faqih-e-shahr sey mai ka jawaz kya poochhein*
*Ke chaandni ko bhi hazrat haram kahtey hain*

What validation do we ask for wine from the jurist?
That grandee proclaims even moonlight as forbidden

*Rung pairahan ka, khushbu zulf lahraney ka naam*
*Mausam-e-gul hai tumharey baam par aaney ka naam*

Colour implies the attire; fragrance signifies the fluttering of tresses
The season of flowers is the name of your emergence on the roof

*Mohtasib ki khair ooncha hai usi key faiz sey*
*Rind ka, saaqi ka, mai ka, khum ka, paimaney ka naam*

May the watchdog stay on well for whose influence has held high
The name of the boozer, the cup-bearer, the wine, the vessel and the goblet

*Hum ney jo tarz-e-fughan ki hai qafas mein ijaad*
*Faiz gulshan mein wohi tarz-e-bayan thahri hai*

The style of lamentation that I've devised in the prison
O Faiz! That has turned into the style of expression in the garden

By the time the third anthology, *Zindan Nama* appeared, Faiz was acknowledged as the leading poet of both nazm and ghazal. His poetic style had become a rage across the Indian subcontinent and many minor poets started unabashedly copying his style. In the fifteen ghazals, Faiz sticks to his soft, melodious and symbolic manner of writing ghazals with a subtle difference that can be discerned only by those who look for it; and that is while dealing with the political issues he seems to be more forthright. A long and unjustified period of imprisonment could have registered its impact on his thought process and consequently on his poetic expression. He seems to be acerbic, though not bitter, in some of the ghazals that have couplets with a political undercurrent.

*Har ik qadam ajal thha, har ik gaam zindagi*
*Hum ghoom phir key koocha-e-qatil sey aaye hain*

Each step was death, each pace was life
I have gone and turned back from the lane of the slayer

*Sitam ki rasmein bahut thein lekin, na thi teri anjuman sey pahley*
*Saza, khata-e nazar sey pahley, itaab jurm-e-sukhan sey pahley*

There were many rites of persecution but such weren't prior to your assemblage
Punishment before the slipup of the glance, wrath prior to the crime of speech

*Jo chal sako to chalo ki raah-e-wafa bahut mukhtaser hui hai*
*Muqaam hai ab koi na manzil, faraz-e-daar-o-rasan sey pahley*

If you can walk, then walk for the road to the fidelity has become short
Now there is neither a place nor a destination prior to the elevation of the gallows

The entire ghazal is full of political realities of the then Pakistan that was mainly characterised by persecution and oppression of democratic and socialist forces and the establishment was mired in depravity.

*Rah-e-khizan mein talash-e-bahar kartey rahey*
*Shab-e-siyah sey talab husn-yaar kartey rahey*

On the path of autumn I searched for springtime
From the dark night I called for the beauty of the beloved

*Dil na-umeed to nahin na-kaam hi to hai*
*Lambi hai gham ki sham magar sham hi to hai*

The heart is not without hope, it is just failed
The nightfall of grief is long yet it is merely nightfall

*Muqaam Faiz koi raah mein jacha hi nahein*
*Jo koo-e-yaar sey nikley to soo-e-daar chaley*

O Faiz! No locale on the way fascinated in the least
I left the lane of the beloved and walked to the gallows

*Bedaad garon ki basti hai, yaan daad kahan, khairat kahan*
*Sar phodti phirti hai nadaan faryaad jo dar dar jaati hai*

It is the town of the oppressors, there's no justice or alms here
The unwise plaint shatters its head as it moves from door to door

The ghazals contained in *Dast-e-Tah-e-Sang* are, like many of Faiz's ghazals deeply steeped in romantic vocabulary, expressions, symbols and metaphors. He sings in praise of the beauty of the beloved (it may be revolution, hope for a better tomorrow or the archetypal darling of the Urdu poets) and hopes for uniting together with it/her. Nevertheless we can also sense a tinge of gloominess, a slight dejection that is probably the upshot of the disagreeable socio-political conditions wherein he lived. Consider a few couplets from his fourth collection:

*Mit jayegi makhlooq to insaf karogey*
*Munsif hai to ab hashr uttha kyon nahin detey*

You'll do justice when all the living beings get wiped out
If you're the judge then why don't you cause a tumult?

*Lo suni gayi hamari, yun phirey hain din ki phir sey*
*Wohi gosha-e-qafas hai, wohi fasl-e-gul ka maatam*

Lo! My plea got answered and the old days have returned
There is the similar seclusion of prison, the same lament of spring

*Ye hamein thhey jin ke libas par sar-e-rah siyahi likhi gayi*
*Yehi daag thhey jo saja ke hum sar-e-bazm-e-yaar chaley gaye*

It was on whose attire the blotches were publicly smeared in black
We went to the assembly of the buddies adorning the same stains

*Jo rukey to koh-e-giran thhey hum, jo chaley to jaan se guzar gaye*
*Rah-e-yaar hum ney qadam qadam tujhey yaadgar bana diya*

When we halted we were like a huge mount, when we moved on we let go our lives

O pathway of the darling! We've turned you into a memorial at every step

In his seventh collection, *Merey Dil Merey Musafir*, Faiz, with the intention of paying tribute to his friend and comrade Makhdoom Mohiuddin, wrote two ghazals in the meter of two of the famous ghazals of the latter. These are two couplets from those ghazals:

*Jo na aaya usey koi zanjeer-e-dar*
*Har sada par bulati rahi raat bhar*

The one who didn't turn up, for him the door-chain
Kept calling on every sound all through the night

*Ghar jo veeran thha sar-e-shaam wo kaisey kaisey*
*Furqat-e-yaar ney aabad kiya aakhir-e-shab*

The home that was deserted in early evening how did it, in myriad ways,
Get inhabited due to the absence of the beloved by the end of the night

The lone Dakhani (Old Urdu) ghazal that Faiz wrote is also included in this collection. He is not very successful in handling the Dakhani dialect. He only made a slight change in the verb that is part of *Radeef* (the part that gets repeated in all couplets after the rhyme word). Consider the *Mutl'a* (opening couplet) of his Dakhani ghazal:

*Kuchh pahley in aankhon aagey kya kya na nazara guzrey thha*
*Kya raushan ho jaati thhi gali jab yaar hamara guzrey thha*

In the standard Urdu of today, the underlined word '*guzrey*' should be *guzra*. Faiz, thought that by making it *guzrey* the couplet would turn into that of Dakhani. The other couplets of the ghazal are also similar wherein minor changes have been made in a word or two to make them sound like Dakhani words. However, he was not very successful in the venture. The noteworthy couplets of oher ghazals of the seventh anthology and of the last one, *Ghubar-e-Ayyam,* are:

*Har ik shab har ghadi guzrey qayamat yun to hota hai*
*Magar har subh ho roz-e-jaza aisa nahin hota*

Each moment of each night ends up as calamitous may be quite likely
But then, every morn turns out to be the Day of Judgment is unlikely

*Karey na jag mein alao to sh'er kis masraf*
*Karey na shahr mein jal-thal to chashm-e-num kya hai*

If it cannot ignite fire in the world, then what is the use of a couplet?

If it cannot inundate the city then what for is a tearful eye?

Faiz's poetry has magnificently done both jobs. What is the usefulness of poetry is a very old and thorny debate. In the contemporary world where business and commerce have come to dominate human life and all sources that bestow serenity, peacefulness, equanimity to mind and soul have been cast out as futile. Consequently, poetry, ideology and all kinds of sublime art are gasping for survival. Nevertheless, those who still believe that the true rationale of life is to appreciate all that is beautiful and dainty and to appreciate all forms of expression, poetry, painting, dance, drama and fiction, amounts to the supreme purpose of human living. Faiz's poetry has a magical quality. The reader does not remain the same person when he reads and deeply comprehends its meanings. He changes for better. He seeks pleasure in the marvels of nature, starts adoring flowers and other beautiful objects around him, he treats everyone as a lover treats his/her darling, he wants peace for himself and for the rest of the world. At the same time he reacts violently when he looks at the exploitation of the helpless, weak, workers, peasants and powerless people by the powerful members of society; he gets upset when he observes economic, political and social corruption and widespread venality. He wants to change the social, economic and political system but feels incapable of doing it. Nonetheless, the poetry of Faiz gives him a new vision, a new philosophy to cherish, a new perspective to look at things. That in itself is worthwhile and for this reason Faiz is counted among the most prominent poets of the Urdu language.

# CHAPTER 8

# Faiz: A Few Poems

Among the Urdu poets, Faiz is one of those few and fortunate Urdu poets whose poetry has been extensively translated into English and many other languages. The other two poets in this category are Ghalib and Iqbal. It was a British historian and a Marxist, Victor Kiernan who first translated Faiz into English. Kiernan was an extraordinary man. He was a reputed historian who wrote scholarly books on Chinese, American and European history applying Marxist tools of analysis in critiquing different phases of these countries, in particular, Western imperialism. All at once he also wrote scholarly tomes about Western literature such as *Shakespeare, Poet and Citizen* (1993), *Eight Tragedies of Shakespeare: A Marxist Study* (1996) and *Horace: Poetics and Politics* (1999) remain among the finest studies on the respective topics. In 1938, he arrived in India to promote Marxist political activities. Once in India, he also got assignments to teach first at the Sikh National College and later at Aitchison College, Lahore. It was in Lahore that he got fascinated with the Urdu language, in particular, its poetry. Having acquired the nuances of Urdu poetry, he translated the works of Ghalib, Iqbal and Faiz.

Once in the Punjab, it was impossible for Kieranan not to know Faiz. On this point Kiernan writes that when Faiz was teaching at Amritsar "where I had the good fortune to get to know him, thirty years agao." (He wrote this in 1971.)[1] It was the time when Faiz, in the company of Sahabzada Mahmood-uz-Zafar and his wife Rasheed Jahan was getting introduced to Marxism and establishing a rapport with the All India Trade Union Congress. Thus, it was obvious that Faiz hit it off with Kiernan readily who was not only a Marxist but also a keen lover of Urdu poetry. In subsequent years, Kiernan was smitten by Faiz's poetry too and made a decision to translate it into English. The first volume of translations was not as exhaustive as the one published in 171. To quote Kiernan from the latter edition:

> This volume is an expansion of a set of verse translation from Faiz which were begun in a forest rest-house on the banks of Woolar Lake in Kashmir in the summer of 1945, continued at intervals over the next dozen years, and published in 1958 at Delhi (later reprinted at Lahore). These translations have now been revised throughout, and also brought into line with the latest editions of the originals: Faiz is a reviser and polisher, as careful literary craftsmen have often been, and has made various alterations over the years...All these, like most of the former set, were chosen by Faiz himself, and all the translations have been discussed with him.[2]

This, rather lengthy citation makes it clear that the poems that Kiernan translated were selected by Faiz himself and all the translations were discussed with the poet himself. These factors largely contributed to make Kiernan's volume of 1971 as the most valuable. It includes almost all of Faiz's significant poems and ghazals that he had composed till the end of the seventh decade of the last century. Besides, the quality of the translations is excellent for two reasons. First it was Kiernan's translating deftness and secondly because of Faiz's revision and suggestions that helped to improve the value of the translations. Many other translations of Faiz appeared afterwards, some of them are really good but none could surpass the benchmark set by Kiernan. *Poems by Faiz* by Kiernan, remains the best volume of Faiz's poetry in English renditions.

For this book, I have selected a few poems by Faiz for translation with a strategy that I have not chosen any poem that has already been translated by Kiernan. I know that I cannot improve upon Kiernan's renditions. Faiz lived another 14 years after Kiernan's volume got published and during those years he also composed some of his finest poems. A few of them are translated here though I have also chosen at least one poem from each of his anthologies.

A word about Faiz's proclivity to use the plural case 'we' instead of 'I' for himself, not only in conversations but in writings too including poetry. While translating the lines wherein the expression, '*hum*' (we) appears, the translator has to be extremely careful to choose either 'we' or 'I'. It is only after meticulously contextualising the usage that I have used the respective case wherever the situation has come up. In this section along with English translations, the original Urdu versions and Nagri transliterations of the poems have also been added for the readers to have a better insight into Faiz's poetry.

## مرگِ سوزِ محبّت

آؤ کہ مرگِ سوزِ محبّت منائیں ہم
آؤ کہ حسنِ ماہ سے دل کو جلائیں ہم

خوش ہوں فراقِ قامت ورخسارِ یار سے
سرو وگل و سمن سے نظر کو ستائیں ہم

ویرانیِ حیات کو ویران تر کریں
لے ناصح آج تیرا کہا مان جائیں ہم

پھر اوٹ لے کے دامنِ ابرِ بہار کی
دل کو منائیں ہم کبھی آنسو بہائیں ہم

سُلجھائیں بے دلی سے یہ اُلجھے ہُوے سوال
واں جائیں یا نہ جائیں، نہ جائیں کہ جائیں ہم

پھر دل کو پاسِ ضبط کی تلقین کر چکیں
اور امتحانِ ضبط سے پھر جی چُرائیں ہم

آؤ کہ آج ختم ہوئی داستانِ عشق
اب ختمِ عاشقی کے فسانے سُنائیں ہم

## मरगे-सोज़े-मुहब्बत

आयो कि मरगे-सोज़े-मुहब्बत मनायें हम
आयो कि हुस्न-ए-माह से दिल को जलायें हम

ख़ुश हों फ़िराके-कामतो-रुख़सारे-यार से
सरवो-गुलो-समन से नज़र को सतायें हम

वीरानी-ए-हयात को वीरानतर करें
ले नासेह आज तेरा कहा मान जायें हम

फिर ओट ले के दामने-अबरे-बहार की
दिल को मनायें हम, कभी आँसू बहायें हम

सुलझायें बे-दिली से ये उलझे हुए सवाल
वां जाएँ या ना जाएँ, न जाएँ कि जाएँ हम

फिर दिल को पासे-ज़ब्त की तलकीन कर चुके
और इम्तहाने-ज़ब्त से फिर जी चुरायें हम

आयो कि आज ख़त्म हुयी दास्ताने-इश्क
जब ख़त्मे-आशिकी के फ़साने सुनायें हम

## Death of the Passion of Love[3]

Come! Let's rejoice the death of the passion of love
Come! Let's burn the heart with the splendor of moon

Let's revel in the parting of the figure and visage of the darling
Let's tease the sight with cypress, flowers and jasmine

Let's make the bleakness of life bleaker
Well, O counselor! Let's heed to your advice today

By taking refuge again in the declivity of clouds of spring
Let's cajole the heart at some point, let's sob at another time

Let's unravel with apathy the knotted queries
Should we go there or not, should we not go or should we

Let's instruct the heart again about adherence of restraint
And let's once again evade the test of restraint

Come! Today the tale of love got terminated
Now, let's recount the stories of extremity of love

## .... تمھارے حُسن کے نام

سلام لکھتا ہے شاعر تمھارے حُسن کے نام
بکھر گیا جو کبھی رنگِ پیرہن سرِ بام
نِکھر گئی ہے کبھی صبح، دوپہر، کبھی شام
کہیں جو قامتِ زیبا پہ سج گئی ہے قبا
چمن میں سرو و صنوبر سنور گئے ہیں تمام
بنی بساطِ غزل جب ڈبو لیے دل نے
تمھارے سایۂ رخسار و لب میں ساغر و جام
سلام لکھتا ہے شاعر تمھارے حُسن کے نام!
تمھارے ہاتھ پہ ہے تابشِ حنا جب تک
جہاں میں باقی ہے دلداری عروسِ سُخن
تمھارا حُسن جواں ہے تو مہرباں ہے فلک
تمھارا دم ہے تو دمساز ہے ہوائے وطن
اگرچہ تنگ ہیں اوقات ؛ سخت ہیں آلام
تمھاری یاد سے شیریں ہے تلخیٔ ایام
سلام لکھتا ہے شاعر تمھارے حُسن کے نام!

## तुम्हारे हुस्न के नाम

सलाम लिखता है शायर तुम्हारे हुस्न के नाम
बिखर गया जो कभी रंगे-पैरहन सरे-बाम
निखर गयी है कभी सुबह, दोपहर, कभी शाम
कहीं जो कामते-ज़ेबा पे सज गई है कबा
चमन में सरवो-सनोबर संवर गये हैं तमाम
बनी बिसाते ग़ज़ल जब डुबो लिए दिल ने
तुम्हारे साया-ए-रुख़सारो-लब में साग़रो-जाम
सलाम लिखता है शायर तुम्हारे हुस्न के नाम
तुम्हारे हाथ पे है ताबिशे-हिना जब तक
जहां में बाकी है दिलदारी-ए-उरूसे-सुख़न
तुम्हारा हुसन जवां है तो मेहरबां है फ़लक
तुम्हारा दम है तो दमसाज़ है हवा-ए-वतन
अगरचे तंग है औकात, सख़्त हैं आलाम
तुम्हारी याद से शीरीं है तलख़ी-ए-अय्याम
सलाम लिखता है शायर तुम्हारे हुस्न के नाम

## ...To Your Beauty[4]

The poet composes greetings to your beauty

Whenever the hues of your attire got strewn at the edge of the roof
At some time the morn and noon got refreshed, at other point the evening
When the attire got adorned on your charming figure
Cypreses and and junipers got embellished in the garden
The scope of *ghazal* got set when the heart dropped
The goblet of wine in the shadows of your phiz and lips

The poet composes greetings to your beauty

As long as the shine of henna stays on your hands
The adoration of the bride of poetry lives on in the world
As long as your beauty is young the destiny is munificent
As long as you are around, pleasant is the environ of the homeland
Though the times are trying, the sorrows are forbidding
Your memory makes sweeter the bitterness of times

The poet composes greetings to your beauty

## یاد

دشتِ تنہائی میں، اے جانِ جہاں، لرزاں ہیں
تیری آواز کے سائے، ترے ہونٹوں کے سَراب
دشتِ تنہائی میں، دوری کے خس و خاک تلے
کِھل رہے ہیں، ترے پہلو کے سمن اور گلاب

اُٹھ رہی ہے کہیں قربت سے تری سانس کی آنچ
اپنی خوشبو میں سُلگتی ہوئی مدھم مدھم
دور- اُفق پار، چمکتی ہوئی؛ قطرہ قطرہ
گر رہی ہے تری دلدار نظر کی شبنم

اس قدر پیار سے، اے جان □ جہاں، رکھا ہے
دل کے رخسار پہ اس وقت تیری یاد نے ہات
یوں گماں ہوتا ہے، گرچہ ہے ابھی صبحِ فراق
ڈھل گیا ہجر کا دن، آ بھی گی وصل کی رات

## याद

दशते-तनहायी में, ऐ जाने-जहां, लरज़ां हैं
तेरी आवाज़ के साये, तिरे होठों के सराब
दशते-तनहायी में, दूरी के ख़यो-ख़ाक तले
खिल रहे हैं तिरे पहलू के समन और गुलाब

उठ रही है कहीं कुरबत से तिरी सांस की आंच
अपनी ख़ुशबु में सुलगती हुयी मद्धम-मद्धम
दूर-उफ़क पार, चमकती हुई, कतरा-कतरा
गिर ही है तिरी दिलदार नज़र की शबनम

इस कदर प्यार से, ऐ जाने-जहां, रक्खा है
दिल के रुख़सार पे वक्त तिरी याद ने हाथ
यूं गुमां होता है, गरचे है अभी सुबहे-फ़िराक,
ढल गया हिजर का दिन, आ गई वसल की रात

## Remembrance[5]

O my love! In the desert of solitude there quiver
The mistiness of your voice, the illusions of your lips
In the desert of solitude, below the straw and trash of separation
There bloom the jasmines and roses of your body

There rises from somewhere close by the flame of your breath
Burning slowly in its own aroma
Faraway__beyond the horizon, sparkling drop by drop
The dew of your gracious sight is falling

O my beloved! At present with so much love your remembrance
Has placed its hand on the countenance of my heart
That I presume, though it is the morn of separation,
The day of parting has declined; the night of union has arrived

## مُلاقات

یہ رات اُس درد کا شجر ہے
جو مجھ سے، تجھ سے عظیم تر ہے
عظیم تر ہے کہ اس کی شاخوں
میں لاکھ مشعل بکف ستاروں
کے کارواں، گھر کے کھو گئے ہیں
ہزار مہتاب، اس کے سائے
میں اپنا سب نُور، رو گئے ہیں

یہ رات اُس درد کا شجر ہے
جو مجھ سے تجھ سے عظیم تر ہے
مگر اسی رات کے شجر سے
یہ چند لمحوں کے زرد پتے

گرے ہیں، اور تیرے گیسوؤں میں
الجھ کے گلنار ہو گئے ہیں
اسی کی شبنم سے خامُشی کے
یہ چند قطرے، تری جبیں پر
برس کے، ہیرے پرو گئے ہیں

۲

بہت سیہ ہے یہ رات لیکن

اِسی سیاہی میں رُونما ہے

وہ نہر خوں جو مری صدا ہے

اسی کے سائے میں نُور گر ہے

وہ موجِ زر جو تری نظر ہے

وہ غم جو اس وقت تیری باہوں

کہ گلستاں میں سُلگ رہا ہے

(وہ غم، جو اس رات کا ثمر ہے)

کچھ اور تپ جائے اپنی آہوں

کی آنچ میں تو یہی شرر ہے

ہر اک سیہ شاخ کی کماں سے

جگر میں ٹوٹے ہیں تیر جتنے

جگر سے نوچے ہیں، اور ہر اک

کا ہم نے تیشہ بنا لیا ہے

۳

الم نصیبوں، جگر فگاروں

کی صبح، افلاک پر نہیں ہے

جہاں پہ ہم تم کھڑے ہیں دونوں
سحر کا روشن اُفق یہیں ہے
یہیں پہ غم کے شرار کِھل کر
شفق کا گلزار بن گئے ہیں
یہیں پہ قاتِل دکھوں کہ تیشے
قطار اندر قطار کرنوں
کہ آتشیں ہار بن گئے ہیں

یہ غم جو اس رات نے دیا ہے
یہ غم سحر کا یقیں بنا ہے
یقیں جو غم سے کریم تر ہے
سحر جو شب سے عظیم تر ہے

## मुलाक़ात

1

यह रात उस दर्द का शजर है
जो मुझसे तुझसे अज़ीमतर है
अज़ीमतर है कि उसकी शाख़ों में

लाख मशाल-बकफ़ सितारों
के कारवाँ, घिर के खो गए हैं
हज़ार महताब उसके साए
में अपना सब नूर, रो गए हैं
यह रात उस दर्द का शजर है
जो मुझसे तुझसे अज़ीमतर है
मगर उसी रात के शजर से
यह चंद लमहों के ज़र्द पत्ते
गिरे हैं और तेरे गेसुओं में
उलझ के गुलनार हो गए हैं
इसी की शबनम से, .ख़मुशी के
यह चंद कतरे, तेरी ज़बीं पर
बरस के, हीरे पिरो गए हैं

2

बहुत सियाह है यह रात लेकिन
इसी सियाही में रूनुमा है
वो नहरे-ख़ूँ जो मेरी सदा है
इसी के साए में नूर गर है
वो मौजे-ज़र जो तेरी नज़र है

वा ग़म जो इस वक्त तेरी बाँहों
के गुलिसताँ में सुलग रहा है
(वो ग़म जो इस रात का समर है)
कुछ और तप जाए अपनी आहों
की आँच में तो यही शरर है
हर इक सियह शाख़ की कमाँ से
जिगर में टूटे हैं तीर जितने
जिगर से नीचे हैं, और हर इक
का हमने तीशा बना लिया है

3

अलम नसीबों, जिगर फ़िगारों
की सुबह अफ़्लाक पर नहीं है
जहाँ पे हम-तुम खड़े हैं दोनों
सहर का रौशन उफ़क़ यहीं है
यहीं पे गम के शरार खिल कर
खफ़ाक का गुलजार बन गए हैं
यही पे क़ातिल दुखों के तीशे
क़तार अंदर क़तार किरनों
के आतशीं हार बन गए हैं

यह ग़म जो इस रात ने दिया है
यह ग़म सहर का यक़ीं बना है
यक़ी जो गम से करीमतर है
सहर जो शब से अज़ीमतर है

## The Meeting[6]

This night is the tree of the agony
That is greater than you and I
It's greater for in its branches
The caravans of lakhs of torch-wielding
Stars have got lost
Thousands of moons, under its shadow
Have moaned their glow

This night is the tree of the agony
That is greater than you and I
Yet, from the tree of this night alone
Have dropped the pale leaves of these moments
Have dropped and in your hair
Got entwined and turned into scarlet flowers
From its dew alone, these scarce
Drops of silence, on your forehead,
Poured down and have transfixed the diamonds

### II

This night is too dark, yet
There manifests in this darkness alone
The channel of blood that's my voice
In its shadow alone there illumines
The surge of gold that is your vision

The anguish that currently blazes
In the garden of your arms
(The anguish that is the crop of this night)
If it smolders a little more in its sighs's
Fire , this alone is the sparkle

(Released) from each dark bough
The arrows that got stuck in the heart
We have plucked them and made
An adze out of each one of them

**III**

The morn of ill-fated, heartbroken
Souls is not in the heavens
Where both, you and I stand
The bright horizon of the dawn is here alone
Here alone, the sparkles of the anguish got unfolded
And turned into the garden of redness of twilight
Here alone the killer adzes of pains,
Rows after rows, have turned into
The blazing garlands of beams

The anguish that this night has handed over
This anguish has developed into the certainty of the dawn
The certainty that's more gracious than agony
The dawn that is greater than night!

## ہم جو تاریک راہوں میں مارے گئے

(ایتھل اور جولیس روزنبرگ کے خطوط سے متاثر ہو کر لکھی گئی)

تیرے ہونٹھوں کی پھولوں کی چاہت میں ہم
دار کی خشک ٹہنی پہ وارے گئے
تیرے ہاتوں کی شمعوں کی حسرت میں ہم
نیم تاریک راہوں میں مارے گئے

سُولیوں پر ہمارے لبوں سے پرے
تیرے ہونٹوں کی لالی لپکتی رہی
تیری زلفوں کی مستی برستی رہی
تیرے ہاتھوں کی چاندی دمکتی رہی

جب گھلی تیری راہوں میں شامِ ستم
ہم چلے آئے، لائے جہاں تک قدم
لب پہ حرفِ غزل، دل میں قندیلِ غم
اپنا غم تھا گواہی تیرے حسن کی
دیکھ قائم رہے اس گواہی پہ ہم
ہم جو تاریک راہوں میں مارے گئے

نارسائی اگر اپنی تقدیر تھی،
تیری اُلفت تو اپنی ہی تدبیر تھی
کس کو شکوہ ہے گر شوق کے سلسلے
ہجر کی قتل گاہوں سے سب جا ملے

قتل گاہوں سے چُن کر ہمارے علَم
اور نکلیں گے عشّاق کے قافلے

جن کی راہِ طلب سے ہمارے قدم
مختصر کر چلے درد کے فاصلے
کر چلے جن کی خاطر جہاں گیر ہم
جان گنوا کر تری دلبری کا بھرم
ہم جو تاریک راہوں میں مارے گئے

## हम हो तारीक राहों में मारे गए

(ईथेल और जूलियस रोजनबर्ग के खतों
से मुतासिर होकर लिखी गई)

तेरे होटों के फूलों की चाहत में हम
दार की ख़ुश्क टहनी पे वारे गए
तेरे हाथों की शम्माओं की हसरत में हम
नीमतारीक राहों में मारे गए

सूलियों पर हमारे लबों से परे
तेरे होटों की लाली लपकती रही
तेरी जुल्फ़ों की मस्ती बरस्ती रही
तेरे हाथों की चाँदी चमक़ती रही

जब धुलि तेरी राहें में शामे-सितम
हम चले आए, लाए जहाँ तक क़दम
लब मे हर्फ़े-ग़जल, दिल में क़दीले-ग़म

अपना ग़म था गवाही तेरे हुस्न की
देख क़ायम रहे इस गवाही पे हम
हम जो तारीक राहों में मारे गए

नारसाई अगर अपनी तक़दीर थी
तेरी उल्फ़त तो अपनी ही तदबीर थी
किसको शिकवा है गो शौक के सिलसिले

हिज्र की क़त्लगाहों से सब जा मिले
क़त्लगाहों से चुन कर हमारे अलम
और निकलेंगे उश्शाक़ के क़ाफ़िले
जिनकी राहे तलब से हमारे क़दम
मुख़्तसर कर चले दर्द के फ़ासिले

कर चले जिनकी .खातिर जहाँगीर हम
जाँ गँवा कर तेरी दिलबरी का भरम
हम जो तारीक राहों में मारे गए

## We, Who Got Slain in the Dark Alleys[7]

(Having inspired by the correspondence between Ethel and Julius Rosenberg)

For the yearning of the roses of your lips
We were slain on the parched stalk of the gallows
In the wistfulness of your glittering hands
We got slain in the dimly-lit alleys

On the gallows, beyond our lips
The rosiness of your lips kept swooping
The bliss of your tresses kept streaming
The glisten of your hands kept glimmering

When the dusk of coercion got dissolved in your pathways
We arrived where our steps brought us
With a *ghazal* on our lips, a lamp of grief in the heart
Our sorrow was the testimony of your beauty
Look! We have held out on the testimony
We, who got slain in the dark alleys

If letdown was our destiny
Your love was after all our own ploy
Who should find fault if the links of affection
Led to the execution place of separation

Having gathered our standards from the killing fields
The caravans of the devotees would move on further
For the sake of their expedition our footfalls
Have cut down the painful distances
For their sake we have made extensive,
Having given up our lives, the repute of your love
We, who got slain in the dark alleys

## جب تیری سمندر آنکھوں میں

## (گیت)

یہ دھُوپ کنارا، شام ڈھلے
ملتے ہیں دونوں وقت جہاں
جو رات نہ دن، جو آج نہ کل
پل بھر میں امر، پل بھر میں دھواں
اِس دھوپ کنارے، پل دو پل
ہونٹھوں کی لپک
باہوں کی چھنک
یہ میل ہمارا، جھوٹ نہ سچ
کیوں زار کرو، کیوں دوش دھرو
کس کارن جھوٹی بات کرو
جب تیری سمندر آنکھوں میں
اس شام کا سورج ڈوبے گا
سُکھ سوئیں گے گھر دَر والے
اور راہی اپنی رہ لے گا

## जब तेरी समंदर आँखों में

ये धूप किनारा, शाम ढले
मिलते हैं दोंनो वक़्त जहाँ
जो रात न दिन, जो आज न कल
पल भर में अमर, पल भर में धुआँ
इस धूप किनारे, पल दो पल
होठों की लपक, बाँहों की खनक
ये मेल हमार झूठ न सच
क्यों रार करो, क्यों दोष धरो
किस कारन झूठी बात करो
जब तेरी समंदर आँखों में
इस शाम का सूरज डूबेगा
सुख सोएँगे घर-दर वाले
और राही अपनी राह लेगा

## When in the Sea of Your Eyes[8] (Lyric)

This edge of the sunshine, the evening falls
When both the times run into
It's neither night nor day; neither it's today nor tomorrow
For a moment eternal, the next moment turns into haze
At the bank of this sunshine, for a moment or two
The swoop of lips
The clank of arms
This meeting of ours, neither untrue nor true
Why whimper, why accuse
For what reason tell lies

When in the sea of your eyes
The sun of this evening will set
The dear ones will happily sleep in the home
And the traveller will move on

## اِنتساب

آج کے نام

اور

آج کے غم کے نام

آج کا غم کہ ہے زندگی کے بھرے گلستاں سے خفا

زرد پتّوں کا بن

زرد پتّوں کا بن جو میرا دیس ہے

درد کی انجمن جو میرا دیس ہے

کلرکوں کی افسردہ جانوں کے نام

کرم خوردہ دلوں اور زبانوں کے نام

پوسٹ مینوں کے نام

تانگے والوں کے نام

ریل بانوں کے نام

کارخانوں کے بھوکے جیالوں کو نام

بادشاہِ جہاں، والی ماسواء، نائب اللہ فی الارض

دہقاں کے نام

جس کے ڈھوروں کو ظالم ہنکالے گئے

جس کی بیٹی کو ڈاکو اُٹھالے گئے

ہاتھ بھر کھیت سے ایک انگشت پٹوار نے کاٹ لی ہے

دوسری مالیے کے بہانے سے سرکار نے کاٹ لی ہے
جس کی پگ زور والوں کے پاؤں تلے
دھجیاں ہو گئی ہے

ان دکھی ماؤں کو نام
راتم میں جن کو بچّے بلکتے ہیں اور
نیند کی مار کھائے ہوئے بازوؤں میں سنبھلتے نہیں
دکھ بتاتے نہیں
منتوں زاریوں سے بہلتے نہیں

ان حسیناؤں کے نام
جن کی آنکھوں کے گل
چلمنوں اور دریچوں کی بیلیوں پہ بیکار کھِل کھِل کے
مُرجھا گئے ہیں
ان بیاہتاؤں کے نام
جن کے بدن
بے محبّت ریاکار سیجوں پہ سج سج کے اکتا گئے ہیں
بیواؤں کے نام
"کٹڑیوں" اور گلیوں، محلّوں کے نام
جن کی ناپاک خاشاک سے چاند راتوں

کو آ آ کے کرتا ہے اکثر وضو

جن کے سایوں میں کرتی ہے آہ وبُکا

آنچلوں کی حنا

چوڑیوں کی کھنک

کاکلوں کی مہک

آرزومند سینوں کی اپنے پسینے میں جلنے کی بُو

پڑھنے والوں کے نام

وہ جو اصحابِ طبل و علم

کے دروں پر کتاب اور قلم

کا تقاضا لیے، ہاتھ پھیلائے

پہنچے، مگر لوٹ کر گھر نہ آئے

وہ معصوم جو بھولپن میں

وہاں اپنے ننھے چراغوں میں لو کی لگن

لے کے پہنچے جہاں

بٹ رہے تھے، گھٹاٹوپ، بے انت راتوں کے سائے

اُن اسیروں کے نام

جن کو سینوں میں فردا کے شب تاب گوہر

جیل خانوں کی شوریدہ راتوں کی صرصر میں

جل جل کے انجم نما ہو گئے ہیں

آنے والے دنوں کے سفیروں کے نام

وہ جو خوشبوئے گُل کی طرح

اپنے پیغام پر خود فدا ہو گئے ہیں

(ناتمام)

## इंतिसाब

आज के नाम
और
आज के ग़म के नाम

आज का ग़म कि है ज़िन्दगी के भरे गुलिसतां से .ख़फ़ा
ज़रद पत्तों का बन जो मेरा देस है
दर्द की अंजुमन जो मेरा देस है
किलरकों की अफ़सुरदा जानों के नाम
किरमख़ुरदा दिलों और जवानों के नाम
पोसटमैनों के नाम
तांगेवालों के नाम
रेलबानों के नाम
कारखानों के भोले जियालों के नाम
बादशाहे-जहं, वालिए-मासिवा, नायबुल्लाहे-फ़िल-अरज़, दहकां के नाम
जिके ढोरों को ज़ालिम हंका ले गये
हाथ-भर खेत से एक अंगुशत, पटवार ने काट ली है
दूसरी मालिये के बहाने से सरकार ने काट ली है
जिसकी पग ज़ोरवालों के पांव तल
धज्जीया हो गई है
उन दुखी मायों के नाम
रात में लिके बच्चे बिलखते हैं और
नींद की मार खाए हुए बाज़ुयों से संभलते नहीं
दुख बताते नहीं
मिन्नतों ज़ायों से बहलते नहीं

उन हसीनायों के नाम

जिनकी आंखों के गुल
चिलमनों और दरीखें की बेलों पे बेकार खिल-खिल के
मुरझा गये हैं
उन बयाहतायों के नाम
जिनके बदल
बे-मुहब्बत रियाकार सेजों पे सज-सज के उकता गये हैं
बेवायों के नाम
कटड़ियों और गलियों, मुहल्लों के नाम
जिनकी नापाक ख़ाशाक से चांद रातों
को आ-आ के करता है अकसर वज़ू
जिनके सायों में करती है आहो-बुका
आचलों की हिना
चूड़ियों की खनक
काकुलों की महक
आरज़ूमन्द सीनों की अपने पसीने में जलने की बू

तालिबइलमों के नाम
वो जो असहाबे-तबलो-अलम
के दरों पर किताब और कलम
का तकाज़ा लिये, हाथ फैलाये
पहुंचे, मगर लौट कर घर न आये
वो मासूम जो भोलेपन में
वहों अपने ननहें चिराग़ों में लौ की लगन
ले के पहुंचे, जहां
बंट रहे थे घटाटोप, बेअंत रातों के साये
उन असीरों के नाम
जिनक सीनों में फ़रदा के शबताब गौहर

जेलखानों की शोरीदा रातों की सरसर में
जल-जल के अंजुम-नुमां हो गये हैं

आनेवाले दिनों के सफ़ीरो के नाम
वो जो खुशबू-ए-गुल की तरह
अपने पैग़ाम पर .ख़ुद फ़िदा हो गये हैं

(अधूरी)

## Dedication[9]

For today
And
For the name of today's grief
Today's grief that is annoyed with the entire garden of life
The forest of pale leaves
The forest of pale leaves that is my homeland
The congregation of pain that is my homeland

For the dejected souls of clerks
For moth-eaten hearts and tongues
For postmen
For *tonga* drivers
For train drivers
For the starving braves of the factories

For the king of the world, the sovereign of the beyond,
The deputy of God on earth, the peasant
His cattle have been driven away by the persecutors
His daughter has been abducted by the dacoits
From his field of a hand's length a slice has been cut off by the village registrar
Another one has been severed by the government in the name of revenue
His turban, under the feet of the strong,
Has been reduced to tatters

For the tormented mothers
Whose children wail during nights and
Cannot be supported by the sleepless arms

Don't express their pain
Cannot be cheered by
Entreaties and lamentations

For those beautiful lasses
The flowerets of whose eyes
Got withered away
After having bloomed
On the vines of screens and windows

For the married women
Whose bodies got bored to death for
Adorning the loveless, phony beds

For widows
For precincts and streets, for neighborhoods
With whose dirty garbage the moon often
Arrive during nights to perform ablution
And from under whose shadows ascend the howls and cries
Of the hues of veils
The clink of bangles
The scent of tresses
The stench of the burning of aspiring hearts

For students
The ones who approached
The abodes of the rich and powerful
Beseeching for books and pens
However, never returned home
Those innocuous beings
Who because of their naivety

Reached there, with the longing
Of lighting their little lamps,
Where the shadows of dark and endless nights
Were being handed out

For those inmates
In whose hearts the glittering jewels of the future
Have been reduced, in tempest of the dismal prison nights,
To star-like objects by constant burning

For the envoys of the forthcoming days
The ones who, like the scent of a flower,
Fell in love with the message of their own

(Incomplete)

## لہو کا سُراغ

کہیں نہیں ہے کہیں بھی نہیں لہو کا سُراغ
نہ دست و ناخنِ قاتل نہ آستیں پہ نشاں
نہ سرخیٔ لبِ خنجر نہ رنگِ نوکِ سناں
نہ خاک پر کوئی دھبّا نہ بام پر کوئی داغ
کہیں نہیں ہے کہیں بھی نہیں لہو کا سراغ
نہ صرفِ خدمتِ شاہاں کہ خوں بہا دیتے
نہ دیں کی نذر کہ بیعانۂ جزا دیتے
نہ رزم گاہ میں برسا کہ معتبر ہوتا
کسی عَلم پہ رقم ہو کے مشتہر ہوتا
پکارتا رہا، بے آسرا، یتیم لہو
کسی کو بہرِ سماعت نہ وقت تھا نہ دماغ
نہ مدّعی، نہ شہادت، حساب پاک ہُوا
یہ خونِ خاک نشیناں تھا، رزقِ خاک ہُوا

## लहू का सुराग़

कही नहीं है, कही भी नहीं लहू का सुराग़

न दस्तो-नाख़ुने-कातिल न आसतीं पे निशां
न सुरख़ी-ए-लब-ए-ख़ंजर, रंगे-नोके-सनां
न ख़ाक पर कोई धब्बा न बाम पर कोई दाग़
कहीं नहीं है, कहीं भी नहीं लहू का सुराग़
न सरफ़े-ख़िदमते-शाहां कि ख़ूंबहा देते
न दीं की नज़र कि बयाना-ए-जज़ा देते
न रज़मगाह में बरसा कि मोतबर होता
किसी अलम पे रकम हो के मुशतहर होता
किसी अलम पे रकम हो के मुशतहर होता
पुकारता रहा बे-आसरा यतीम लहू
किसी को बहरे-समाअत न वक़्त था न दिमाग़
न मुद्दई, न शहादत, हिसाब पाक हुआ
ये ख़ूने-ख़कनशीनां था रिज़के-ख़ाक हुआ

## Trace of Blood[10]

There is nowhere, there is nowhere at all the trace of blood
It is neither on the hands and nails of the assassin nor on his sleeve
It is neither on the blade of the dagger nor on the point of the spear
There is no smudge on the ground nor there is a stain on the roof
There is nowhere, there is nowhere at all the trace of blood

It neither got used up in the duty of the kings so that it would fetch compensation
Nor it was spent in the service of the faith so as it would bring reward in the hereafter
It was neither shed on the battlefield so that it could turn into reputable
And would have been flaunted on some standard so that it would come to be famed

The hopeless, forsaken blood kept on calling
None had either the time or mentality to listen to
Neither there is the plaintiff nor any witness, the accounts have been squared
This blood has been the dweller of the grime, got consumed by the dust

## یہاں سے شہر کو دیکھو

یہاں سے شہر کو دیکھو تو حلقہ در حلقہ
کھنچی ہے جیل کی صورت ہر ایک سمت فصیل
ہر ایک راہ گزر گردشِ اسیراں ہے
نہ سنگِ میل، نہ منزل، نہ مخلصی کی سبیل

جو کوئی تیز چلے رہ تو پوچھتا ہے خیال
کہ ٹوکنے کوئی للکار کیوں نہیں آئی
جو کوئی ہاتھ ہلائے تو وہم کو ہے سوال
کوئی چھنک، کوئی جھنکار کیوں نہیں آئی ؟

یہاں سے شہر کو دیکھو تو ساری خلقت میں
نہ کوئی صاحبِ تمکیں، نہ کوئی والیِ ہوش
ہر ایک مردِ جواں مجرمِ رسن بہ گلو
ہر اِک حسینۂ رعنا، کنیزِ حلقہ بگوش

جو سائے دُور چراغوں کے گرد لرزاں ہیں
نہ جانے محفلِ غم ہے کہ بزمِ جام و سبُو
جو رنگ ہر در و دیوار پر پریشاں ہیں
یہاں سے کچھ نہیں کُھلتا یہ پھول ہیں کہ لہو

## यहां के शहर को देखो

यहां के शहर को देखो हलका-दर-हलका
खिंची है जेल की सूरत हर एक सिमत फ़सील
हरेक राहगुज़र गरदिशे-असीरां है
न संगे-मील, ना मंज़िल, न मुख़लिसी ही सबील

जो कोई तेज़ चले रह, तो पूछता है ख़्याल
कि टोकने कोई ललकार कयूं नहीं आई
जो कोई हाथ हिलाये तो वहम को है सवाल
कोई छ़नक, कोई झंकार कयूं नहीं आई

यहां से शहर को देखो तो सारी ख़लकत में
न कोई साहबे-तमकीं न कोई वाली-ए-होश
हरेक मरदे-जवांमुजरिमे-रसन-ब-गुलू
हर इक हसीना-ए-राना कनीज़े-हलका-ब-गोश

जो साये दूर चिराग़ों के गिरद लरज़ां हैं
न जाने महफ़िले-ग़म है कि बज़्में-जामो-सुबू
जो रंग हर दरो-दीवार पर परीशां है
यहां से कुछ नहीं खुलता-ये फूल है कि लहू

## Look at the City From This Point[11]

Look at the city from this point there appears, ring after ring,
A rampart like in a jail spread out in all directions
Every path is like a spherical corridor for the inmates
Neither a milestone, nor a destination, nor an egress

If someone walks briskly, then the thought quizzes
Why no call of challenge has come to hinder the steps
If someone shakes hand then the whim inquires
Why there is no tinkling, no jingling?

Look at the city from this point there appears among all the people
None with serenity, none with senses
Every young man seems to be a convict to be hanged
Every exquisitely beautiful girl looks like a faithful servant

The shadows that quiver faraway near the lamps
Nobody knows whether it is a crowd of mourning or a gathering of drinkers
The colour that is distressed on every wall
One can't make out from this point if it is flower or blood

## گیت

چلو پھر سے مُسکرائیں

چلو پھر سے دل جلائیں

جو گزر گئی ہیں راتیں

انہیں پھر جگا کے لائیں

جو بسر گئی ہیں باتیں

انہیں یاد میں بُلائیں

چلو پھر سے دل لگائیں

چلو پھر سے مسکرائیں

کسی شہ نشیں پہ جھلکی

وہ دھنک کسی قبا کی

کسی رگ میں کسمسائی

وہ کسک کسی ادا کی

کوئی حرفِ بے مُروّت

کسی کُنجِ لب سے پھُوٹا

وہ چھنک کے شیشۂ دل

تہِ بام پھر سے ٹوٹا

یہ مِلن کی نا مِلن کی -

یہ لگن کی اور جلن کی

جو سہی ہیں وارداتیں

جو گزر گئی ہیں راتیں

جو بسر گئی ہیں باتیں

کوئی ان کی دُھن بنائیں

کوئی ان کا گیت گائیں

چلو پھر سے مسکرائیں

چلو پھر سے دل جلائیں

## गीत

चलो फिर से दिल जलाएं
चलो फिर से मुस्कुराएं

जो गुज़र गई हैं रातें
उनहें फिर जगा के लाएं
जो बिसर गई हैं बातें
उनहें याद में बुलाएं
चलो फिर से दिल लगाएं
चलो फिर से मुस्कुराएं

किसी यह-नशीं पे झलकी
वो धनक किसी कबा की
किसी रग में कसमसाई
वो कसक किसी अदा की
कोई हरफ़े-बे-मुरव्वत
किसी कुंजे-लब से फूटा
वो छनक के शीशा-ए-दिल
तहे-बाम फिर से टूटा

ये मिलन की, नामिलन की
ये लगन की और जलन की
जो सही हैं वारदातें
जो गुज़र गई है रातें
जो बिसर गई हैं बातें
कोई इनकी धुन बनाएं
कोई इनका गीत गाएं
चलो फिर से मुस्कुराएं
चलों फिर से दिल जलाएं

## Lyric[12]

Well! Let's smile once again
Well! Let's afire the heart again

The nights that've gone by
Let's stir and relive them
The gabs that've been forgotten
Let's recall them yet again
Well! Let's link up the heart yet again
Well! Let's smile once again

In certain balcony showed off
The rainbow of someone's attire
In certain vein twitched
The pang of someone's elegance
A certain insensitive word
Came forth from certain lips
The glass of heart, with a tinkle sound,
Got splintered below the balcony

These events of__________
Meetings and no meetings
Love and heart aches
That we've lived through
The nights that've gone by
The chats that've been forgotten
Let's make some tune out of them
Let's sing some lyric of them
Well! Let's smile once again
Well! Let's afire the heart again

## ڈھاکہ سے واپسی پر

ہم کہ ٹھہرے اجنبی اتنی ملاقاتوں کے بعد
پھر بنیں گے آشنا کتنی ملاقاتوں کے بعد
کب نظر میں آئے گی بے داغ سبزے کی بہار
خون کے دھبّے دھُلیں گے کتنی برساتوں کے بعد
تھے بہت بے درد لمحے ختمِ دردِ عشق کے
تھیں بہت بے مہر صبحیں مہرباں راتوں کے بعد
دل تو چاہا پر شکستِ دل نے مہلت ہی نہ دی
کچھ گلے شکوے بھی کر لیتے مناجاتوں کے بعد
اُن سے جو کہنے گئے تھے فیضؔ جاں صدقہ کیے
اَن کہی ہی رہ گئی وہ بات سب باتوں کے بعد

## ढाका से वापसी पर

हम कि ठहरे अजनबी इतनी मुदारातो के बाद
फिर बनेंगे आश्ना कितनी मुलाकातों के बाद
कब नज़र में आएगी बे-दाग़ सब्ज़े की बहार
ख़ून के धब्बे धुलेंगे कितनी बरसातों के बाद
थे बहुत बेदर्द लम्हे ख़त्म-ए-दर्द-ए-इश्क़ के
थी बहुत बे-मेहर सुब्हे मेहरबां रातो के बाद
दिल तो चाहा पर शिकस्त-ए-दिल ने मोहलत ही न दी
कुछ गिले शिकवे भी कर लेते मुनाजातो के बाद
उन से जो कहने गए थे 'फ़ैज़' जो सदक़े किए
अन-कही ही रह गई वो बात सब बातों के बाद

## On Return from Dhaka[13]

We have been classed as strangers after so many meetings
We will be friends again after how many meetings

When will the spring of unblemished verdure be visible again
The blood stains will be washed away after how many rainfalls

The painful moments of ending of love were too merciless
The morns were too callous after the caring nights

While the heart yearned for yet the rout of heart didn't give the respite
That we could exchange a few grievances after the supplications

O Faiz! The thought that we went to express to them, we let go the life instead
That subject stayed unexpressed after all the conversations

## لینن گراڈ کا گورستان

سرد سِلوں پر

زرد سِلوں پر

تازہ گرم لہو کی صورت

گلدستوں کے چھینٹے ہیں

کتبے سب بے نام ہیں لیکن

ہر اک پھول پہ نام لکھا ہے

غافِل سونے والے کا

یاد میں رونے والے کا

اپنے فرض سے فارِغ ہو کر

اپنے لہو کی تان کے چادر

سارے بیٹے خواب میں ہیں

اپنے غموں کا ہار پرو کر

امّاں اکیلی جاگ رہی ہے

## लेनिनगराड का गोरिस्तान

सर्द सिलों पर

ज़रद सिलों पर

ताज़ा गरम लहू की सूरत

गुदलस्तों के छींटे हैं

कतबे सब बे-नाम हैं लेकिन

हर इक फूल पे नाम लिखा है

ग़ाफ़िल सोनेवाले का

याद में रोनेवाले का

अपने फ़रज़ से फ़ारिग़ होकर

अपने लहू की तान के चादर

सारे बेटे ख़्वाब में हैं

अपने गमों का हार पिरोकर

अंमां अकेली जाग रही है।

## The Cemetery of Leningrad

On the cold slabs of stones
On the pallid slabs of stones
In the form of fresh, warm blood
There are drops of bouquets
All the epitaphs are nameless yet
The name is inscribed on each flower
Of the one who's soundly asleep
Of the one whose memory causes wailing
Having performed their duties
Having covered themselves with the sheets of own blood
All sons are fast asleep
Having interweaved the chain of her sorrows
The mother alone is wide-awake

## یہ ماتمِ وقت کی گھڑی ہے

ٹھہر گئی آسماں کی ندیا

وہ جا لگی افق کنارے

اُداس رنگوں کی چاندنیاّ

اتر گئے ساحل زمیں پر

سبھی کھویا

تمام تارے

اکھڑ گئی سانس پتّیوں کی

چلی گئیں اُونگھ میں ہوائیں

گجر بجا حکمِ خامُشی کا

تو چپ میں گم ہو گئی صدائیں

سحر کی گوری کی چھاتیوں سے

ڈھلک گئی تیرگی کی چادر

اور اس بجائے

بکھر گئے اس کے تن بدن پر

نراس تنہائیوں کے سائے

اور اس کو کچھ بھی خبر نہیں ہے

کسی کو کچھ بھی خبر نہیں ہے

کہ دن ڈھلے شہر سے نکل کر
کدھر کو جانے کا رُخ کیا تھا
نہ کوئی جادہ، نہ کوئی منزل
کسی مسافر کو
اب دماغِ سفر نہیں ہے
یہ وقت زنجیرِ روز و شب کی
کہیں سے ٹوٹی ہوئی کڑی ہے
یہ ماتمِ وقت کی گھڑی ہے

یہ وقت آئے تو بے ارادہ
کبھی کبھی میں بھی دیکھتا ہوں
اتار کر ذات کا لبادہ
کہیں سیاہی ملامتوں کی
کہیں پہ گل بوٹے الفتوں کے
کہیں لکیریں ہیں آنسوؤں کی
کہیں پہ خونِ جگر کے دھبّے
یہ چاک ہے پنجۂ عدو کا
یہ مہر ہے یارِ مہرباں کی

یہ لعل لب ہائے مہوشاں کے
یہ مرحمت شیخِ بدزباں کی

یہ جامۂ روز و شب گزیدہ
مجھے یہ پیراہنِ دریدہ
عزیز بھی، ناپسند بھی ہے
کبھی یہ فرمانِ جوشِ وحشت
کہ نوچ کر اس کو پھینک ڈالو
کبھی یہ اصرارِ حرفِ اُلفت
کہ چُوم کر پھر گلے لگا لو

## ये मातम-ए-वक्त की घड़ी है

ठहर गई आसमां की नदिया
वो जा ललगी है उफ़क किनारे
उदास रंगों की चांद नैया
उतर गये साहले-ज़मीं पर
सभी खिबैया
तमाम तारे
उखड़ गई सांस पत्तियों की
चल गई ऊंध में हवाएं
गज़र बजा हुक़्में-ख़ामोशी का
तो चुप में गुम हो गई सदाएं
शहर की गोरी की छातियों से
ढलक गई तीरगी की चादर
और इस बजाय
बिखर गये उसके तन-बदन पर
निरास तनहाईयों के साये
और उस की कुछ भी ख़बर नहीं है
किसी को कुछ भी ख़बर नहीं है
कि दिल ढले शहर से निकलकर
किधर को जाने का रुख़ किया था
न कोई जादा, न कोई मंज़िल
किसी मुसाफ़िर को
अब दिमाग़े-सफ़र नहीं है

ये वक़्त ज़ंजीरे-रोज़ो-शब की
कहीं से टूटी हुई कड़ी हैं
ये मातम-ए-वक़्त की घड़ी है
ये वक़्त आये तो बेइरादा
कभी-कभी मैं देखता हूँ
उतारकर ज़रत कर लबादा
कहीं सिपाही मलामतों की
कहीं पे गुल-बूटे उलफ़तों के
कहीं लकीरें हैं आंसूओं की
कहीं पे ख़ूने-जिगर के धब्बे
ये चाक है पंजा-ए-अदू का
ये मुहर है यारे-मेहरबां की
ये लाल लब-हाए-महवशां के
ये मरहमत शैख़े-बदज़ुबां की
ये जामा-ए-रोज़ो-शब-गज़ीदा
मुझे ये पैराहने-दरीदा
अज़ीज़ भी, नापसन्द भी है
कभी ये फ़रमाने-जोशे-वहशत
कि नोचकर इसको फेंक डालो
कभी ये इसरारे-हर्फ़े-उलफ़त
कि चूमकर फिर गले लगा लो

## This Moment is to Mourn the Death of Time[15]

The river of the sky has paused
And near the bank of horizon
The moon-ferry of the gloomy hues has anchored
All the ferryman, all the stars
Have disembarked
On the shore of the earth
The leaves are gasping for breath
The winds are dozing off
The gong has issued the order of silence
Then all voices have lost in quietness
From the bosom of the fairy of dawn
The sheet of darkness has fallen down
And in its place
Have stretched on her body
The shadows of morose solitude
And she isn't even aware of it
Nobody is aware of anything
That at dusk when he left the town
Where had he planned to go
No way, no destination
No traveller now
Has disposition for journey
This time is a broken link of
The chain of day and night
This moment is to mourn the death of time

When such a time arrives
I too, off and on, look over
After shedding the covering of the self

At places the dark patches of reproach
At other place the flowers of love
At some place there are strands of tears
At other place there are blotches of heart's blood
Here is a shred of the hand of a foe
This is the imprint of a loving friend
This ruby is that of the warm lips of the exquisite beauties
These incisions are caused by a foul-mouthed cleric

This attire waned by days and nights
This torn apparel is
Dear to me yet I detest
On occasions wildness commands
Pull it off, discard it
At times love persists gently
Caress it and embrace it tightly

## ہم تو مجبورِ وفا ہیں

تجھ کو کتنوں کا لہو چاہیے اے ارضِ وطن
جو ترے عارضِ بے رنگ کو گلنار کریں
کتنی آہوں سے کلیجہ ترا ٹھنڈا ہوگا
کتنے آنسو ترے صحراؤں کو گلزار کریں

تیرے ایوانوں میں پُرزے ہُوے پیماں کتنے
کتنے وعدے جو نہ آسودۂ اقرار ہُوے
کتنی آنکھوں کو نظر کھا گئی بدخواہوں کی
خواب کتنے تری شاہراہوں میں سنگسار ہُوے

بلاکشانِ محبّت پہ جو ہُوا سو ہُوا
جو مجھ پہ گزری مت اس سے کہو، ہُوا سو ہُوا
مَبادا ہو کوئی ظالم ترا گریباں گیر
لہو کے داغ تو دامن سے دھو، ہُوا سو ہُوا

ہم تو مجبورِ وفا ہیں مگر اے جانِ جہاں
اپنے عشّاق سے ایسے بھی کوئی کرتا ہے
تیری محفل کو خدا رکھے ابد تک قائم
ہم تو مہماں ہیں گھڑی بھر کے، ہمارا کیا ہے

## हम तो मजबूर-ए-वफ़ा हैं

तुझको कितनों का लहू चाहिए ऐ अरज़े-वतन
जो तिरे आरिज़े-बेरंग को गुलनार करें
कितनी आहों से कलेजा तेरा ठंडा होगा
कितने आंसू तिरे सहरायों को गुलज़ार करें

तेरे ऐवानों में पुर्ज़े हुए पैमां कितने
कितने वादे जो न आसूदा-ए-इकरार हुए
कितनी आंखों को नज़र खा गई बदख़ाहों की
ख़्वाब कितने तिरी शाहरायों में संगसार हुए

'बला कशाने मुहब्बत पे जो हुआ सो हुआ
जो मुझ पे गुज़री मत उस से कहो, हुआ सो हुआ
मबादा हो कोई ज़ालिम तेरा गरीबांगीर
लहू के दाग़ तू दामन से धो, हुआ सो हुआ'

हम तो मजबूर-ए-वफ़ा हैं मगर ऐ जाने-जहां
अपने उशाक से ऐसे भी कोई करता है
तेरी महफ़िल को ख़ुदा रक्खे अबद तक कायम
हम तो महमां हैं घड़ी भर के हमारा क्या है

## We are Powerless Owing to Love[16]

O my homeland! You crave for blood of how many folks
That can turn your pale face into cherry red
Your heart needs how many exhalations to cool off
You require how many teardrops to transform your deserts into gardens

In your Houses how many pledges have been broken
How many promises that were never fulfilled
How many eyes were blinded by the evil-eyed louts
How many dreams were stoned to death in your thoroughfares

Let go whatever happened to the lovers suffering from separation
Let go whatever I suffered from, don't tell it to him
Lest a tormenter seizes your robe
Let go whatever happened, wash away the stains of blood from the robe

We are powerless owing to love but O my darling
Does anyone treat one's lovers like this
May God sustain your congregation till the end of the world
We are but the guests here for a while why worry about us

## پیرس

دن ڈھلا، کوچہ و بازار میں صف بستہ ہُوئیں

زرد رُو روشنیاں

ان میں ہر ایک کے کشکول سے برسیں رِم جھم

اس بھرے شہر کی نا سودگیاں

دور پَس منظرِ افلاک میں دھُندلانے لگے

عظمتِ رفتہ کے نشاں

پیش منظر میں

کسی سایہ دیوار سے لپٹا ہُوا سایہ کوئی

دوسرے سائے کی موہُوم سی اُمیدّ لیے

روز مرّہ کی طرح

زیرِ لب

شرحِ بے دردیٔ ایام کی تمہید لیے

اور کوئی اجنبی

ان روشنیوں سایوں سے کتراتا ہُوا

اپنے بے خواب شبستاں کی طرف جاتا ہُوا

## पेरिस

दिन ढला, कूचा-ओ-बाज़ार में सफ़बसता हुई
ज़र्द-रू रौशनियां
इनमें हर एक के कशकोल से बरसें रिम-झिम
इस भरे शहर की नासूदगीयां
दूर पसमंज़रे-अफ़लाक में धुंधलाने लगे
अज़मते-रफ़ता के निशां
पेश मंज़र में
किसी साया-ए-दीवार से लिपटा हुआ साया कोई
दूसरे साये की मौहूम-सी उम्मीद लिये
ज़ेरे-लब शामे-गुज़िसता की तरह
शरहे-बेदर्दी-ए-अय्याम की तमहीद लिये
और कोई अजनबी
इन रौशनियों के सायों से कतराता हुआ
अपने बेख़्वाब शबिसतां की तरफ़ जाता हुआ

## Paris[17]

The day declined, in the streets and the markets have drawn up in rows
Pale lights
From the begging bowl of each one of them rained with ringing noise
The discontentments of this crowded city
Far away in the backdrop of the skies emerged the hazy
Images of the grandeur gone by
In the focal point
A shadow clung to the silhouette of some wall
With the faint hope of uniting with another shadow
Like everyday
In a low voice
Mumbling the summary of hostile times
And some stranger
Evading the lights and shadows
Moving on towards his dreamless boudoir

## ایک نغمہ کربلائے بیرُوت کے لیے

بیروت نگارِ بزمِ جہاں
بیروت بدیلِ باغِ جناں
بچّوں کی ہنستی آنکھوں کے
جو آئنے چکنا چور ہوئے
اب ان کے ستاروں کی لَو سے
اس شہر کی راتیں روشن ہیں
اور رُخشاں ہے ارضِ لبنان
بیروت نگارِ بزمِ جہاں
جو چہرے لہو کے غازے کی
زینت سے سوا پُرنور ہوئے
اب ان کی رنگیں پرتو سے

اس شہر کی گلیاں روشن ہیں
اور تاباں ہے ارضِ لبنان
بیروت نگارِ بزمِ جہاں
ہر ویراں گھر، ہر ایک کھنڈر
ہم پایہء قصرِ دارا ہے
ہر غازی رشکِ اسکندر

ہر دختر ہمسر لیلیٰ ہے

یہ شہر ازل سے قائم ہے

یہ شہر ابد تک دائم ہے

بیروت نگارِ بزمِ جہاں

بیروت بدیلِ باغِ جناں

## एक नग़मा करबला-ए-बेरूत के लिये

बेरूत निगारे-बज़्मे-जहां
बेरूत बदीले-बाग़े-जिनां

बच्चों की हंसती आंखों के
जो आईने चकनाचूर हुए
अब उनके सितारों की लौ से
इस शहर की रातें रौशन हैं

जो चेहरे लहू के ग़ाज़े की
ज़ीनत से सिवा पुरनूर हुए
अब उनकी दमक के परतव से
इस शहर की गलियां रौशन हैं
अब जगमग है अरज़े-लबनां

बेरूत निगारे-बज़्मे-जहां
बेरूत बदीले-बाग़े-जिनां

हर कुशता मकां हर इक खंडर
हम-पाया-ए-कसरे-दारा है
हर ग़ाज़ी रशके-इसकन्दर
हर दुख़तर कामते-लैला है
ये शहर अज़ल से कायम है
बेरूत दिले-अरज़े-लबनां

बेरूत निगारे-बज़्मे-जहां
बेरूत बदीले-बाग़े-जिनां

## A Song for the Calamity Called Beirut[18]

Beirut, the beloved of the world
Beirut, the replica of Garden of Eden
The mirrors of the cackling eyes of the children
That got shattered
Now with the illumination of their stars
The nights of this city are bright
And resplendent is the land of Lebanon

Beirut, the beloved of the world
The faces with the rouge of blood
Have got illumined with this adornment
Now with their multihued shadow
The streets of this city are set alight
And illuminated is the land of Lebanon

Beirut, the beloved of the world
Each abandoned house, each ruin
Is equal to the palace of Dara
Each warrior is Alexander's envy
Each daughter is comparable to Laila
This city exists from the beginning
This city will survive till the end of the world

Beirut, the beloved of the world
Beirut, the replica of Garden of Eden

# Appendix

## THE UNICORN AND THE DANCING GIRL

(Faiz wrote this poem in blank verse in the 1960s as a script for a documentary on Mohenjodaro that was never made.)

In Pakistan as elsewhere in Asia
Of the timeless sea
And written within this eternity of silence
The music of time began
In the leap of a lonely spring
Out of the encrusted womb of a wilderness of rocks
The joyous limbs of the dancing girl
Defying the motionless unicorn
And dancing waters on their festival
March to the sea.
Thus time was born
And cities arose on the plains
Attracting an unending caravan
Of human feet arching in and
Out of the timeless mountains

Arabs, Tartars, Turks, and White Men
But as time unwound its first
The unicorn which is the past
Grabbed it in its blind hoofs
And spun it round and imprisoned it within itself.
And time became
The endless drone of the waterwheel
The hum of the spinning wheel
The closed spectrum of light and shadow
The heat and cold of the seasons
Although men matched their strength
Against the wheel
To fight and create
Much that was good and beautiful

And Africa time past is time present
And in the past–the past
There was no time
Only timelessness
The timelessness of the city of dead
And the graves of nameless saints
With their tattered flags
Which never rallied anyone to any cause
And their earthen lamps which shed no
Light on the mysteries of human darkness.
The timelessness of the unicorn
Presiding over pots and pans
Over weapons and vanities
Of the city of dead
Who is not even a unicorn
Is not even a legend

For even a legend is a memory
And the memory is in time
But the past is timeless
Like the eternal snows of
Timeless mountains
The eternal sands
Of timeless deserts
And the waters
Of the timeless sea
And written within this eternity of silence
The music of time began
In the leap of a lonely spring
Out of the encrusted womb of a wilderness of rocks
The joyous limbs of the dancing girl
Defying the motionless unicorn
And dancing waters on their festival
March to the sea
Thus time was born
And cities arose on the plains
Attracting an unending caravan
Of human feet arching in and
Out of the timeless mountains
Parthians, Bactrians, Huns and Scythians
Arabs, Tartars, Turks, and White Men
But as time unwound its first thread
The unicorn which is the past
Grabbed it in its blind hoofs
And spun it round and imprisoned it within itself.
And time became
The endless drone of the waterwheel
The creaking of the wooden cart

The hum of the spinning wheel
The closed spectrum of light and shadow
The heat and cold of the seasons
Although men matched their strength
Against the wheel
To fight and create
Much that was good and beautiful
Buildings
Gardens
Paintings
Carpets
Ornaments
Music
But everything moved within
Its own remorseless orbit
Even the dance of the dancing girl
Imprisoned within the circular whirl
Of her own limbs
And the gaze of eager eyes in a close-set circle
For the wheel was fate
And custom
And the will of the unknown powers
Which predestined all beauty
To death and decay after its span
And mighty cities to dust
And small men gave up
The fight
And accepted the yoke
To circumambulate their
Allotted round of days
Like blindfold oxen

And the wheel was fate
And the yoke was karma
And fear and want and pain
And withering of age
And death with its mercy
And the tyrant with no mercy in his heart
Until the present
And then the striving and the strain
The sorrows and dreams and passions and yearnings
Of numberless beings
Over untold centuries
Snapped the yoke
And broke the wheel
To unleash an orgy of frenzied movement
The wheel clanking away on steel tracks
Speeding on metalled roads
Whirling on airfields
In giant factories
Explosives ripping up the timeless
Mountains to release power
Earthmovers ploughing through timeless sands to admit water
Men and women
Boys and girls
Unyoked from fate and 'karma', and
Custom and the dream of an unknown will
The joyousness of the dancing girl
Rippling in abandon through the young flesh
Of countless limbs
And the unicorn reduced
At last to a mere design on a fabric
A mere decoration on the wall

And yet
Time present is still time past
In faces
In places
In custom and ritual and the grave of the nameless saint
In hunger and want and pain and the withering of age
The birth of time out of timelessness
Is beset like all births
With travail, and hope, and joy and apprehension
And its birth in Pakistan as elsewhere in
The newly liberated countries of Asia
And Africa
Is as yet only a small flag of freedom
Raised against
The bannered and embattled host of
Fear and want and hunger and
Pain
And the death of human hearts.

# Notes and References

## CHAPTER 1

1. Most of the events reported here in the life of Sultan Muhammad Khan (Faiz's father) particularly during his stay in Afghanistan are based on Lillias Hamilton, *A Vizier's Daughter: A Tale of the Hazara War,* Gale and The British Library, Detroit, MI, 1900.

## CHAPTER 2

1. In an interview given to Mirza Zafarul Hasan, *Sham-e-Shar-e-Yaran,* (*Nuskha Hai Wafa*), Farid Book Depot Pvt. Ltd., Delhi, p. 489.
2. Ibid., p. 491.
3. Ibid., p. 492.
4. Ibid., p. 493.
5. T. Eagleton, *Marxism and Literary Criticism,* University of California, Berkeley, p. 1976.
6. Excerpts translated from the original Urdu Presidential Address of Premchand by the author, cited in Khalil-ur-Rehman Azmi, *Urdu Mein Tarraqui Pasand Adabi Tahreek,* Educational Book House, Aligarh, 2015, pp. 41-45.
7. Alys Faiz, *Over My Shoulder*, Sang-e-Meel Publications, Lahore, 2015, p. 18.
8. Ibid. p. 20.

9. Ibid., p. 21.
10. Ibid., p. 22.
11. https://amedleyofpotpourri.blogspot.com/2014/08/mahatma-gandhi.html.
12. *The Pakistan Times*, Lahore, February 2, 1948.
13. *The Pakistan Times*, Lahore, April 1948.
14. *The Pakistan Times*, Lahore, March 23, 1949.
15. G. Allana, *Pakistan Movement Historical Documents* (Karachi: Department of International Relations, University of Karachi, 1969), pp. 407-411.

## CHAPTER 3

1. *https://www.revolvy.com/topic/*1951 *in Pakistan.*
2. Alys Faiz, op. cit., p. 31.
3. See Mohammad Ayub Khan, *Friends, Not Masters,* Oxford University Press, London, 1967, pp. 32ff.
4. See Faiz Ahmed Faiz, *Saleebein Merey Dareechey Mein*, Shaikh Muhammad Usman Book Seller, Srinagar, 1974, pp. 33-34.
5. Alys Faiz, op. cit., p. 31.
6. Once Faiz divulged to a friend: "In July 1947, I got hold of a sensitive and revealing letter of the Chief of CID, Mr. W.N.P. Jain. I was in my office of *The Pakistan Times* when an unknown man came to meet me. Handing over a sealed envelop he told me that the CID Chief asked him to deliver it personally to the Governor of Punjab. Since he thought it might contain something of significance he brought it to me." Faiz opened the envelope skilfully without damaging the seal. In the letter the CID Chief had expressed that partition of India would in no way endanger the interests of the British; the decisions of the Boundary Commission would, however, rattle the Muslims. "First I got the copies of the letter made and then sealed the envelope as it was. The man took it to deliver to its addressee. I made up my mind to show the letter to the Prime Minister, Liyaqat Ali Khan, at the appropriate time, i.e. sometime after August 14, 1947. Thus, I reached Karachi. I got the chance to meet him after waiting for three days. Having read the letter the Prime Minister said that he was aware of the

circumstances and that he knew everything. He then advised me to go back to Lahore and do my work. I went back to Lahore and got busy editing the *Pakistan Times.* I waited for a while expecting a reaction from the Prime Minister. When nothing came from any quarter, then I published the letter verbatim in the *Pakistan Times* on September 4, 1947, along with the editorial entitled as 'Spy Ring'. In response many people wrote letters that I published in the newspaper. However, the Government did nothing. No official bothered." Except the Governor Mr. Jenkins who ordered an inquiry. (Quoted in Ayub Mirza, *Faiz Nama,* Khuda Bakhsh Oriental Public Library, Patna, 2002, pp. 93-94).

## CHAPTER 4

1. Faiz Ahmed Faiz, *Saleebein Merey Dareechey Mein,* Shaikh Muhammed Usman Book Seller, Srinagar, 1974, p. 152.

   Though 25 original letters written in English have survived and they are now available in a volume published in 2011, titled as *Two Loves.* Salima Hashmi, Faiz's daughter writes in the Foreword: "In 2009, when we had embarked upon the project 'Faiz Ghar'— setting up a small Museum in a house leased to us by a friend and admirer of Faiz—we commenced sorting Faiz's belongings, papers and books. It was not a massive collection by any means, given his nomadic, rather spartan life, but an interesting one. My mother was instrumental in saving and sorting what little there was: a smart grey lounge suit, a fur cap, his scarf, his pen, and a reasonably large cache of photographs, letters, certificates and medals. After my mother's death, all this had been packed away in cartons in my house, waiting for just the sort of opportunity that the Faiz Ghar project afforded. Sifting through his papers, I came across a plastic bag containing some scraps of paper. On a closer look, I deciphered Faiz's writing, and the unmistakable stamp of the censor from Hyderabad Jail. These few letters were in poor shape but readable. It is surprising that they were there at all. Alys and Faiz had moved to Beirut in 1978. Their home in Lahore was closed for almost three years. On return, all seemed to be in order except our cupboard, which had been attacked by termites. Here too, the termites had spared all but one small wicker basket, where

Alys had stored all of Faiz's correspondence from the Rawalpindi Conspiracy Case days. Alys was inconsolable, but Faiz reminded her that the Urdu translation existed: '*Saleebein Meray Dareechay Mein*', published in 1972. The termite-ridden, now salvaged remnants were conserved with the help of Dr. Asma Ibrahim and transcribed by Kyla Pasha and were published under the title *Two Loves* in 2011. We decided to bring out the volume accompanied by photographs of some of the cells and other bits and pieces.

"... Going through these letters—only 25 had survived from the originals—I was struck by two things: Firstly the comparison with the Urdu translation, and I realise what a commendable job Faiz had done of translating his own letters. And secondly, the things he had chosen to omit in the translation, in the published translation. (These were largely bits of juicy gossip, and also certain bits of intimate sentences written to his wife and the way that he chose to mention us, the two daughters, calling us "pigeons" and "funny faces".

2. Faiz Ahmed Faiz, op. cit., p. 25.
3. Ibid., p. 26.
4. Ibid., p. 132.
5. Ibid., p. 42.
6. Ibid., p. 83.
7. Ibid., pp. 91-92.
8. Ibid., pp. 31-32.
9. Ibid., p. 33.
10. Ibid., p. 108.
11. Ibid., pp. 220-221.
12. Ibid., p. 222.
13. Ibid., p. 27.
14. Later Poshni published an account of his days with Faiz in jail. He writes: "After finishing dinner in the cell of Sajjad Zaheer we would without fail spend some time reciting poetry, singing qawwalis and songs. I would always be forced to be the lead singer of qawwalis. Though many ghazals and poems had been rattled off in these sessions, the most popular of these was the revolutionary

Song that Faiz had penned in the Hyderabad Central Jail. The Song was liked so much by all of us that we would sing it at least once in each session and often would keep singing it for more than half an hour. It is the kind of protest that is full of resolve and optimism and also communicates the prophecy of the ultimate victory of truth and justice.

15. Ex Major Muhammad Ishaq, 'Rudad-e-Qafas', included as Introduction to *Zindan Nama, Nuskha Hai Wafa*, op. cit., p. 199.
16. Ibid., p. 204.
17. In an interview given to Prof. Muhammad Hasan, the famous critic, Faiz edifies us about his 'concept of pain': "There is probably no equivalent in the English language for *'dard'* the Urdu word for pain. Pain in the English language normally suggests only physical pain, unless it is qualified by some other phrase pain of love, pain of bereavement, etc. Physical pain, however violent and acute, is an ephemeral and subjectively a very superficial experience because it is almost completely effaced the moment it is over. It does not even leave in memory any precise image of its physiological manifestation. All that one can recall is a vague emotive or affective state of discomfort or unpleasantness. For mental or subjective pain there are other words, such as anguish, agony, suffering, etc. each with a limited connotation.

   "The Urdu word *'dard'*, however, is not only inclusive of both physical and mental pain but is connotative of a whole spectrum of human emotions, love, passion, sympathy, sorrow, yearning, etc.

   "In poetry we also use it interchangeably with *'gaham'* which stands for care or grief. Pain in this pervasive sense is a primary element in all significant human experience even the happiest and most pleasurable. Firstly, because unlike pleasure, its penetration into consciousness is deeper and more incisive. Secondly, even the happiest moment when recalled brings with it not only the glow of happiness past but also the nostalgia of paradise lost. Pain thus becomes an antennae of sensitivity for sensory perception, a dynamo that electrifies human experience and transforms it into creative activity.

"This concept of pain, however, should not be confused with masochistic self-pity or wallowing in misery for misery's sake–the stock in–of so much decadent poetry. It should, on the other hand, be conceived as the elan vital of what is called revolutionary romanticism. It is the element which in the Turkish poet Nazim Hikmat's phrase 'keeps bright the jewelled heart'." [Cited in Mirza, Ayub, Faiz Nama, op. cit., pp. 33-34].

## CHAPTER 5

1. See References 17 of the previous chapter.
2. Translated from the original Urdu by the author. Ibid.
3. Alys Faiz, op. cit., p. 50.
4. Alys Faiz, op. cit., p. 58.
5. Ibid., pp. 58-59.
6. Cited in Ali Madeeh Hashmi, *Love and Revolution: Faiz Ahmed Faiz*, Rupa, New Delhi, pp. 200-201.
7. Faiz's address that he delivered in Urdu while accepting the Lenin Peace Prize. Translated from the original Urdu by the author.
8. As reported in Ayub Mirza, in *Faiz Nama*, op. cit.
9. Walt Whitman in *Song of Myself*, Section 51.
10. Ali Madeeh Hashmi, op. cit., pp. 191-192.
11. Philip Charles Habib (1920-1992) was an eminent American diplomat. He was Ronald Reagan's special envoy to the Middle East. He was successful to avert an Israel-Syria war and also Israel-PLO war in the early 1980s.
12. Alys Faiz, op. cit., p. 82.

## CAHAPTER 6

1. Faiz Ahmed Faiz, *Meezan*, Maghrabi Bengal Urdu Academy, Kolkata, Second edition, 1982, 2002, p. 13.
2. Ibid., pp. 18-19.
3. Ibid., p. 31.
4. Ibid., p. 68.
5. Ibid., p. 69.
6. Ibid., p. 71.

7. Ibid., pp. 71-72.
8. Ibid., pp. 72-73.
9. Ibid., p. 92.
10. Karl Marx, *Theses on Feuerbach* (third thesis) http://www.marxists.org/archive/marx/works/1845/theses/index.htm.
11. *Meezan,* op. cit., p. 97.
12. Ibid., p. 106.
13. Ibid., p. 110.
14. Ibid., p. 123.
15. Ibid., pp. 123-124.
16. Ibid., pp. 130-131.
17. Ibid., p. 147.
18. Ibid., p. 151.
19. Ibid., p. 204.
20. "Patras Bukhari". *amazingpakistanis.com*. Retrieved October 15, 2016.
21. *Meezan,* op. cit., p. 221.
22. Ibid., p. 226.
23. Ibid., p. 244.

## CHAPTER 7

1. Kuldeep Kumar, *The Hindu*, March 24, 2017.
2. Baqar Mehdi's article, Faiz-Ek Naya Tajziya, in Shahid Mahuli (ed.), *Faiz Ahmed Faiz: Aks aur Jahtein*, Me'ayar Publications, Delhi, 2011, p. 138.
3. Major Muhammed Ishaq, Rudad-e-Qafas in *Zindan Nama,* in *Nuskha Haay Wafa* (Collected Works), Farid Book Depot Pvt. Ltd., Delhi, 1997, pp. 228-229.
4. Quoted in Khalil ur Rehman Azmi, *Urdu Mein Tarraqi Pasand Adabi Tahreek*, Educational Book House, Aligarh, 2015, p. 97.
5. Baqar Mehdi, op. cit., p. 150.
6. Kalimuddin Ahmed's article, Faiz, included in, Shahid Mahuli (ed.), op. cit., p. 23.
7. Ibid., pp. 27-28.
8. Quoted in Ali Madeeh Hashmi, op. cit., pp. 106-07.

9. Baqar Mehdi's article in Shahid Mahuli, op. cit., p. 142.
10. Aal-e Ahmed Suroor cited in Shahid Naqvi's article, 'Tarraqi Pasand Tahreek ki Aabru Faiz: Ek Shuhra-e Aafaq Sahaer', in *Bedar Shuaein*, Karachi, October 2002, p. 122.
11. Faiz az Faiz, *Dast-e- Tah-e Sang*, in *Nuskha Hai Wafa*, Farid Book Depot Pvt. Ltd., Delhi, 1997, pp. 314/20.
12. Shamsur Rehman Faruqi's article, 'Faiz aur Classiki Ghazal', included in Shahid Mahuli (ed.), op. cit., p. 236.
13. Ibid., p. 239.

## CHAPTER 8

1. Victor G. Kiernan, *Poems by Faiz*, George Allen & Unwin, London, 1971, p. 21.
2. Ibid., p. 9.
3. *Naqsh-e Faryadi*, in *Nuskha Hai Wafa*, Farid Book Depot Pvt. Ltd., Delhi, 1997, pp. 69-70 (77-78).
4. *Dast-e Saba*, in Ibid., pp. 40-41 (136-137).
5. Ibid., pp. 88-89 (136-137).
6. *Zindan Nama*, in Ibid., pp. 58-61 (248-251).
7. Ibid., pp. 76-78 (266-268).
8. *Dast-e Tah-e Sang*, in Ibid., pp. 69-70 (363-364).
9. *Sar-e Wadi-e Sina*, pp. 19-23 (393-397).
10. Ibid., pp. 27-28 (401-402).
11. Ibid., pp. 31-32 (405-406).
12. *Shaam-e Shahr-e Yaran*, in Ibid., pp. 54-56 (532-534).
13. Ibid., p. 60 (538).
14. Ibid., pp. 73-74 (551-552).
15. *Merey Dil Merey Musafir* in Ibid., pp. 34-37 (640-643).
16. Ibid., pp. 38-39 (644-645).
17. Ibid., pp. 43-44 (649-650).
18. Ghubar-e-Ayyam in Ibid., pp. 10-11 (698-699).

# Index

## Also by the Same Author

*Vrindavanlal Verma (Tr.)*
*Off the Spotlight*
*Talmihat-e-Faiz (Urdu)*
*Portrait of a Pragmatist (Tr.)*
*Secularism and Its Indian Version*
*Reading History (Ed.)*
*What Ails Indian Muslims (Jointly edited with Murzban Jal)*
*Secularism under Siege (Ed.)*
*Mata-e-Nazar (Urdu)*
*Khilafat in History and Indian Politics*